THE COMPLETE BOOK OF
ITALIAN
COOKING

THE COMPLETE BOOK OF
ITALIAN
COOKING

CUISINES OF THE
MEDITERRANEAN

NEW
BURLINGTON
BOOKS

A QUINTET BOOK

First published by New Burlington Books in 2002
6 Blundell Street
London N7 9BH

ISBN 1-86155-382-X

This book was designed and produced by
Quintet Publishing Limited
6 Blundell Street
London N7 9BH

Art Director: Silke Braun
Designer: James Lawrence
Senior Editor: Laura Sandelson
Editor: Anne Hildyard

Creative Director: Richard Dewing
Publisher: Oliver Salzmann

Typeset in Great Britain by Type Technique, London W1
Manufactured in Hong Kong by Regent Publishing Services Ltd
Printed in China by Leefung-Asco Printers Ltd

Contents

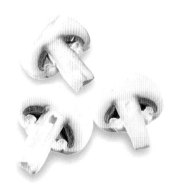

Pasta

Pasta is one of man's earliest culinary inventions, dating back to over 3,000 years ago when the ancient Greeks recorded it in manuscripts and paintings, showing it to be one of the staple foods in their diet. Greece and Italy are not the only countries with a history of pasta making – the tradition also exists in Spain, Israel, and even Russia.

Dried pasta (which means paste in Italian) is generally made from semolina, durum, or hard wheat mixed with water and/or oil and sometimes eggs. The dough is kneaded and rolled or extruded commercially to produce a myriad of shapes and sizes. Dried pasta will keep for up to a year if stored in a covered container in a dry, cool place.

Fresh pasta is available in many different varieties, not only from delicatessens (where the pasta is often made on the premises) but also from major supermarkets, where it can be found in packages in the chilled cabinets. Fresh pasta is easy to make at home and will keep for up to 5 days in the refrigerator or for 6 months in the freezer.

Nutrition

Contrary to popular belief, pasta is not a fattening food. It is healthful and nutritious, providing protein, fiber, B vitamins, and minerals such as potassium and iron.

The type of complex carbohydrates found in pasta makes it a good energy food, providing the body with a steady flow of energy as the carbohydrates are broken down during the process of digestion

Mix and Match

It is a case of personal preference when it comes to choosing a particular pasta shape to match your favorite sauce. You may prefer small gnocchi (shells) to scoop up a rich tomato sauce, and tagliatelle or linguini for serving with a thick, creamy sauce, where each strand of pasta can be evenly coated in the sauce for a perfect combination of flavor and texture. Thicker sauces are best served with ridged or hollow pasta shapes such as penne, while spiral shapes are good with meat or vegetable sauces.

If you don't have the pasta that is called for in a recipe, just substitute a similar shape.

Cooking Pasta

Pasta should be cooked in enormous quantities of boiling water. Although you can get away with less water than the volume which is always suggested for authentic recipes (which means using a stock pot or catering-size kettle when cooking enough for four people), you need a large saucepan which holds 4–4½ quarts to cook ¾–1 pound of pasta. If

Gefäß, das gut 4 l Wasser fasst. Wenn Sie über einen Suppentopf oder einen großen Schnellkochtopf verfügen, der ohne Deckel verwendet werden kann, umso besser.

Füllen Sie den Topf zu drei Vierteln mit Wasser. Fügen Sie Salz hinzu und bringen Sie das Wasser zum Kochen. Etwas Öl verhindert ein Schäumen des Wassers und schnelles Überkochen. Ein Zusammenkleben der Pasta in einem zu kleinen Topf wird allerdings auch durch Öl nicht vermieden. Verwenden Sie einen ausreichend großen Topf. Dann klebt die Pasta auch nicht zusammen. Geben Sie die Pasta erst ins Wasser, wenn es richtig kocht. Rühren Sie um und bringen Sie das Wasser schnell wieder zum Kochen. Halten Sie sich bereit, die Hitze zu reduzieren, sonst schäumt das Wasser über. Frische Nudeln und ungefüllte Pasta sollten etwa 3 Minuten kochen. Gefüllte Pasta braucht länger, damit die Füllung gart. Getrocknete Pasta kochen Sie entsprechend den Angaben auf der Packung.

Nach dem Kochen sollte die Pasta „al dente" (mit Biss) sein, d. h. fest, aber doch zart und nicht weich oder verklebt. Gießen Sie die Pasta sofort in ein großes Sieb ab, das sie über dem Spülbecken schwenken. Die Pasta in eine heiße Schüssel füllen und die Sauce darüber geben. Anschließend sofort servieren!

Vorbereitete Pasta kühl stellen

Die Pasta mit viel Mehl einstäuben und in einem großen luftdichten Behälter in den Kühlschrank stellen. Wenn Sie sie nicht innerhalb von 2 Tagen kochen wollen, sollten Sie sie sofort einfrieren. Unausgerollter Teig kann eingewickelt und 1 bis 2 Tage kühl gehalten werden.

Pastareste

Reste an einem kühlen Ort in einem geschlossenen Behältnis aufbewahren. Wärmen Sie Pasta in der Mikrowelle, in einer Sauce auf dem Herd oder im Backofen auf.

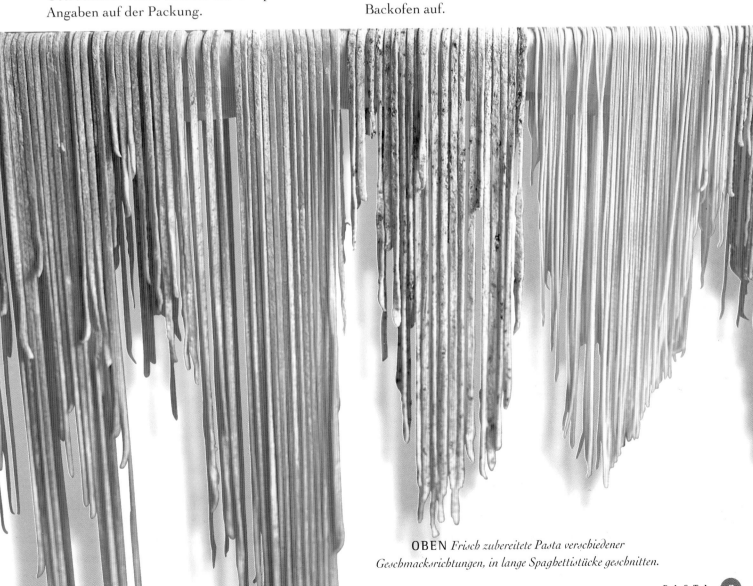

OBEN *Frisch zubereitete Pasta verschiedener Geschmacksrichtungen, in lange Spaghettistücke geschnitten.*

Equipment for making Pasta Dough

ABOVE *Hand-turned pasta machine, being used to roll dough.*

You do not need any special equipment for making pasta. A large area of work surface helps, but it is not essential as you can always roll the dough in two or more batches. A mixing bowl, spoon, and rolling pin are the basics, and an extra-long rolling pin is useful (make sure an ordinary one does not have knobs at the ends as they indent the dough and make rolling out difficult). You may also wish to invest in some of the following:

Pastry Wheel A fluted pastry wheel for cutting out ravioli.

Ravioli Pan A small metal pan with round or square hollows. Lay a sheet of pasta over the pan, press it in neatly and spoon mixture into the hollows. Brush with egg, cover with a second sheet of dough, and roll the top to seal before cutting out the ravioli.

Pasta Machine A small but heavy metal machine for rolling pasta. Fitted with plain rollers which can be set at different distances apart, this basic, inexpensive machine is terrific. Once the dough is briefly kneaded, rolling it through the machine several times on the widest setting will complete the kneading.

Set the rollers at the narrow width for rolling out sheets of dough or substitute cutting rollers to make noodles or spaghetti. A ravioli filler attachment makes very small, neat ravioli by feeding the pasta and filling through a hopper-like attachment.

Electric Pasta Machines Large, expensive machines are available for mixing, kneading, rolling, and extruding pasta. Unless you are an avid pasta eater, such a machine is an unlikely piece of equipment for the average domestic kitchen.

Pasta Dryer A small wooden rack on which to hang cut noodles or sheets of pasta as they are rolled out.

Pasta Dough

MAKES ABOUT 1¼ POUNDS PASTA

There is no great mystery involved in making simple, Italian-style pasta dough. All it takes is a touch of muscle power for the kneading and rolling – unless, of course, you have a pasta machine which will make light work of pounding the ingredients to a smooth, pliable dough. It really is worth making your own dough, if only for filled pasta such as tortellini and ravioli; apart from the variety of fillings which you can introduce, homemade filled pasta is infinitely superior to the average (or even slightly better) bought alternatives. Remember that you can make a large batch of shapes when the mood takes you, fill them and freeze them for future use.

12 oz hard flour

1 tsp salt

3 eggs

4 tbsp olive oil

1 tbsp water

Mix the flour and salt together in a large bowl. Make a well in the middle, then add the eggs, olive oil, and water. Use a spoon to mix the eggs, oil, and water, gradually working in the flour. When the mixture begins to bind into clumps, scrape the spoon clean and knead the dough together with your hands.

Press the dough into a ball and roll it around the bowl to leave the bowl completely clean of the mixture. Then place the dough on a lightly floured, clean surface and knead it thoroughly until it is smooth. Follow the notes on kneading (see page 11), keeping the dough moving and adding the minimum extra flour required to prevent it sticking as you work. Wrap the dough in a plastic bag and leave it to rest for 15–30 minutes before rolling it out. Do not chill the dough as this will make it difficult to handle.

ABOVE *Fresh pasta noodles ready for freezing.*

Pasta-making Techniques

Mixing and Kneading

1 *Kneading pasta dough.*

Unlike pastry, pasta dough needs a firm hand and a positive approach to mixing and kneading. The dough will seem very dry and prone to crumbling at first but as you knead it, the oil and egg combine fully with the flour and the ingredients bind together.

1 Mix the ingredients in the bowl, using a spoon at first, then your hand.

2 Begin the kneading process in the bowl, bringing the dough together and "wiping" the bowl clean of any crumbs.

3 Place the dough on a lightly floured, clean surface and knead it into a ball. Add a little flour to the work surface to prevent the dough sticking, but try to keep this to the minimum during kneading.

4 Once the dough has come together, knead it firmly and rhythmically, pressing it down and out in one movement, then pulling the edge of the dough back in toward the middle in the next movement. Keep turning the dough as you knead it, so that you work it around in a circle rather than constantly pressing and pulling one side. Keep the dough moving and it will not stick to the surface.

5 The dough is ready when it is smooth and warm. Wrap it in a plastic bag or plastic wrap and set it aside for 15–30 minutes if possible before rolling it out.

Rolling Out

2 *Rolling out pasta dough.*

When rolling the dough, try to keep it in the shape you want to end up with. Press the dough flat, forming it into an oblong or square, then roll it out firmly. Lift and "shake out" the dough a few times initially to insure it does not stick to the surface. As the dough becomes thinner you have to handle it more carefully to avoid splitting it. However, pasta dough is far more durable than pastry and the smoother it becomes as it is rolled, the tougher it is. It can be rolled out very thinly – until you can almost see through it – without breaking, but this is not essential for the majority of pasta dishes. Dust the surface under the dough with a little flour occasionally, as necessary, and dust the top, rubbing the flour over the dough with one hand. Continue rolling until the dough is thin and even – a common mistake is to leave the dough too thick, so that it becomes unpleasantly solid when cooked. For noodles, or pasta which is to be eaten plain or topped with sauce, try to roll out to the thickness of a piece of brown wrapping paper: this makes excellent noodles.

Make sure the surface under the dough is sifted with flour, then cover the dough completely with plastic wrap and leave for 10 minutes. This relaxes the dough before cutting – it is not essential but does prevent the dough from shrinking as it is cut.

Cutting Pasta

You need a large, sharp knife and a large floured platter or tray on which to place the pasta (a clean roasting pan will do). Flour the dough lightly before cutting. Once cut, keep the pasta dusted

3 *Pasta shapes made with cookie cutters.*

with flour to prevent it sticking together. Pasta may be dried before cooking by hanging it on a rack or spreading it out. I have, before now, draped pasta between two chair backs (covering them with paper towels first). Quite honestly, I have not found any great advantage to drying the pasta and have always felt that it is thoroughly inconvenient and unhygienic. It seems to cook well if it is added to boiling water straight after rolling.

Sheets Trim the dough edges so that they are straight, then cut the pasta into squares or oblongs. This is basic lasagne, so cut the dough to suit the size of dish.

Noodles Dust the dough well with flour, then roll it up. Use a sharp knife to cut the roll into ¼-inch wide slices. Shake out the slices as they are cut and they fall into long noodles. Keep the noodles floured and loosely piled on the tray to prevent them from sticking together. Cover loosely with plastic wrap.

Circles or shapes Use cookie cutters and aspic cutters to stamp out circles and shapes.

ABOVE *Fresh pasta squares.*

ABOVE *Fresh pasta bows.*

Squares Trim the dough edges, then use a clean, long ruler to cut the dough into wide strips. Cut these across into squares.

Small squares Use a ruler to cut the dough into 1-inch wide strips, then cut these across into squares. The small squares may be cooked and treated as bought pasta shapes.

Other shapes If you have the time, you can make other shapes by hand. Cut the dough into strips, then into small oblongs or squares. By twisting, pleating or pinching you can make bows and funny little twists and, I am sure, lots of clever alternatives. Frankly, I feel inclined to leave this to the manufacturers as it is very time-consuming.

Flavored Pastas

There is a wide choice of flavored pasta products, and the quality is equally varied, but then this is true of all food products. The information that follows applies to the dried pastas that I tried. Some of the flavored fresh pastas, particularly the less expensive brands, can be rather coarse and raw in taste. By way of contrast, some of the best fresh pastas really are a treat.

Glossary of Flavored Pasta

Porcini Pasta (1)

Delicious pasta flavored with dried ceps or porcini. A distinctly flavored pasta that will stand alone if dressed with a little butter, oil, cream, or other very simple sauce. Clever mushroom shapes enhance the image. Would be terrific in a hearty mushroom soup (it was a shame to drain away the cooking water), or in hotpots and moist stews. The expensive Italian brand I tried really was worth it.

Corn and Spinach Pasta (2)

The combination of corn and spinach was good in flavor and color. Good spinach color.

Black Squid (3a & b)

Cuttlefish or squid ink is used to enrich rather than strongly flavor the pasta. Although squid ink pastas do not have a "fishy" flavor, they are tinged with seafood, and I would not serve them with a poultry sauce or meat. Best for seafood or vegetable-based sauces.

Asparagus (4)

At first taste, a bit "grassy," but better when tossed with melted butter. Serve with a light, creamy, or milky sauce.

Smoked Salmon (5)

The pasta smelled strongly of smoked salmon, but the flavor had diminished markedly after boiling. For the price, I recommend buying plain pasta, and spending the price difference on fresh smoked salmon to toss into it.

Corn, Tomato, and Chili (6)

Quite distinctly tasted of chili, but the tomato does not come through. Good in flavor and texture.

Champignon (7)

From a French range, the "pâtes aux oeufs frais aromatisées" that I tried were flavored with dried "trompettes de mort" mushrooms. A good flavor, milder than porcini pasta. Serve plain with butter, oil or cream and cheese. Toss with sautéed mushrooms to accentuate the flavor, or toss with butter, and serve as a base for creamy chicken mixtures or milk-based seafood sauces. Take care not to drown the delicate mushroom pasta.

Basil (8)

Quality is important when buying herb-flavored pasta. I tried a French-made brand of tagliatelle that had a good, mild basil flavor. Good tossed with oil or butter as a base for a topping or simply with cheese.

Spinach (9)

Qualities vary widely, but expensive types are worth the extra for a good spinach flavor.

Garlic and Chili (10)

The Italian brand I tried was good (spaghetti), with a pronounced pep coming from the chili.

Chianti Speciality (11)

Novelty pasta in the shapes of red grapes (beet), white grapes (plain) and leaves (spinach). This was very good, and the spinach flavor was the best of all the spinach pastas that I tried specifically for this chapter. Looks terrific!

Black and White Spaghetti (12)

Flavored with black squid ink and plain. A good combination that makes an elegant base for seafood. A smart option for appearance rather than flavor.

Black Olive Spaghetti (13)

This is good! A light flavor of black olives that is just sufficient to assert itself. Ideal for tossing with olive oil and garlic, and topping with Romano. Would be lost with a strong (meat-type) sauce, milk, or cream. Diced fresh tomatoes or sun-dried tomatoes would go well, especially with fresh basil or parsley.

Tomato (14)

As for spinach, the quality varies significantly, and some pink pasta tastes rather bland.

Garlic and Tomato 15)

The garlic tends to overpower the tomato, so the latter contributes color rather than flavor.

Fasta Pasta

There is a wide range of quick-cook pasta, instant noodles, and sauced pasta. Here are just a few of them.

Boil-in-the-bag pasta

Perforated boiling bags containing slim spirals (or other shapes) that cook in about 7–8 minutes. Easy to drain, but the texture is not as good as "proper" pasta.

Instant Chinese noodles

These are soaked in freshly boiled water instead of having to be boiled. They are great: a real boon for a-meal-in-a-hurry dishes.

Instant or very speedy pastas

These are usually in cake form, like Chinese dried noodles, and vary considerably in quality and flavor. In general I find that the more they offer in the way of flavoring, the less like real food they tend to be.

Quick-cook pastas

Spaghetti in a major Italian range cooks in 3 minutes to give excellent results, but some larger shapes tend to have a slightly slimy texture. Quick-cook macaronis vary: some are ready in 3 minutes, others in 7 minutes. I found the latter to be excellent.

Sauced dried pasta

There is an ever-increasing and changing range of dehydrated sauce and pasta mixes, rather like flavored rice mixes. Frankly, with fresh pasta so readily available, I would opt for a bowl of pasta topped with a little oil or butter and some grated cheese.

Pasta Soups

Minestrone

Vegetable and Fresh Cilantro Soup

Egg Pasta and Pea Soup

Egg Noodle Soup

Floret Soup

Sprout Soup with Almonds

Clear Cep Soup

Cream of Mushroom Soup

Shrimp and Pasta Bisque with Rouille

Red Pepper Soup

Tomato Pasta Soup

Chicken Noodle Soup

Seafood Chowder

Minestrone

Minestrone makes a warming meal, served with plenty of fresh bread and Parmesan cheese. Try serving the soup with olive bread as an accompaniment.

⅔ cup dried navy beans

2 tbsp olive oil

2 cups chopped, rindless bacon

2 garlic cloves, crushed

2 onions, chopped

6 celery stalks, sliced

2 large carrots, cut in large dice

2 large potatoes, cut in chunks

2 quarts chicken or bacon broth

1 bouquet garni

2 × 14 oz cans chopped tomatoes

4 oz green beans, cut into short lengths

2 small zucchini, halved lengthwise and sliced

3 cups shredded cabbage

1 cup soup pasta

salt and ground black pepper

4–6 tbsp chopped parsley

freshly grated Parmesan cheese, to serve

● Soak the navy beans overnight in cold water to cover.

● Next day, drain the beans, put them in a saucepan, and add plenty of fresh cold water to cover. Bring to a boil, and boil for 10 minutes; then reduce the heat, and cover the pan. Simmer the beans for 30 minutes.

● Meanwhile, heat the oil in a large saucepan. Add the bacon, garlic, onions, celery, and carrots. Cook, stirring all the time, for 15 minutes, or until the bacon is cooked. Then add the potatoes, broth, and bouquet garni. Stir in the drained navy beans. Bring the soup to a boil, reduce the heat, and cover the pan. Simmer for 1 hour.

● Stir in the tomatoes, green beans, zucchini, cabbage, and pasta, and bring back to a boil. Add salt and pepper to taste. Cook for a further 10 minutes, or until the vegetables are cooked, and the pasta is just tender. Taste for seasoning before stirring in the parsley and serving with Parmesan cheese.

Vegetable and Fresh Cilantro Soup

SERVES 4-6

A light, fresh-tasting soup that is ideal either as a starter or as a light lunch.

2 pt vegetable broth

¾ cup dried pasta (any shape)

dash of olive oil

½ cup carrots, thinly sliced

¾ cup frozen peas

6 tbsp chopped fresh cilantro

salt and freshly ground black pepper

● Bring the vegetable broth to a boil in a large saucepan and add the pasta with a dash of olive oil. Cook for about 5 minutes, stirring occasionally, then add the sliced carrots.

● Cook for 5 minutes, then add the peas and cilantro. Season with salt and freshly ground black pepper, and simmer gently for about 10 minutes, stirring occasionally, until the pasta and carrots are tender. Serve the soup with finely grated cheese, if wished.

Egg Pasta and Pea Soup

SERVES 4

½ carrot, chopped

½ onion, chopped

½ stalk of celery, chopped

1 tbsp chopped parsley

1 tbsp butter

1 tbsp tomato paste

salt and pepper

¾ cup shelled young peas

¾ cup small egg pasta shapes

½ cup grated parmesan

Gently fry the chopped vegetables and parsley in a pan with the butter until golden brown. Add the tomato paste diluted with 2 tablespoons water, season and cook for 10 minutes. Pour on 2½ pt water, bring to a boil and add the peas. Cook for 25 minutes, add the pasta and cook for a further 25 minutes. Serve at once, handing the grated cheese separately.

Egg Noodle Soup

SERVES 4

3 eggs

3 tbsp fine semolina

1 tbsp chopped parsley

¼ cup grated parmesan

3 pt meat broth

salt

nutmeg

In a bowl, beat the eggs with the semolina and parsley, and half the parmesan. Pour on a cup of cold broth, season with salt and nutmeg, and whisk. Bring the remaining broth to a boil, pour in the semolina mixture and stir for 3–4 minutes over a moderate heat until fine shreds of egg form. Serve at once and pass the remaining cheese round.

Floret Soup

A pretty and delicately flavored soup for a dinner-party menu. Make it in advance and reheat to serve.

2 tbsp butter

2 garlic cloves, minced

¾ lb tiny broccoli, cauliflower, and romanesco florets

½ cup dried pastina (any tiny shapes)

5 cups vegetable broth

salt and ground black pepper

Melt the butter in a large saucepan, and sauté the garlic for about 2 minutes. Add the tiny florets to the garlic and cook for about 5 minutes, stirring occasionally, until tender.

Stir the pastina into the floret mixture, cook for 1–2 minutes, then add the vegetable broth. Season with salt and freshly ground black pepper, cover, and bring to a boil. Simmer for about 10 minutes, until the pastina is cooked and the florets have softened. Serve with warm, fresh bread.

Sprout Soup with Almonds

SERVES 4-6

A warming soup with a subtle flavor, this makes an excellent starter for a dinner party. Made up to two days in advance, this soup can be reheated just before serving.

¼ cup butter

1 garlic clove, minced

2 tsp chopped fresh rosemary

½ lb Brussels sprouts, finely shredded

1¼ cups dried ditalini rigati (tiny, short, ridged tubes)

scant ½ cup toasted, flaked almonds

6½ cups vegetable broth

salt and ground black pepper

4 tbsp light cream

freshly grated Parmesan cheese, to serve

Melt the butter in a large saucepan, and sauté the garlic and rosemary for about 2 minutes. Add the shredded Brussels sprouts and cook for a further 3–4 minutes, stirring occasionally. Add the ditalini rigati with the flaked almonds. Stir and cook for 1–2 minutes, then stir in the vegetable broth and season with salt and ground black pepper.

Cover the soup and simmer for about 10 minutes, stirring occasionally. Stir in the cream, then serve in individual bowls with freshly grated Parmesan cheese.

Clear Cep Soup

SERVES 4

*T*his is a formal soup for special occasions. It has a strong mushroom flavor with the delicate addition of vegetables and pasta to create the contrasting textures.

1 oz dried ceps

2½ cups warm water

1 leek

1 carrot

1 cup conchigliette piccole (tiny pasta shells), cooked

salt and ground black pepper

flat parsley leaves, to garnish

Place the ceps in the warm water, and leave to soak for about 30 minutes. Drain the ceps, reserving the liquid in a saucepan.

Slice the ceps, and shred the leek and carrot. Add the vegetables to the mushroom stock and cook over medium heat for about 10 minutes, until the vegetables are tender. Add the cooked pasta shells, and season with salt and ground black pepper. Cook for a further minute. Serve garnished with parsley leaves.

Clear Cep Soup ▶

Hearty Cream of Mushroom Soup

SERVES 4

*P*erfect for a cold winter's night or even a filling lunchtime dish. Serve with warm, crusty garlic bread for a more substantial meal.

2 tbsp butter

1 onion, finely chopped

¾ lb mushrooms, finely chopped

1 tbsp all-purpose flour

2½ cups vegetable broth

1¼ cups milk

salt and ground black pepper

½ cup cooked tiny pasta shapes

pinch of freshly grated nutmeg

Melt the butter in a large saucepan, and sauté the onion for about 3 minutes until softened. Add the chopped mushrooms, cover, and cook for a further 5 minutes.

Stir in the flour, then gradually add the broth and milk, stirring well after each addition. Cover, and cook for 15–20 minutes, stirring occasionally. Season with salt and ground black pepper. Stir in the pasta shapes and grated nutmeg. Cook for another 2–3 minutes, then serve.

Shrimp and Pasta Bisque with Rouille

SERVES 4

*U*ncooked shrimp are sold frozen and sometimes fresh or defrosted with their heads removed. As the shrimp are poached, their shells turn pink.

FOR THE BISQUE

¼ cup butter

1 onion, finely chopped

1 small carrot, diced

1 celery stalk, diced

1 bay leaf

1 sprig of parsley

1½ cups diced potato, peeled

12 uncooked jumbo shrimp, heads removed

4 tbsp brandy

1¼ cups dry white wine

2½ cups water

salt and ground black pepper

1 cup soup pasta shells or other soup pasta

⅔ cup light cream

FOR THE ROUILLE

2 garlic cloves, peeled

1–2 red chilies, seeded and chopped (see Cook's Tip)

2 egg yolks

2 tbsp fresh white bread crumbs

2 tbsp lemon juice

generous ¾ cup olive oil

TO GARNISH

paprika

chopped parsley

TO SERVE

1 short French bread stick

COOK'S TIP

Chilies vary considerably in strength, and personal preferences also differ widely, so adjust the number of chilies accordingly.

To prepare chilies, cut off the stalk end and scrape out the seeds (which are especially hot) and pith from inside; then rinse the shells well before slicing or chopping them.

Take care when rinsing the chilies, wash your hands thoroughly after handling them, and avoid touching your eyes while working with them. The juices are a severe irritant to delicate skin and eyes.

Make the rouille first. Purée the garlic, chilies, egg yolks, bread crumbs, and lemon juice in a food processor or blender. Alternatively, the ingredients may be gradually pounded to a paste in a mortar; then the yolks and lemon juice beaten in. Gradually trickle in the olive oil, with the machine running, to make a thick, fiery mayonnaise. Transfer to a serving bowl, cover, and chill.

Next, make the bisque. Melt the butter in a saucepan. Add the onion, carrot, celery, bay leaf, parsley, and potato. Cook, stirring, for 5 minutes. Then add the shrimp. Cook, stirring gently, for 5 minutes. Add the brandy, and pour in the wine. Heat until simmering; then simmer gently for 5 minutes.

Remove the pan from the heat, and use a slotted spoon to lift out the shrimp. Shell the shrimp, and return the shells to the pan. Slice the flesh, and set it aside.

Pour the water into the soup, add plenty of seasoning, and bring it back to a boil. Reduce the heat, cover the pan, and let simmer for 20 minutes.

Purée the soup in a blender or food processor; then press it through a fine strainer to remove any large bits of shell. Rinse out the saucepan; then pour the soup back into it, and bring it to a boil. Add the pasta, reduce the heat, and cover the pan. Simmer for 15 minutes, or until the pasta is cooked.

Slice the French bread fairly thinly, and toast the slices until golden on both sides. Taste the soup for seasoning; then stir in the reserved shrimp flesh, and heat for a few seconds. Stir in the cream, and heat for a few seconds without boiling; then garnish with a little sprinkling of paprika and parsley. Offer the toasted bread and rouille with the soup.

Red Pepper Soup

SERVES 4

This delicious, wholesome, filling soup can be served with your favorite pasta shapes.

14 oz can pimientos, drained

2½ cups vegetable broth

salt and ground black pepper

1 tbsp ground coriander

½ lb cooked pasta shapes, such as tortelloni, shells, or bows

fresh cilantro, to garnish

Place the pimientos in a food processor or blender, and purée until smooth. Transfer to a large saucepan and add the vegetable broth, salt and pepper, and ground coriander. Stir and cook over gentle heat for about 10 minutes. Add the cooked pasta shapes and cook for a further 2–3 minutes, until heated through. Serve garnished with fresh cilantro.

◀ *Red Pepper Soup*

Tomato Pasta Soup

SERVES 4

1 onion, peeled and sliced

1 leek, washed and sliced

1 celery stalk

1 tbsp oil

1 tbsp butter

1 tbsp flour

3¾ cups broth

1½ cups canned tomatoes

4 tomatoes, skinned and chopped

1 tbsp tomato paste

1 stalk parsley

1 tbsp chopped fresh or 1 tsp dried basil

1 bay leaf

salt and ground black pepper

½ cup small pasta shapes

2 tbsp heavy cream

Prepare the vegetables making sure that the leek is trimmed, cut with a cross, and thoroughly washed before chopping. Remove the strings from the celery with a sharp knife and slice.

Heat the oil and butter in a large saucepan and toss the vegetables in the fat over a low heat for 4 minutes.

Sprinkle with flour and mix well before adding the broth and tomatoes. Mix well with a wooden spoon before adding the herbs and seasoning. Bring to a boil and simmer for 35 minutes. Allow the soup to cool slightly before sieving or blending.

Return to the saucepan, taste for seasoning, bring to a boil, and add the small pasta shapes. Cook by simmering for a further 5 minutes or until pasta is cooked. Stir in the cream and serve.

Chicken Noodle Soup

SERVES 4-6

1 large, boneless chicken breast, skinned

1 tbsp oil

½ oz fresh root ginger, peeled and cut into thin strips

1 carrot, cut into fine matchstick strips

¼ cup canned bamboo shoots, cut into fine matchstick strips

4 scallions, shredded diagonally

1 quart chicken broth

salt and freshly ground black pepper

about 6 fresh spinach leaves, washed and finely shredded (optional)

½ cup fresh wheat noodles or Chinese egg noodles

Cut the chicken into thin slices, then cut these into fine strips. Heat the oil in a skillet and stir-fry the chicken with the ginger until lightly browned. Add the carrot, bamboo shoots, and scallions. Stir for a few seconds before stirring in the broth.

Bring to a boil, reduce the heat, and cover the pan. Simmer the soup for 30 minutes. Season, add the spinach, if using, and noodles and cook for a further 10 minutes. Taste for seasoning before serving.

Seafood Chowder

SERVES 4

2 tbsp oil

2 leeks, sliced

1 small onion, halved and thinly
   sliced

1 carrot, diced

1 celery stick, diced

1 potato, diced

1 pint fish broth

1 bouquet garni

1 lb cod fillet, skinned

1 pint milk

8 scallops, shelled

½ cup quick-cook macaroni

salt and freshly ground black
   pepper

1¼ cups shelled, cooked mussels

1 cup peeled, cooked shrimp

4 tbsp chopped fresh parsley

freshly grated Parmesan cheese,
   to serve

Heat the oil in a large saucepan. Add the leeks, onion, carrot, celery, and potato. Cook, stirring, until the leeks have reduced and the onion has softened slightly but not browned. Pour in the broth, then bring to a boil. Add the bouquet garni, reduce the heat and cover the pan. Simmer for 20 minutes.

Meanwhile, place the cod in a saucepan and add the milk. Heat gently until the milk is just about to simmer, then poach the fish for 2–3 minutes, until it is barely cooked. Remove the fish from the milk and set it aside on a plate. Poach the scallops in the milk for 2–3 minutes, until just cooked. Set the milk aside.

Flake the cod, discarding any bones, and slice the scallops. Add the macaroni and salt and pepper to the soup, and bring back to a boil. Then, reduce the heat, cover and cook for about 7 minutes, or until the macaroni is just tender. Pour in the poaching milk and heat, stirring all the time.

Taste the soup for seasoning, then add the cooked cod, scallops, mussels, and shrimp. Gently stir in the parsley and heat for 2–3 minutes, or until the seafood is hot. Serve at once, with freshly grated Parmesan cheese.

Pasta Sauces

Crayfish and Tasso in Cream Sauce over Fettuccine

Leek and Turkey Sauce

Chicken in Blue

Spicy Tomato Sauce

Red Bell Pepper and Herb Paste

Pesto

Sun-dried Tomato and Black Olive Sauce

Cardamom Fish Sauce

Quick Tomato Sauce

Almond and Parsley Paste

Lemon Anchovy Butter

Pasta Carbonara

Garlic and Olive Oil Sauce

Pasta with Fresh Tomatoes

Shrimp Butter

Sweet-and-sour Sauce

Greek Yogurt Topping

Bolognese Sauce

Light Cheese Dressing

Clam and Chili Sauce

Ragù

Spring Vegetable and Cream Sauce

Butter and Tomato Sauce

Crayfish and Tasso in Cream Sauce over Fettuccine

SERVES 4-6

This quick-and-easy dish makes a rich, creamy, yet spicy sauce. It's also good made with large shrimp instead of crayfish tails.

3 oz butter

8–10 scallions, chopped

3 garlic cloves, finely chopped

½ cup dry white wine

½ cup fish broth or clam juice

5 oz diced Tasso

1 oz all-purpose flour

8 oz cooked and shelled crayfish tails

2 cups light cream

salt

hot cooked fettuccine, to serve

In a large frying pan, melt the butter. Sauté the scallions and garlic about 2 minutes. Add the wine, ¼ cup fish broth, and the Tasso and cook until bubbly. Reduce the heat and simmer until the liquid is reduced slightly, about 10 minutes.

Dissolve the flour in the remaining ¼ cup fish broth, then add to the sauce and stir until smooth. Stir in the crayfish tails and the light cream. Mix well and heat just until bubbly. Taste and adjust the seasoning. Serve with fettuccine.

COOK'S TIP

Tasso is a richly seasoned piece of pork which is smoked and used to flavor beans, pastas, and eggs.

Spicy Tomato Sauce

This sauce is made hot and spicy by the use of fresh jalapeño chilies. Dried crushed chilies can be substituted; use ¼–½ teaspoon depending on how hot you like it.

FOR THE SAUCE

1½ lb fresh plum tomatoes

3 tbsp virgin olive oil

1–2 garlic cloves, peeled and minced

1–2 jalapeño chilies, seeded and finely chopped

2 tbsp tomato paste

1 tbsp roughly chopped fresh oregano

salt and ground black pepper

TO SERVE

1 lb fresh pasta

freshly grated Romano cheese

Make a small cross in the top of each tomato and place in a large bowl. Cover with boiling water and leave for 2–3 minutes. Drain and peel. Cut into quarters, discard the seeds, then roughly chop the flesh.

Heat the oil in a pan and gently sauté the garlic and chilies for 3 minutes, taking care not to let the garlic or chilies burn. Add the chopped tomatoes and tomato paste blended with 2 tablespoons water. Bring to a boil, reduce the heat, and simmer for 15 minutes or until a sauce consistency is reached. Add the chopped oregano with seasoning to taste and let simmer while you cook the pasta.

Cook the pasta in plenty of boiling salted water for 1–2 minutes or until "al dente." Drain and toss with the sauce. Serve immediately, handing the grated cheese separately.

Pesto

Perhaps one of the best-loved and well-known of all the sauces is used in many other dishes as well as pasta. Originating in the Liguria region of Italy, where the Genoese grow the tiny sweet basil leaves to make their world-famous pesto.

FOR THE SAUCE

2 oz fresh basil leaves

8 tbsp extra virgin olive oil

¼ cup pine nuts

2–3 garlic cloves, peeled

salt

½ cup freshly grated Parmesan cheese

1 tbsp freshly grated Romano cheese

TO SERVE

1 lb fresh pasta

extra grated cheese

fresh basil leaves

Place the fresh basil leaves, extra virgin olive oil, pine nuts, and garlic in a food processor and blend the ingredients together until smooth. Spoon into a bowl and stir in salt to taste and the freshly grated cheeses.

Meanwhile, cook the pasta in plenty of boiling salted water for 1–2 minutes or until "al dente." Drain and toss with the pesto sauce. Serve immediately with extra freshly grated cheese and a few basil leaves to garnish.

Cardamom Fish Sauce

SERVES 4

*L*emon and cilantro pep up plain white fish in this delicious sauce. It is particularly good with spirals or small pieces of pasta, such as squares or cut-up spaghetti; saffron or turmeric pasta is ideal if you are making your own. For a first course, serve half quantities of sauce in small rings of saffron or turmeric noodles.

¼ stick (2 tbsp) butter	¼ cup all-purpose flour
1 small onion, finely chopped	1¼ cups fish broth
1 red bell pepper, seeded and diced	salt and ground black pepper
6 green cardamoms	1½ lb white fish fillet, skinned and cut into chunks
1 bay leaf	1¼ cups light cream
grated zest of 1 lemon	2 tbsp chopped cilantro leaves

Melt the butter in a saucepan. Add the onion, bell pepper, cardamoms, bay leaf, and lemon zest. Press the cardamoms to split them slightly, then cook gently for 20 minutes, until the onion and bell pepper are well cooked. Stir often, so that the bay and spices give up their flavor and the onions do not brown.

Stir in the flour, then gradually pour in the broth, stirring all the time, and bring to a boil. Reduce the heat, if necessary, so that the sauce just simmers – it will be too thick at this stage. Add seasoning and the fish. Stir lightly, then cover the pan and cook gently for 20 minutes, or until the fish is cooked. Gently stir in the cream, then heat through without boiling. Taste for seasoning before serving sprinkled with the cilantro.

Almond and Parsley Paste

SERVES 4

A food processor or blender makes this a simple recipe, but it can be made by hand by first passing the nuts through a mouli grater, which will grind them, then pounding them to a paste with finely chopped parsley and finely grated cheese. Then the oil can be slowly pounded into the mixture. Toss this paste with pasta verde or tomato-flavored pasta to make a delicious, light meal.

8 oz blanched almonds	about a scant cup olive oil
½ cup parsley	3 tbsp snipped chives
4 oz Jarlsberg cheese	salt and ground black pepper

Grind the almonds and parsley together in a food processor (or see left if making by hand) until quite fine. Cut the Jarlsberg cheese into chunks, add these to the nuts, and process the mixture until it begins to bind into a stiff paste. Add a little of the oil, and process to a thick paste; then gradually trickle in the remaining oil as the machine is running.

Stir in the chives and seasoning to taste; then let the paste sit for at least an hour before serving.

Pasta Carbonara

SERVES 4

The pasta must be freshly drained and piping hot when added to this creamy, lightly scrambled egg mixture. Regular cooked ham or finely shredded bacon (though it must be well cooked before the eggs are added) can be used instead of expensive prosciutto. This is a favorite sauce for long pasta, such as spaghetti or tagliatelle.

1 lb pasta

salt and ground black pepper

12 oz prosciutto

8 eggs

⅔ cup light cream

¼ cup butter

3 tbsp finely chopped parsley

Cook the pasta in boiling salted water until just tender.

Meanwhile, trim any excess fat from the ham, and cut it into fine shreds. Beat the eggs with the cream, a little salt, and plenty of pepper.

Melt the butter in a large, heavy-bottomed skillet or saucepan. Add the ham, and cook, stirring, for 3 minutes. Then pour in the egg mixture, and cook over a low heat, stirring all the time, until the eggs are very lightly scrambled, but not setting into lumps.

Drain the pasta, and add it to the pan; then turn it in the sauce for a few seconds. Stir in the parsley, and serve at once.

◀ *Pasta Carbonara*

Pasta with Fresh Tomatoes

SERVES 4

Make this when ripe plum tomatoes are available, or use full-flavored home-grown fruit. Serve with olive bread.

2 tbsp olive oil

¼ cup butter

1 small onion, finely chopped

1 garlic clove, minced

1½ lb plum tomatoes, peeled, seeded, and cut into chunks

1 tsp superfine sugar

salt and ground black pepper

4 tbsp chopped fresh parsley

2 tbsp chopped fresh tarragon or 1 tbsp chopped fresh thyme

3 large sprigs of basil, shredded

Heat the olive oil and butter together in a saucepan. Add the onion and garlic. Cook, stirring, for 15 minutes, or until the onion has softened. Stir in the tomatoes and sugar, and salt and pepper to taste. Cook, stirring, until the tomatoes are hot. Then stir in the parsley and tarragon or thyme. Toss the mixture with freshly cooked pasta; then gently toss in the basil.

Sweet-and-sour Sauce

Sweet-and-sour Sauce is the classic accompaniment for won tons. It is also good with egg noodles, which are cooked, then drained and stir-fried for a few minutes in a little oil and sesame oil, then tossed with the sauce for a flavorsome side dish.

2 tbsp oil

1 tsp sesame oil

1 large onion, roughly chopped

1 large green bell pepper, seeded and cut into large dice

1 large carrot, cut into matchstick strips

6 tbsp tomato ketchup

⅔ cup dry sherry

2 tbsp sugar

4 tbsp cider vinegar

4 tbsp soy sauce

8 oz can pineapple rings in syrup

2 tsp cornstarch

Heat both oils in a saucepan. Add the onion, green bell pepper, and carrot. Stir-fry the vegetables for 5 minutes, until they are lightly cooked, but still crunchy.

Stir in the tomato ketchup, sherry, sugar, vinegar, and soy sauce. Drain the pineapple, and mix a little of the syrup with the cornstarch to make a smooth, thin paste. Add the remaining syrup; then pour this mixture into the sauce.

Bring to a boil, stirring all the time, then reduce the heat, and simmer for 5 minutes. Cut the pineapple rings into chunks, and add them to the sauce. Remove from the heat, and use as required.

Sweet-and-sour Sauce ▶

Bolognese Sauce

This is a favorite sauce for serving with all types of pasta, particularly spaghetti. It is also used in a variety of other dishes, including baked lasagne. The sauce freezes well for at least 3 months.

2 tbsp olive oil

1 large onion, chopped

2 garlic cloves, minced

2 celery stalks, diced

1 green bell pepper, seeded and diced

1 bay leaf

2 cups lean ground beef

2 cups lean ground pork

2 tbsp tomato paste

2 tbsp chopped fresh oregano or marjoram

1 large sprig of thyme

1 tbsp all-purpose flour

salt and ground black pepper

scant 2 cups robust red wine

2 × 14 oz cans chopped tomatoes

2½ cups sliced small button or crimini mushrooms

Heat the oil in a heavy-bottomed saucepan or flameproof casserole. Add the onion, garlic, celery, green bell pepper, and bay leaf. Stir well, then cover, and cook for 15 minutes.

Stir in the ground beef and pork, and cook, stirring, for 5 minutes. Add the tomato paste, oregano or marjoram, thyme, and flour. Stir well, then season well, and pour in the wine and tomatoes. Bring to a boil, stirring occasionally, then lightly mix in the mushrooms, and reduce the heat so that the sauce just simmers. Cover and cook for 1 hour, or until the meat is tender.

Remove the lid, and simmer for a further 30 minutes, until the liquid has reduced slightly, and the sauce is full-flavored. Taste for seasoning before serving.

Clam and Chili Sauce

When cooking clams use the same rule as for mussels. Discard those that are open before cooking and those that remain closed after cooking.

FOR THE SAUCE

2 lb fresh clams

4 tbsp olive oil

1 garlic clove, peeled and minced

2 shallots, peeled and chopped

1 jalepeño chili, seeded and finely chopped

1¼ cups dry white wine

salt and ground black pepper

4 tbsp light whipping cream (optional)

TO SERVE

1 lb fresh pasta

2 tbsp chopped fresh flat leaf parsley

Scrub the clam shells and soak in cold water at least 30 minutes, discarding any that remain open. (If you tap an open clam before cooking and it closes, you can use it.) Drain the clams just before using. Heat the oil in a large pan and gently sauté the garlic, shallots, and chili for 5 minutes or until softened. Add the wine and simmer gently for 5 minutes.

Add the drained clams, cover with a lid, and steam for 5 minutes or until all the clams have opened. Carefully shake the pan occasionally until the clams have opened. Discard any that remain closed. Remove from the heat and stir in the seasoning and cream.

Meanwhile, cook the pasta in plenty of boiling salted water for 1–2 minutes or until cooked to almost "al dente." Drain the pasta thoroughly and reserve.

Add the pasta to the clam pan and place over a medium heat. Continue to cook for 1–2 minutes or until the pasta has finished cooking. Remove from the heat and add the parsley. Stir and serve immediately.

Spring Vegetable and Cream Sauce

MAKES 2 CUPS

You can generally buy most vegetables all year round. However, when home-grown produce first comes into the stores or the new baby vegetables first appear, make the most of them in this sauce.

FOR THE SAUCE

3 oz young asparagus, trimmed

3 oz new or baby carrots, trimmed

½ cup shelled fava beans

½ cup snow peas

4 tbsp unsalted butter

2 shallots, peeled and chopped

¾ cup diced zucchini

scant cup heavy whipping cream

salt and ground black pepper

4 tbsp freshly grated Parmigiano Reggiano cheese

TO SERVE

1 lb fresh pasta

sprig of opal basil, to garnish

Cut the asparagus into short lengths. Blanch in lightly salted boiling water for 2 minutes. Drain and refresh in cold water, then drain again.

Slice long carrots or cut baby carrots in half. Cook in lightly salted boiling water for 2–3 minutes or until almost tender. Drain and refresh in cold water, then drain again. Blanch the fava beans for 3 minutes and the snow peas for 1 minute. Refresh in cold water and drain.

Melt the unsalted butter in a large pan and gently sauté the shallots for 5 minutes. Add the zucchini and sauté for a further 1 minute. Add all the drained, refreshed vegetables and the heavy whipping cream and cook gently, stirring, for about 5-8 minutes or until the cream has reduced slightly.

Melt the unsalted butter in a large pan and gently sauté the shallots for 5 minutes. Add the zucchini and sauté for a further 1 minute. Add all the drained, refreshed vegetables and the heavy whipping cream and cook gently, stirring, for about 5-8 minutes or until the cream has reduced slightly.

Leek and Turkey Sauce

SERVES 4

Boneless turkey breast fillets are versatile and inexpensive when combined with bulky vegetables and pasta. This is a sauce to serve with any type of pasta or it can be used in baked dishes or with lasagne.

12 oz boneless turkey breast fillet, skinned and diced

4 tbsp all-purpose flour

salt and ground black pepper

2 tbsp oil

1 lb leeks, sliced

2 tbsp chopped sage

1¼ cups dry cider

1¼ cups turkey or chicken broth

2 tbsp freshly grated Parmesan cheese

2 oz mozzarella cheese, chopped

⅔ cup strained plain yogurt

a little paprika

Coat the turkey with the flour and plenty of seasoning. Heat the oil in a large saucepan. Add the turkey and cook, stirring often, until lightly browned. Add the leeks and sage, stir well, then cover the pan and cook for 15 minutes, stirring once or twice, until the leeks are greatly reduced in volume.

Stir in the cider and broth, then bring to a boil, stirring, and reduce the heat. Cover and simmer for 15 minutes, until the leeks are cooked. Stir in the Parmesan and mozzarella, and taste for seasoning. When the cheeses have melted, stir in the yogurt and remove the pan from the heat. Serve at once, poured over pasta or tossed with it. Dust with a little paprika.

Chicken in Blue

SERVES 4

*B*lue cheese makes a rich sauce for chicken or turkey. Serve large quantities of plain fresh pasta noodles to balance the full flavor of the sauce. The recipe uses Danish blue but any other blue cheese may be substituted – dolcelatte, for example, or tangy Gorgonzola for a really powerful flavor.

2 tbsp olive oil

1 garlic clove, minced

1 red bell pepper, seeded and diced

1 lb boneless chicken, skinned and diced

salt and ground black pepper

8 oz small button mushrooms

4 tbsp dry white wine

⅔ cup light cream

8 oz Danish blue cheese, cut into small pieces

2 scallions, finely chopped

2 tbsp chopped fresh parsley

Heat the oil in a large skillet. Add the garlic, red bell pepper, and chicken with some seasoning – go easy on the salt at this stage as the blue cheese can make the sauce quite salty. Cook, stirring often, for about 20 minutes, or until the diced chicken is lightly browned and cooked.

Add the mushrooms and cook for 2 minutes, then pour in the wine and bring to a boil. Turn the heat to the lowest setting and make sure the mixture has stopped boiling before pouring in the cream and stirring in the cheese. Stir over low heat until the cheese has melted. Do not allow the sauce to simmer or it will curdle.

When the cheese has melted, taste the sauce, then pour it over the pasta and sprinkle with the scallions and parsley. Serve at once.

Red Bell Pepper and Herb Paste

MAKES ABOUT 1¼ CUPS

A light, slightly tangy and mild cheese makes the ideal base for this paste of sweet red bell peppers and fresh, summery herbs. This is good with hot pasta, and also makes a tasty dressing for cold pasta – an ideal way of using up leftovers. Simply serve the pasta on a base of salad greens; and top with the paste.

2 garlic cloves, peeled

2 large red bell peppers

4 oz New York State Cheddar or
    similar crumbly cheese

½ cup olive oil

salt and ground black pepper

4 tbsp finely chopped parsley

4 tbsp snipped chives

1 tbsp chopped fresh tarragon

🔴 Blanch the garlic cloves in boiling water for 2 minutes; then drain. Skewer one of the bell peppers on a large metal fork, and rotate it over a gas flame until the skin is charred. Then rub off the skin under cold water. Repeat with the second bell pepper. Alternatively, char both peppers under a hot broiler, turning them until the skin is blistered on all sides.

🔴 Seed and cut up the bell peppers; then purée them in a food processor or blender with the garlic, cheese, and a little of the olive oil. Gradually pour in the remaining oil while the machine is running to make a smooth paste. Stir in salt and pepper to taste, the parsley, chives, and tarragon, and serve.

Sun-dried Tomato and Black Olive Sauce

MAKES 1 CUP

This is a robust sauce and is ideally suited to the thicker ribbons of pasta, such as tagliatelle, or shapes such as penne or garganelli.

FOR THE SAUCE

2 tbsp olive oil

8 sun-dried tomatoes in oil, finely chopped

1 medium onion, peeled and finely chopped

2 garlic cloves, peeled and minced

2 celery stalks, trimmed and finely chopped

2 oz pancetta, chopped

½ cup pitted and chopped black olives

1 tbsp tomato paste

1¼ cups vegetable broth

few sprigs of marjoram

salt and ground black pepper

TO SERVE

1 lb fresh pasta

fresh basil leaves

freshly grated Parmesan cheese

Heat the olive oil and 1 tablespoon of the sun-dried tomato oil in a pan and sauté the onion, sun-dried tomatoes, garlic, celery, and pancetta for 5 minutes. Stir in half of the olives.

Blend the tomato paste with a little of the broth, then stir into the pan with the remaining broth and the marjoram. Bring to a boil and simmer for 10 minutes. Cool, then pass through a food processor and return to the pan. Add seasoning to taste with the remaining olives. Cover with a lid and remove from the heat.

Meanwhile, cook the pasta in plenty of boiling salted water for 1–2 minutes or until "al dente." Drain well, then add the tomato sauce and toss lightly. Serve immediately, scattered with basil leaves and Parmesan cheese.

Quick Tomato Sauce

MAKES 1 CUP

This sauce is ideal when time is critical and you are relying on pantry ingredients. It is also an excellent sauce to use for filled pasta as well as layered dishes.

FOR THE SAUCE

2 tbsp olive oil

1 large onion, peeled and grated

14 oz can chopped tomatoes

salt and ground black pepper

few dashes hot pepper sauce

TO SERVE

1 lb fresh pasta

freshly shaved Parmesan cheese

Heat the oil in a large pan and sauté the onion for 5 minutes. Add the contents of the can of tomatoes and sauté gently for 10 minutes. Add seasoning and hot pepper sauce to taste, cover with a lid, and remove from the heat.

Meanwhile, cook the pasta in plenty of boiling water for 1–2 minutes or until "al dente." Drain thoroughly, then return to the pan. Add the tomato sauce to the cooked pasta. Heat through for 2 minutes, tossing lightly, then serve immediately, sprinkled with shavings of fresh Parmesan cheese.

Lemon Anchovy Butter

SERVES 4

oss this butter with freshly cooked pasta, and serve with lemon wedges so that diners can add a little juice to their pasta if liked. The butter is especially well suited to serving with black squid ink pasta, but other fresh pasta also tastes superb served this way.

Pound, mash or process the anchovies with the oil from the can to make a smooth paste. Mix in the garlic and lemon. Soften the butter; then gradually beat in the anchovy mixture. Add ground black pepper and Worcestershire sauce to taste. Finally, mix in the parsley.

2 oz can anchovy fillets in olive oil

1–2 garlic cloves, minced and chopped

grated zest of 1 lemon

½ cup unsalted or lightly salted butter

ground black pepper

dash of Worcestershire sauce

4 tbsp chopped fresh parsley

Garlic and Olive Oil Sauce

MAKES ²/₃ CUP

One of the simplest of sauces yet one of the most delicious. As with good wines, the better the olive oil used the better the taste, so don't skimp on the quality of the oil.

FOR THE SAUCE

2–4 garlic cloves, peeled

6–8 tbsp extra virgin olive oil

salt and ground black pepper

1 tbsp roughly chopped fresh
   flat leaf parsley

TO SERVE

1 lb fresh pasta

Finely chop the garlic. Place in a pan with the oil and sauté gently for 5 minutes. Add seasoning to taste with the parsley, cover the pan with a lid, and remove from the heat.

Meanwhile, cook the pasta in plenty of boiling salted water for 1–2 minutes or until "al dente." Drain and add the garlic sauce. Toss lightly, then serve immediately.

Shrimp Butter

SERVES 4

Toss this with freshly cooked pasta to make a delicious supper dish. Spaghetti, mafaldine, tagliatelle, small to medium pasta shells, or any long or small pasta shapes are good with this butter coating them.

¾ cup unsalted butter

1 small onion, very finely chopped

½ tsp ground mace

1¾ cups peeled, cooked, finely chopped shrimp

3 tbsp chopped fresh dill

salt and ground black pepper

Melt a quarter of the butter in a small saucepan. Add the onion, and cook gently for about 20 minutes, or until it is well cooked and softened, but not browned. Stir in the mace and cook for 1 minute; then remove the pan from the heat.

Mix the cooked onion with the remaining butter. If most of the butter is quite soft, then let the onion mixture cool; if not, it will soften the bulk of the butter ready for mixing in the shrimp. Beat in the shrimp; then add the dill and seasoning to taste.

LITTLE PASTA COCKTAILS

Toss freshly cooked soup pasta with Shrimp Butter; then serve in shell dishes on a base of finely shredded lettuce and cucumber cut into matchstick strips. Garnish with whole, cooked shrimp, lemon wedges (so that guests may squeeze a little juice over their cocktails if liked), and sprigs of dill.

Greek Yogurt Topping

SERVES 4

This is good with garlic-flavored pasta or dough that is seasoned with spices. It is important to use a mild salad onion as a regular onion is too overpowering for this topping.

2-inch length of English cucumber, peeled and finely diced

salt and ground black pepper

1 red or white onion, finely chopped

4 tbsp chopped parsley

2 tbsp chopped fresh tarragon or cilantro leaves

4 firm, ripe tomatoes, peeled, seeded, and diced

2 tbsp chopped capers

2 bottled or canned mild green chilies, chopped

2 cups strained plain yogurt

Put the diced cucumber in a strainer over a bowl. Sprinkle generously with salt, and let sit for 30 minutes. Pat the cucumber thoroughly on doubled pieces of paper towel.

Mix the onion, parsley, tarragon or cilantro, cucumber, tomatoes, capers, and chilies. Then stir in the yogurt and taste for seasoning, adding ground black pepper as required, but the cucumber should contribute sufficient salt. Serve within about 30 minutes of mixing.

Light Cheese Dressing

SERVES 4

This makes a delicious summer supper or lunch. Offer a green salad as an accompaniment. Cut up some crusty Italian bread to mop every last bit of the dressing from the bowls!

1 large garlic clove, finely chopped

1 tbsp olive oil

2 scallions, finely chopped

8 green olives, pitted and chopped

1 cup ricotta cheese

⅔ cup fromage frais

4 large sprigs of basil, finely shredded

salt and ground black pepper

freshly grated nutmeg

● Put the garlic and olive oil in a small saucepan, and heat gently until the garlic is just beginning to sizzle. Cook for 2 minutes, without overheating the oil to the point when the garlic would brown (the aim is to take the raw taste off the garlic, not cook it thoroughly). Remove the pan from the heat, and let cool slightly.

● Scrape the garlic and oil into a bowl. Stir in the scallions, olives, ricotta, fromage frais, and basil. Add salt, pepper, and nutmeg to taste.

Ricotta and Truffle Paste Topping

White truffle paste is superb with ricotta cheese. Mix about 2 tablespoons of the paste into 1 cup cheese.

Ragù

This sauce is native to the Italian city of Bologna. There, every family has its own recipe, which has been passed down through the generations.

FOR THE SAUCE

2 tbsp olive oil

2–4 garlic cloves, peeled and minced

1 onion, peeled and finely chopped

2 celery stalks, trimmed and finely chopped

1 large carrot, peeled and diced

12 oz lean ground beef

1 cup dry white wine

14 oz can chopped tomatoes

1 tbsp tomato paste

salt and ground black pepper

1 tbsp chopped fresh oregano

TO SERVE

1 lb fresh pasta

freshly grated Parmesan cheese

Heat the olive oil in a large pan and sauté the garlic, onion, celery stalks, and diced carrot for 5–8 minutes or until softened but not browned. Add the beef and continue to sauté for 5 minutes or until sealed, stirring frequently to break up any lumps.

Add the wine and the contents of the can of tomatoes. Blend the tomato paste with 2 tablespoons water and stir into the pan. Bring to a boil, cover with a lid, then simmer for 20 minutes or until a thick consistency is reached. Add seasoning to taste with the chopped oregano, cover with a lid, and remove from the heat. Reserve.

Meanwhile, cook the pasta in plenty of boiling salted water for 1–2 minutes or until "al dente." Drain thoroughly and return to the pan. Add the sauce and toss lightly. Either stir in the grated Parmesan cheese or pass the cheese separately. Serve immediately.

Butter and Tomato Sauce

MAKES 2 CUPS

Always use unsalted butter when cooking, as it imparts a far better flavor. You can also control the salt content far better.

FOR THE SAUCE

1½ lb ripe beefsteak tomatoes, peeled

6 tbsp unsalted butter

6 shallots, peeled and finely chopped

3 tbsp fresh basil leaves

salt and ground black pepper

TO SERVE

1 lb fresh pasta

basil leaves

freshly grated Parmigiano Reggiano cheese

Seed and dice the tomatoes. Melt the butter in a large pan and gently sauté the shallots for 5 minutes or until softened but not browned. Add the tomatoes and continue to sauté gently for 5–8 minutes or until the tomatoes have begun to break down. Stir in the basil leaves with seasoning to taste. Cover with a lid and remove from the heat.

Meanwhile, cook the pasta in plenty of boiling salted water for 1–2 minutes or until "al dente." Drain thoroughly and add to the tomato sauce. Toss lightly and serve immediately, garnished with extra basil leaves. Hand some freshly grated Parmigiano Reggiano cheese separately.

Pasta Salads

Avocado with Lime-dressed Pasta

Warm Pasta Salad

Pasta Platter

Pasta Salad and Fresh Dates

Pasta and Waldorf Salad

Farfalle and Mixed Vegetable Medley

Ravioli Salad

Coronation Turkey Pasta

Salad of Smoked Haddock with
Lemon-dressed Tagliatelle

Pasta Niçoise with Balsamic Dressing

Pasta and Yogurt Salad

Pasta Salad with Bacon and Pesto

Salami and Pasta Salads

Farfalle with Marinated Bell Peppers

Melon Smoked Chicken and Pasta Salad

Minty Crab, Pear and Pasta Salad

Smoked Salmon, Pasta and Raspberry Salad

Spicy Chicken and Pasta Salad

Fig Pasta and Proscuitto Salad

Winter Salad

Pasta with Tomato Tapenade

Salad of Pasta and Roasted Peppers

Wild Mushroom and Pasta Salad

Black-eyed Pea and Pasta Salad
with Zesty Dressing

Pasta and Duck Salad

Avocado with Lime-dressed Pasta

An attractive and palate-refreshing pasta salad goes well with creamy avocado. Serve warmed plain crackers or Melba toast as a crunchy accompaniment.

¾ cup soup pasta

salt and ground black pepper

grated zest and juice of 1 lime

½ tsp superfine sugar

4 tbsp olive oil

4 black olives, sliced

1 scallion, finely chopped

½ cup chopped Romano cheese

3 sprigs of basil, shredded

2 ripe avocados

sprigs of basil and lime slices, to garnish

Cook the pasta in boiling salted water for 5–10 minutes, or according to the instructions on the package, until tender. Drain well, and set aside to cool.

Whisk the lime rind and juice with the superfine sugar, and salt and pepper to taste. When the sugar has dissolved, whisk in the oil. Add the olives, scallion, Romano, and basil. Mix the pasta with the other ingredients until well coated in dressing.

Halve the avocados, remove their pits, and place in dishes. Fill with the pasta mixture, and garnish with sprigs of basil and lime slices. Serve at once.

Pasta Platter

A pasta hors-d'oeuvre, this is an attractive first course that allows diners to opt for a light or satisfying starter, and it is easy to prepare ahead. Add to the ingredients according to your taste and pocket, and increasing the amount turns this dish into an ample meal.

8 oz novelty pasta shapes or flavored pasta or one or two types (for example, try pasta flavored with porcini or tri-colored pasta)

salt and ground black pepper

6 tbsp pesto

1¼ cups sour cream

4 tbsp snipped chives

8 quails' eggs

8 oz mozzarella cheese, sliced

1 cup chopped or finely crumbled Romano cheese

8 oz salami (include a couple of different types)

8 oz tomatoes, peeled and slcied

1 red onion, halved and thinly sliced

1 cup black olives

good-quality virgin olive oil

warmed, fresh Italian bread, to serve

ALTERNATIVE OR ADDITIONAL INGREDIENTS

Canned or bottled artichoke hearts
Dress them with olive oil and a squeeze of lemon juice, adding some chopped fresh marjoram if liked.

Fennel or green beans
Cut the fennel into fine slices, or, if using beans, leave them whole. Blanch whichever vegetable you have chosen in boiling water for 1 minute. Drain and toss with a little lemon juice.

Garbanzo beans
Drain canned garbanzo beans, and mix them with chopped parsley, finely chopped garlic, and some olive oil.

Cook the pasta in boiling salted water for about 15 minutes, or according to the instructions on the package, until tender. Drain well, and rinse under cold water. Let drain.

Put the pesto into a small bowl. Mix the sour cream and chives in another bowl.

Place the quails' eggs in a saucepan, and add cold water to cover. Bring to a boil; then cook for 3 minutes. Drain, rinse under cold water, and remove the shells.

Arrange these and all the remaining ingredients, except the oil, on a huge platter, overlapping the slices of mozzarella, piling up the Romano, folding or overlapping the tomato slices. Sprinkle the onion in a small mound. Put the olives into a small bowl. Place the olive oil and a pepper mill on the table.

Diners help themselves to pasta, and dress it to taste with a little pesto or sour cream with chives, or trickle olive oil over. The other ingredients are eaten with the pasta. Plenty of warmed, fresh Italian bread is an essential accompaniment.

Pasta with Waldorf Salad

This recipe is based on the famous Waldorf salad, and every serious cook has their own interpretation. Try this salad as it gives an exciting new twist to the original recipe.

FOR THE SALAD

2 red apples, rinsed, cored, and thinly sliced

2 ripe pears, peeled, cored, and sliced

juice of 1 lemon

4 celery stalks, trimmed and sliced

½ cup pecan halves

8 oz fresh pasta, such as tri-colored brandelle

1 small head romaine lettuce

freshly shaved Romano cheese

FOR THE DRESSING

3 tbsp reduced calorie mayonnaise

2 tbsp yogurt

1–2 tsp medium hot curry powder

Place the apples and pears in a bowl, pour over the lemon juice, and toss lightly. Add the sliced celery and pecan halves, and mix lightly.

Cook the pasta in plenty of boiling salted water for 1–2 minutes or until "al dente." Drain and add to the celery.

Blend together the mayonnaise, yogurt, and curry powder to taste, reserve. Rinse the lettuce and use to line a salad bowl. Pile the prepared salad into the center and drizzle over the dressing. Sprinkle with the freshly shaved Romano cheese.

Pasta with Waldorf Salad ▶

Ravioli Salad

For this dish you do need good quality fresh flat leaf parsley, as the sprigs of parsley are encased in the pasta then cooked and tossed in a herb vinaigrette.

FOR THE SALAD

8 oz Pasta Dough (page 9)

small bunch flat leaf parsley, rinsed

2 oz can anchovy fillets, drained (and soaked, optional)

2 tbsp capers (soaked if preferred)

4 hard-cooked eggs, shelled and sliced

FOR THE DRESSING

6 tbsp extra virgin olive oil

2 garlic cloves, peeled and minced

2 shallots, peeled and finely chopped

1 tbsp chopped fresh flat leaf parsley

1 tbsp chopped fresh basil

salt and ground black pepper

1 tbsp balsamic vinegar

Using your pasta machine, roll out the pasta dough to form strips about 5 inches wide. Place sprigs of the flat leaf parsley on half the dough, dampen edges, and fold over the other half of the pasta.

Using a square fluted cutter, cut out squares ensuring that each square contains a sprig of parsley. Sprinkle with a little flour and let dry for about 1 hour.

For the salad dressing, heat the oil in a pan, and gently fry the garlic and shallots for 5 minutes or until softened. Remove the pan from the heat and stir in the herbs, seasoning, and vinegar. Cover and reserve.

Cook the ravioli squares in plenty of boiling salted water until "al dente." Drain and return to the pan. Pour over the prepared dressing and toss lightly. Arrange the ravioli in a warmed serving bowl. Top with the anchovy fillets, capers, and sliced hard-cooked eggs, then serve.

Salad of Smoked Haddock with Lemon-dressed Tagliatelle

SERVES 4

strong, lemony dressing matches the robust flavor of the smoked fish.

1½ lb smoked haddock

grated zest and juice of 2 lemons

12 oz fresh tagliatelle verde

salt and ground black pepper

1¼ cups sour cream

1 tsp Dijon mustard or other mild mustard

4 tbsp chopped fresh parsley

2 tbsp chopped fresh dill

8 oz fresh, thin green beans, cut in half or shorter lengths

1 red bell pepper, seeded, quartered, and cut crosswise into thin slices

Place the fish on a heatproof plate that fits over a large saucepan. Bring some water to a boil in the saucepan, sprinkle the fish with the lemon juice, and cover tightly with foil. Cook over the boiling water for 15 minutes, or until just cooked; then remove from the pan and let cool, covered. You may have to do this in two batches if you do not have a sufficiently large plate.

Cook the tagliatelle in boiling salted water for about 3 minutes, or until tender. Drain well, and rinse under cold water; then drain again.

Mix the lemon zest with the sour cream, mustard, parsley, and dill. Add salt and pepper to taste; then toss this lemon dressing with the pasta. Transfer to a serving bowl or individual plates or dishes.

Add the green beans to a saucepan of boiling salted water. Bring back to a boil, and cook for 1 minute. Add the red bell pepper, and boil for a further 30–60 seconds; then drain well.

Flake the smoked haddock flesh off the skin in fairly large pieces, discarding any stray bones as you do so. Lightly mix the fish with the beans and bell pepper, taking care not to break up the flakes. Serve the fish mixture on the pasta base, so that it may be tossed with the pasta before being eaten.

Pasta Salad with Bacon and Pesto

SERVES 4

8 oz short pasta spirals

salt and ground black pepper

2 large oranges

8 oz baby spinach leaves, washed and shredded

4 scallions, finely chopped

1 bunch of watercress, leaves only

6 arugula leaves, shredded

4 large sprigs of parsley, roughly chopped

3 cups diced, rindless bacon

6 tbsp pesto

Cook the pasta in boiling salted water for about 15 minutes, or according to the instructions on the package, until just tender. Drain, and rinse briefly under cold water; then leave to drain completely.

Cut the top and bottom off each orange. Then sit the orange on a board, and cut off all the peel and pith, working down the side in overlapping strips. Holding the orange over a bowl to catch the juices, use a serrated knife to cut between the membranes dividing the sections, removing each section of orange.

Mix the spinach, scallions, watercress, arugula, and parsley. Place this salad base in a bowl or on plates.

Dry-fry the bacon, stirring occasionally, until the pieces have browned, and are crisp. Drain on paper towels.

Toss the orange and bacon with the pasta, and add pepper to taste; then pile it on top of the salad leaf base. Top with pesto, and serve (the pesto is mixed with the pasta and leaves, as the salad is eaten, to act as a dressing).

Farfalle with Marinated Bell Peppers

SERVES 4

Skinning the peppers before marinating ensures that the peppers quickly absorb the flavor of the marinade. The peppers are far easier to digest once skinned and the flesh is sweeter too.

FOR THE SALAD

2 red bell peppers, seeded

2 yellow bell peppers, seeded

2 green bell peppers, seeded

6 tbsp olive oil

1–2 garlic cloves, peeled and minced

1 jalapeño chili, seeded and finely chopped

2 tbsp lemon juice

grated zest of ½ lemon

1 tbsp chopped fresh basil

2 slices thick white bread

TO SERVE

8 oz fresh pasta, such as farfalle

salad greens

freshly shaved Parmesan cheese

extra grated lemon zest

Preheat a broiler to high and line the broiler rack with foil, or use a barbecue. Cut the peppers into quarters and place skin side up on the broiler rack. Broil for 10 minutes or until skins have blistered and blackened. Remove from the heat and place in a plastic bag and leave until cool.

Once cool, skin the peppers and slice thinly. Place the peppers in a shallow dish and pour over the oil. Sprinkle with the minced garlic, chili, lemon juice and zest, and basil. Cover and leave in the refrigerator for at least 2 hours, turning occasionally.

Cut the bread into cubes. Drain the peppers and reserve both peppers and marinade. Heat 3 tablespoons of the marinade in a skillet and fry the bread cubes until golden, stirring frequently. Drain on paper towels; reserve.

Cook the pasta in plenty of boiling salted water for 1–2 minutes or until "al dente." Drain and return to the pan. Mix the marinated peppers with the cooked pasta.

Arrange the salad greens in a serving bowl. Pile the pepper and pasta mix on top of the salad greens. Pour over the marinade and scatter over the croûtons. Serve with freshly shaved Parmesan cheese and grated lemon zest.

Minty Crab, Pear, and Pasta Salad

SERVES 4

I found the dressing used in this recipe while looking through an old cookbook. I have updated it by using a flavored vinegar and oil, and I am sure that once you have tried this recipe it will quickly become a firm favorite.

FOR THE SALAD

8 oz cooked fresh pasta, such as tri-colored spaghetti

7 oz white crab meat, flaked

2 oranges, peeled and cut into sections

2 pink grapefruit, peeled and cut into sections

2 tbsp chopped fresh mint

½ cup pecan halves

FOR THE DRESSING

2 ripe pears

½ cup walnut oil

4 tbsp extra virgin olive oil

1 tbsp orange or raspberry vinegar

salt and ground black pepper

Place the cooked pasta in a bowl and add the flaked crab meat, orange and grapefruit sections, chopped mint, and pecan halves. Toss lightly and spoon into a serving bowl.

For the dressing, peel and core the pears, then place in a food processor. Gradually blend the pears with the walnut oil and then the olive oil. Add the vinegar with seasoning and blend for 30 seconds or until smooth. Pour over the salad, toss lightly, and serve.

Spicy Chicken and Pasta Salad

SERVES 4

8 green cardamom pods

1 tbsp ground coriander

1 tsp ground turmeric

1 tbsp grated fresh ginger

½ onion, grated

2 garlic cloves, minced

2 tbsp oil

grated zest and juice of 1 lemon

salt and ground black pepper

3 boneless chicken breasts, skinned

8 oz pasta spirals or twists

⅔ cup mayonnaise

⅔ cup ricotta cheese

4 scallions, chopped

1 large ripe, but firm, mango

½ head of chicory

1 green bell pepper, seeded, quartered, and cut across into very fine slices

a little chopped fresh cilantro

Preheat the oven to 400°F.

Split the cardamom pods over a mortar; then carefully scrape out the tiny black seeds from inside. Crush the seeds to a powder; then mix with the coriander, turmeric, ginger, onion, and garlic. Heat the oil in a small saucepan. Add the spice paste, and cook, stirring, for 5 minutes. Remove the pan from the heat, and add the lemon zest and juice. Season well.

Place the chicken in an ovenproof dish, and spread with the spice paste. Cover, and bake in the preheated oven for 30–40 minutes, until cooked through. Let cool, covered, in the dish.

Cook the pasta in plenty of boiling salted water for about 15 minutes, or according to the instructions on the package. Drain, and rinse under cold water.

Mix together the mayonnaise, ricotta, and scallions. Dice the chicken, and add it to the dressing with all the cooking juices and spice paste. Mix well, and taste for seasoning. Peel the mango, and cut the flesh off the pit in large slices. Then slice these across into small pieces. Shred the chicory, and toss it with the bell pepper; then place on a serving platter or in a large salad bowl.

Mix the pasta with the chicken until thoroughly combined. Add the mango to the pasta, and mix it in very lightly; then pile the salad on the bed of chicory. Sprinkle with a little chopped fresh cilantro, and serve at once.

Winter Salad

SERVES 4-6

8 oz elbows or ditali or small gnocchi

salt and ground black pepper

1¾ cups diced carrots

¾ cup diced rutabaga

2 celery stalks, sliced

1 leek, sliced

1 cup frozen peas

4 oz cauliflower, divided into small florets

1¼ cups shredded white cabbage

1 small onion, finely chopped

1¼ cups mayonnaise

4 tbsp plain yogurt

Cook the pasta in plenty of boiling salted water for about 15 minutes, or according to the instructions on the package, until tender. Drain, and rinse under cold water. Let drain.

Bring a large saucepan of water to a boil. Add the carrots, and boil for 1 minute; then add the rutabaga, and continue to boil for 2 minutes. Next add the celery, and cook for 2 minutes; then add the leek, frozen peas, and cauliflower. Bring back to a boil, and cook for a further 2 minutes. By this time all the vegetables should be tender, and none should be too soft. Drain the cooked vegetables, and rinse them under cold water to prevent further softening; then drain well.

Mix the cabbage, onion, and pasta in a large bowl. Add the mayonnaise, yogurt, and salt and pepper to taste. Toss the ingredients well until thoroughly combined; then lightly mix in the cooked vegetables.

Salad of Pasta with Roasted Bell Peppers

SERVES 4

*F*usilli col buco (long spirals) are good in this dish, but short spirals or twists can be substituted. Long pasta, such as spaghetti, is not suitable.

8 oz fusilli col buco

salt and ground black pepper

2 red bell peppers

2 green bell peppers

2 yellow bell peppers

1 red or white salad onion, thinly sliced

4–6 large sprigs of basil, shredded

3 tbsp balsamic vinegar

1 tsp superfine sugar

1 tsp mild, wholegrain mustard

1 tbsp chopped fresh marjoram

2 tbsp walnut oil

½ cup good virgin olive oil

Cook the pasta in boiling salted water for about 15 minutes, or according to the instructions on the package, until tender. Drain, and rinse under cold water; then let drain.

Peel the bell peppers by charring them individually over a gas flame, or place them all under a very hot broiler. When the outside is blistered and blackened, rinse under cold water, and rub off the skin.

Cut out the stalk and core of the peppers from the top; then carefully remove any remaining seeds from inside. Rinse out, and dry the peppers on paper towels. Slice the peppers; then layer them in a wide, shallow dish, with the pasta, onion, and basil (it is a good idea to start with a thin layer of peppers, then add half the pasta, then most of the remaining peppers, reserving a few rings to go on top of the last layer of pasta, but it is not essential to follow this pattern).

Whisk the balsamic vinegar with plenty of salt and pepper, the sugar, mustard, and marjoram until the sugar has dissolved. Then whisk in the walnut and olive oils. Trickle the dressing over the salad, cover, and let sit for 1–2 hours before serving.

Black-eyed Pea and Pasta Salad with Zesty Dressing

SERVES 4

FOR THE DRESSING

¼ cup olive oil

2 tbsp tarragon, malt, or balsamic vinegar

1 tbsp Dijon-style mustard

¾ tsp minced garlic

¼ tsp ground cumin

½ tsp sugar

½ tsp salt

½ tsp finely grated orange zest

dash of hot pepper sauce

FOR THE SALAD

8 oz macaroni, pasta twists, or tortellini, cooked "al dente" and rinsed immediately under cold running water

15 oz can black-eyed peas, rinsed and drained

1 medium tomato, seeded and diced

⅔ cup ripe black or green olives, sliced (optional)

⅔ cup chopped red bell pepper

⅔ cup chopped green bell pepper

5 oz jicama or water chestnuts, diced

½ cup sliced scallions

¼ cup chopped fresh cilantro

This Creole salad tastes great with any jerked dish and can be be made up to a day ahead.

In a blender, food processor, or bowl, combine the oil, vinegar, mustard, garlic, cumin, sugar, salt, orange zest, and hot pepper sauce. Blend until smooth.

Place the pasta, black-eyed peas, tomato, olives, peppers, jicama or water chestnuts, scallions, and cilantro in a large serving bowl. Add the dressing and toss gently to mix and coat. Cover and chill.

Warm Pasta Salad

SERVES 4

This salad combines the saltiness of green olives, the crunch of walnuts, and the goodness of fresh vegetables. Use fresh grated Parmesan cheese, not the packaged kind; you'll notice a big difference in flavor. The flavors are enhanced when this salad is served warm, but if you have cold leftovers, add a splash of vinaigrette for flavor.

8 oz pasta shapes

4 oz asparagus

4 tbsp extra virgin olive oil

4 tbsp freshly grated Parmesan cheese plus extra for sprinkling

1 zucchini, finely shredded

4 scallions, sliced

1 oz walnuts, chopped

8 green olives, pitted

salt and ground black pepper

Cook pasta according to directions on package. While the pasta is cooking, blanch the aspsragus for 2–3 minutes in boiling water. Drain asparagus, and cut into 1-inch pieces.

When the pasta is cooked, drain but do not rinse, then put it in a large mixing bowl. Pour olive oil over pasta, and toss with two forks. Add the Parmesan, and toss again. Stir in the asparagus, zucchini, scallions, walnuts, and green olives. Add salt and pepper to taste. Serve with a sprinkling of Parmesan over the top.

Pasta Salad with Fresh Dates

SERVES 4

8 oz pasta shapes (such as porcini-flavored mushroom shapes, penne, or rigatoni)

salt and ground black pepper

4 celery stalks, sliced

4 tbsp pine nuts

½ cup roughly chopped walnuts or pecan nuts

8 oz fresh dates, pitted and sliced

1 bunch of watercress, leaves only

4 tbsp chopped fresh parsley

1 tbsp chopped fresh mint

handful of fresh basil leaves, shredded

3 tbsp balsamic vinegar

1 garlic clove, minced

1 tbsp walnut oil

½ cup olive oil

Cook the pasta in boiling salted water for about 15 minutes, or according to the instructions on the package, until tender.

Blanch the celery in boiling salted water for 1 minute; then drain well.

Dry-roast the pine nuts in a small, heavy-bottomed saucepan over a low to medium heat, and shake it often or stir, so that they have browned lightly and evenly.

Mix the walnuts or pecans, pine nuts, dates, watercress, parsley, mint, and basil in a large bowl.

Whisk the balsamic vinegar, garlic, and salt and pepper to taste in a bowl; then slowly whisk in the walnut and olive oils. Pour the dressing over the nut and date mixture.

Drain the cooked pasta, and add it to the bowl; toss well, and cover until cooled before serving.

Farfalle and Mixed Vegetable Medley

SERVES 4–6

When cooking pasta, you may find that sometimes you have leftover pasta. This is ideal to use as the basis of a delicious salad. The short pastas and shapes are better suited for this dish.

FOR THE SALAD

1 cup snow peas

6 scallions, trimmed

1 small bunch radishes, trimmed

¾ cup canned baby corn

1 cup cherry tomatoes

2 oz arugula, rinsed

10 oz cooked fresh farfalle

FOR THE DRESSING

5 tbsp reduced calorie mayonnaise

3 tbsp lemon juice

2 tbsp chopped fresh basil

Cut the snow peas in half, then blanch in lightly salted boiling water for 1 minute. Drain and plunge into cold water, drain again, and place in a serving bowl.

Slice the scallions diagonally and add to the peas. Cut about 4–5 radishes into roses if liked and leave in cold water to open. Slice the remaining radishes and add to the bowl. Cut the baby corn and tomatoes in half; add to the bowl with the arugula and cooked farfalle. Toss ingredients lightly together.

Place the dressing ingredients in a screw top jar and shake vigorously. Pour over the salad, toss lightly, and serve garnished with the radish roses.

Coronation Turkey Pasta

SERVES 4–6

This makes a delicious, filling salad. Ideal for entertaining or for when a more substantial meal is required.

FOR THE DRESSING

2 tbsp olive oil

1 small onion

1 tbsp medium hot curry powder

⅔ cup dry white wine

½ cup ready-to-eat dried apricots, chopped

4 tbsp reduced-calorie mayonnaise

2 tbsp sour cream

FOR THE SALAD

8 oz diced cooked turkey meat

10 oz cooked fresh pasta, such as brandelle

¼ cup sliced toasted almonds

salad greens

fresh apricot slices

For the salad dressing, heat the olive oil in a pan and gentle sauté the onion for 5 minutes or until softened. Add the medium hot curry powder and sauté for 2 minutes, stirring frequently. Pour in the dry white wine with 3 tablespoons of water, add the chopped apricots, and simmer gently for 10 minutes or until the apricots are soft and pulpy.

Remove from the heat and blend in a food processor to form a smooth purée. Mix the mayonnaise, sour cream, and apricot purée together. Stir the diced turkey meat, cooked pasta, and almonds into the dressing.

Arrange the salad greens in the base of a serving platter, then pile the pasta mixture on top. Garnish with the apricot slices and serve.

Pasta Niçoise with Balsamic Dressing

SERVES 4–6

The pungent sweetness of balsamic vinegar adds a new dimension to this traditional salad.

FOR THE SALAD

6 oz French green beans, trimmed

7 oz can tuna, drained

10 oz cooked fresh pasta, such as fusilli

2 tbsp chopped fresh flat leaf parsley

2 large tomatoes, sliced

2 medium hard-cooked eggs, shelled and sliced

2 oz can anchovy fillets, drained (soaked if preferred)

⅓ cup pitted black olives

FOR THE DRESSING

5 tbsp extra virgin olive oil

1 tsp liquid honey

1 tsp wholegrain mustard

salt and ground black pepper

2 tbsp balsamic vinegar

Cook the French green beans in a pan of lightly salted boiling water for 4–5 minutes or until just cooked. Drain and plunge into cold water. Drain again and reserve. Divide the drained tuna into small chunks.

Mix the pasta and chopped parsley together and place in the base of a shallow serving platter or dish. Arrange the cooked beans, sliced tomatoes, tuna, eggs, drained anchovies, and olives attractively on top of the pasta.

Place the dressing ingredients in a screw top jar and shake vigorously. Pour over the salad just before serving.

Pasta and Yogurt Salad

SERVES 4

There are many different ingredients that can be used as salad dressings. Yogurt makes an ideal base for a salad dressing, and with more people watching their intake of fat, it is an obvious choice.

FOR THE SALAD

2 oranges

1 tbsp olive oil

2 cups sliced leeks

¼ cup pine nuts

2 tbsp roughly chopped fresh
   flat leaf parsley

1 cup broccoli florets

1 cup chopped young carrots

4 oz mortadella, sliced into strips

⅔ cup low-fat plain yogurt

salt and ground black pepper

radicchio leaves

TO SERVE

8 oz fresh pasta, such as
   tricolored farfalle

Remove the zest from one of the oranges, then peel and divide both oranges into sections. Reserve the zest and orange sections.

Heat the oil in a skillet and sauté the leeks for 5 minutes or until just softened. Add the orange zest and pine nuts, and continue to sauté for 2 minutes. Remove from the heat, stir in the parsley, and place in a bowl.

Divide the broccoli into smaller florets and blanch in lightly salted boiling water for 2 minutes. Drain and plunge into cold water. Drain again, and add to the leeks.

Cook the carrots in lightly salted boiling water for 5 minutes or until just cooked. Drain and add to the vegetables.

Cook the pasta in plenty of boiling salted water for 1–2 minutes or until "al dente." Drain and return to the pan.

Add the mortadella to the pasta with the vegetables and orange sections. Stir in the yogurt with seasoning to taste. Mix lightly together. Line a serving bowl with the radicchio leaves. Spoon the salad into the bowl.

Salami and Pasta Salads

SERVES 4

These make a satisfying lunch, or they can be served in smaller portions and divided between shell dishes or glasses for a light first course. Serve with warmed crusty bread.

8 oz small pasta shapes, such as elbows or ditali	1 red onion or other mild salad onion, chopped
salt and ground black pepper	10 stuffed green olives, thickly sliced
8 oz good-quality Italian salami (see Cook's Tip, below)	4 tbsp pine nuts
1 small zucchini, very lightly peeled, halved, and thinly sliced	8 quails' eggs
	good olive oil
1 bunch watercress, leaves only	1 lemon, cut into large wedges

COOK'S TIP

To make this salad special, it is essential to buy good-quality salami from a good deli or Italian grocery store. If you do buy from a specialty store, you will find a fantastic range, including coarse-textured and extremely spicy types. If you are limited for choice to a poor selection at a small local supermarket, then have a look at the packed meats – you may find that either bresaola (cured beef) or prosciutto is a preferable alternative.

Cook the pasta in boiling salted water for about 10 minutes, or following the instructions on the package, until tender. Drain well.

Meanwhile, cut the salami into strips, and mix them with the zucchini, watercress, onion, and olives.

Dry-roast the pine nuts in a small, heavy-bottomed saucepan over a low to medium heat, and shake it often so that they cook evenly until lightly browned.

Place the quails' eggs in a saucepan, and pour in cold water to cover them. Bring to a boil; then cook for 3 minutes. Drain, rinse under cold water, and remove the shells.

Toss the hot pine nuts with the freshly drained pasta, and trickle over a little olive oil. Mix well, and put into a bowl. Cover, and leave until warm. Lightly toss the salami mixture with the pasta, and divide it between four plates. Halve the quails' eggs, and arrange them on the salad. Garnish with lemon, and serve at once, offering extra olive oil to trickle over the salad to taste.

Melon, Smoked Chicken, and Pasta Salad

SERVES 4

FOR THE SALAD

12 oz assorted melon slices

6 oz smoked chicken meat

8 oz cooked fresh mushroom
pasta

1 large orange, peeled and cut
into sections

fresh spinach leaves

2 tbsp grated Gruyère cheese

orange zest to garnish

◀ *Melon, Smoked Chicken, and Pasta Salad*

FOR THE DRESSING

4 tbsp sour cream

1 tsp wholegrain mustard

3 tbsp extra virgin olive oil

2 tbsp champagne or white wine
vinegar

*U*se a selection of melons in this refreshing salad. The different colors of the melons make this an attractive dish.

● Discard the seeds and skin from the melons and cut into small dice. Place in a bowl.

● Cut the smoked chicken into strips and add to the melon with the pasta and orange sections; mix lightly. Arrange the fresh spinach leaves on a serving platter.

● For the dressing, place the sour cream in a bowl and beat in the mustard. Gradually beat in the olive oil, then the vinegar. Pour over the pasta and toss lightly. Spoon onto the spinach-lined platter, sprinkle with the grated cheese, garnish, and serve.

Smoked Salmon, Pasta, and Raspberry Salad

SERVES 4

*T*he combination of sweet and savory is especially pleasing if the sweet food is fruit. Here, sweet ripe raspberries are used with smoked salmon to give an interesting and stunning taste sensation.

FOR THE DRESSING

4 tbsp raspberry vinegar

3 tbsp extra virgin olive oil

1 tbsp walnut oil

pinch of mustard powder

4 tbsp sour cream

FOR THE SALAD

8 oz fresh pasta, such as mixed
herb fusilli

6 scallions, trimmed

4 oz smoked salmon

1 cup fresh raspberries

1 cup watercress sprigs, rinsed

freshly shaved Romano cheese

● For the dressing, blend the vinegar with the oils and mustard powder until thoroughly mixed, then stir in the sour cream. Cover and leave in the refrigerator for 30 minutes.

● Cook the pasta in plenty of boiling salted water for 1–2 minutes or until "al dente." Drain and return to the pan.

● Meanwhile, diagonally slice the scallions, cut the smoked salmon into strips, and pick over the fresh raspberries. Add the scallions, smoked salmon, raspberries, and watercress sprigs to the cooked pasta. Add the salad dressing and toss lightly. Serve, sprinkled with the freshly shaved cheese.

Fig, Pasta, and Prosciutto Salad

SERVES 4

$\mathcal{M}$ake the most of fresh figs when they are available. Whether it is the green or purple variety, their soft flesh, delicate flavor, and attractive appearance make them an ideal salad ingredient

FOR THE SALAD

3-in piece cucumber

salt

4 oz prosciutto, sliced

2 ripe pears

1 tbsp fresh orange juice

half a small head arugula

8 oz cooked fresh pasta, such as fusilli

4 fresh ripe figs

edible flowers such as pansies, nasturtiums, and primroses (optional)

FOR THE DRESSING

3 tbsp orange juice

4 tbsp extra virgin olive oil

1 tsp liquid honey

1–2 tsp Dijon-style mustard

ground black pepper

Peel the cucumber and slice thinly. Sprinkle with salt and leave for 30 minutes. Rinse well in cold water and pat dry with paper towels. Place in a bowl with the prosciutto.

Rinse the ripe pears and peel if preferred. Core and slice thinly. Sprinkle with the fresh orange juice and add to the bowl. Tear the arugula into small pieces if large leaves and add to the bowl with the cooked pasta. Toss lightly together until mixed.

Slice the figs and add to the bowl. Spoon onto a serving platter.

Place the dressing ingredients into a screw top jar and shake vigorously until well blended. Pour over the pasta. Garnish the salad with the edible flowers and serve.

Fig, Pasta, and Prosciutto Salad ▶

Pasta with Tomato Tapenade

SERVES 4

$\mathcal{T}$apenade can be found throughout the Mediterranean and is delicious spread on toast as a tasty snack. It also can form the basis of an interesting salad, as this recipe illustrates.

FOR THE TAPENADE

1½ cups black olives, pitted

6 sun-dried tomatoes

1½ oz capers (soaked if preferred)

1 tbsp chopped fresh parsley

2 garlic cloves, minced

1 tsp wholegrain mustard

2 oz can anchovy fillets (soaked if preferred)

⅔ cup extra virgin olive oil

ground black pepper

TO SERVE

8 oz fresh pasta, such as mixed herb farfalle

romaine lettuce

sprigs of watercress

2 tbsp freshly made croûtons

½ cup halved cherry tomatoes

For the tomato tapenade, blend the black olives, sun-dried tomatoes, capers, chopped fresh parsley, garlic, wholegrain mustard, and anchovies with their oil to a thick paste in a food processor. With the motor still running, gradually pour in the olive oil in a thin steady stream to form a thick purée. Add black pepper to taste and reserve.

Cook the pasta in plenty of boiling salted water for 1-2 minutes or until "al dente." Drain and return to the pan.

Meanwhile, rinse the lettuce and watercress leaves and use to line a salad bowl. Add the tapenade to the pasta and toss lightly. Serve in the lettuce-lined bowl, sprinkled with the croûtons. Garnish with the cherry tomatoes.

Wild Mushroom and Pasta Salad

SERVES 4

For a more substantial salad, add some shelled shrimp or a mixture of seafood.

FOR THE SALAD

½ cup virgin olive oil

4 shallots, peeled and sliced

2–3 garlic cloves, peeled and sliced

1–2 serrano chilies, seeded and sliced

4 sun-dried tomatoes, chopped

2½ cups assorted wild mushrooms, such as oyster or chanterelle, wiped and sliced

4 tbsp dry white wine

salt and ground black pepper

1–2 tsp truffle oil

assorted bitter salad greens, such as arugula, spinach, watercress, or sorrel

TO SERVE

8 oz fresh rigatoni

few shavings black truffle (optional)

sprigs flat leaf parsley, to garnish

Heat the oil in a skillet and sauté the shallots, garlic and chilies for 2 minutes. Add the sun-dried tomatoes and mushrooms; continue to sauté for 3 more minutes. Add the white wine and seasoning; simmer for 3–4 minutes or until the mushrooms are just tender.

Cook the pasta in plenty of boiling salted water for 1–2 minutes or until "al dente." Drain and return to the pan. Add the truffle oil to the pasta and heat through for 1 minute, stirring lightly. Stir in the sautéed mushroom mixture.

Line a serving bowl with the salad greens and spoon the pasta salad on top. Sprinkle with the freshly shaved truffle, if using, garnish, and serve.

Wild Mushroom and Pasta Salad ▶

Pasta and Duck Salad

SERVES 4

This flavorful salad is ideal for using up leftover roast duck. If you prefer, you can pan-fry duck breasts, drain thoroughly, then slice.

8 oz fresh farfalle

4 tbsp virgin olive oil

4 oz pancetta or smoked bacon, rinded and cut into strips

3 tbsp dry white wine

1 tbsp white wine vinegar

salt and ground black pepper

8 oz roast duck, cut into strips

1 cup diced Gruyère cheese

1 large orange, peeled and cut into sections

roughly chopped fresh flat leaf parsley

salad greens

halved kumquats (optional), to garnish

Cook the farfalle in salted boiling water for 1–2 minutes or until "al dente." Drain and place in a bowl. Pour over the olive oil and toss lightly.

Meanwhile, place the pancetta or bacon in a non-stick skillet and cook gently until crisp. Add the white wine and vinegar and simmer for 2 minutes, stirring occasionally.

Add the pancetta and liquid to the pasta with seasoning to taste, the duck strips, Gruyère cheese, orange sections, and chopped parsley. Toss lightly.

Arrange the salad greens on a platter and spoon on the pasta mixture. Garnish with the kumquat halves and serve.

Pasta Main Dishes

Poached Salmon in Pink Sauce

Thick Macaroni with Seafood Sauce

Spaghettini with Shellfish

Lobster and Spinach Topping

Fettuccine with Shrimp and
Andouille Sausage

Seafood Darioles

Seafood Lasagne

Salmon and Pasta Timbales

Chicken Supreme

Brandied Chicken Livers

Tagliatelle with Meatballs

Piquant Diced Lamb

Chicken and Ham Lasagne

Classic Lasagne Al Forno

Beef and Mushroom Cannelloni

Beef Stew and Pasta

Brandelle with Porcini and Anchovies

Farfalle with Turkey and Porcini

Pasta Lamb Bake

Salmon-Stuffed Shells

Cauliflower and Salami Cannelloni

Turkey, Tomato, and Basil Lasagne

Ravioli with Mixed Mushrooms

Stuffed Lumache

Bacon and Pine Nut Triangles

Turkey Cannelloni with Lemon Sauce

Easy Over Ravioli

Tortelloni with Ricotta and Herbs

Tortelloni with Parma Ham

Rich Pork and Beef Stuffing

Poached Salmon in Pink Sauce

SERVES 4

1½ lb salmon fillet

1¼ cups white wine

⅔ cup water

1 bay leaf

2 tbsp butter

¼ cup flour

2 tbsp tomato paste

finely grated zest of 1 lemon

2 egg yolks

1¼ cups light cream

1 tbsp chopped gherkin

2 tbsp chopped fresh parsley

2 tbsp snipped chives

salt and ground black pepper

fresh herbs, to garnish

Place the salmon fillet in a saucepan, cutting it into pieces as necessary to fit. Pour in the wine and water. Add the bay leaf, and heat, slowly, until just simmering. Remove the pan from the heat, cover, and set it aside until the liquid has cooled. Remove the salmon fillet, and flake the fish off the skin in chunks. Then pour the liquor through a fine strainer and set aside.

Melt the butter in a saucepan. Stir in the flour, and cook, stirring, for 2 minutes. Pour in the salmon cooking liquor, and bring to a boil, stirring all the time. Add the tomato paste and lemon zest. Add the salmon, and allow to heat through very gently.

Beat the egg yolks with the cream; then stir in some of the sauce from the salmon. Pour the cream mixture into the sauce, and heat gently without boiling. Stir in the gherkin, parsley, and chives, and season to taste; then serve promptly, pouring the sauce over some freshly cooked pasta. Garnish with fresh herbs.

Thick Macaroni with Seafood Sauce

SERVES 4

*Y*ou can vary the seafood used in this sauce according to what is available and to personal taste, using the ingredients list below as a guide for your own variations.

1 lb fresh mussels	1¼ cups light red wine
1 lb fresh cockles or small clams (optional)	1 tbsp tomato paste
	salt and ground black pepper
1¼ cups water	4 squid sacs, sliced
2 tbsp olive oil	1 lb white fish fillet, skinned and cut into chunks
1 garlic clove, crushed	
1 onion, chopped	8–12 uncooked jumbo shrimp
2 celery stalks, thinly sliced	8 fresh scallops, shelled and sliced
1 carrot, diced	
1⅓ cups sliced mushrooms	freshly grated Parmesan cheese, to serve
¼ cup all-purpose flour	

COOK'S TIP

This is how to clean and cook live mussels, clams, and cockles.

Thoroughly scrub the shells, and scrape off any barnacles. Discard any open or broken shells which do not close when tapped sharply.

Traditionally, shellfish require purging by leaving them to stand in cold water so that they egest any sand from their shells. Leave the shellfish to soak overnight in a large bucket of cold water with a handful of oatmeal added, leaving the bucket in a cold place.

Next day, drain and rinse the shellfish. Remove the "beards" from the mussels – the group of fine, black hairs that protrude from the shells. Pull them away sharply.

The two important points to remember are, first, to discard opened uncooked shellfish that do not shut when tapped, and, second, to discard any shells that do not open during cooking. In both cases, there is a risk of poisoning as these shellfish are dead, and may contain toxins.

Clean the mussels and cockles or clams, if using (see Cook's Tip, left). Put them in a large saucepan, and pour in the water. Bring the water to a boil, then reduce the heat so that the water simmers, and cover the pan. Cook, shaking the pan occasionally, for about 10 minutes, or until all the shells have opened (discard any that do not open). Reserve a few mussels in their shells for garnishing, if you like, then remove the other mussels and cockles or clams from their shells and set aside.

Strain the cooking liquid through cheesecloth, and boil it to reduce it to about 1¼ cups, if necessary. Set this aside.

Heat the olive oil in a saucepan. Add the garlic, onion, celery, and carrot. Stir well, cover the pan, and cook gently for 20 minutes, shaking the pan occasionally, until the vegetables are tender, but not browned.

Add the mushrooms and stir in the flour. Slowly pour in the strained cooking liquor and wine. Bring to a boil, stirring, and add the tomato paste. Stir in salt and freshly ground black pepper to taste. Add the squid to the sauce, cover, and simmer gently for 15 minutes.

Then add the white fish, and continue to cook, covered, for 10 minutes. Next, add the shrimp, and cook for 5 minutes. Add the scallops, and poach gently for 5 minutes. Lastly, add the cooked mussels and cockles or clams. Heat for a few minutes without simmering or boiling. Taste for seasoning, and serve with freshly cooked thick macaroni. Offer freshly grated Parmesan cheese and garnish with the reserved mussels in their shells, if liked.

Spaghettini with Shellfish

This is a simple dish in which shellfish, vegetables, or herbs add a rich flavor to spaghettini. Use whatever shellfish are available, like winkles, cockles, and whelks.

1 lb fresh unshelled shrimp, a fish head and bones

1 small fennel bulb with fronds

1 onion

5–6 parsley stalks

1 bay leaf

scant 1 cup dry vermouth or white wine

3 tbsp olive oil

2 garlic cloves, finely chopped

1 big ripe tomato, skinned, seeded, and chopped

salt and ground black pepper

1½ tsp paprika

8 saffron strands

2 cups clams or small mussels, cleaned

14 oz spaghettini

1 tsp anis or Pernod

about ¼ cup chopped fresh parsley

lemon wedges, to serve

Peel the shrimp and put the shells, fish head, and bones into a saucepan. Add the outer fennel and hard stalks, chopped, 3 slices of onion, the parsley stalks (snapping them up), bay leaf, and half the vermouth or wine. Add 4¼ cups of water and simmer for 30 minutes, then strain the broth.

Meanwhile, finely chop the remaining onion and soften it in the oil in a paella pan or shallow casserole. Add the garlic. Thinly slice the remaining fennel (reserving the fronds) and add about halfway through, while the onion is softening.

Add the chopped tomato and season with salt, pepper, and paprika. Powder the saffron with your fingers into a little of the broth.

Add the remaining wine, reserved fish broth, and saffron liquid and bring to a boil. Add the clams or mussels and, when they open (discard any that do not), add the pasta and shrimp. Cook for about 10 minutes, stirring halfway through. The pasta should be well done and thickening the liquid slightly. Add the anis or Pernod, check the seasonings, and sprinkle with chopped parsley and fennel fronds. Serve with lemon wedges.

Lobster and Spinach Topping

SERVES 4

This is a good way in which to use the small ready-cooked lobsters that are easily available from supermarkets, and also sold frozen.

2 small, cooked lobsters (about 1 lb each)

¼ cup butter

1 small onion, finely chopped

2¼ lb fresh spinach, trimmed, washed, and left wet

salt and ground black pepper

8 oz oyster mushrooms, halved if large

squeeze of lemon juice

⅔ cup ricotta

2 tbsp freshly grated Parmesan cheese

12 oz dry pasta, any shape

lemon wedges, to serve (optional)

Twist off the lobster claws and legs. Crack the claws with nut crackers, and use a meat skewer to pick out all the meat. Break the legs at the joints, and pick out all the meat. Lay one of the lobsters on a board on its back. Use a sharp, pointed knife to cut through the shell along the tail, underneath the firm bright shell which overlaps the jointed section. Do this along both sides so that you can pull off the softer area of shell covering the tail meat. Lift out the tail meat in one piece; then slice it.

Melt half the butter in a large saucepan. Add the onion, and cook, stirring often, for about 10 minutes, or until it has softened but not browned.

Add the wet spinach, cover the pan, and steam it for about 7 minutes, or until it has reduced and is tender. Stir well; then add salt and pepper to taste. Keep hot over a low heat.

Melt the remaining butter in a large skillet, and add the lobster meat with the oyster mushrooms. Sprinkle in salt and pepper. Cook, turning the mushrooms and lobster gently, until both are piping hot. Add a squeeze of lemon juice, the ricotta cheese, and the Parmesan. Stir well; then remove the pan from the heat to prevent the ricotta cheese curdling.

Give the spinach a stir; then tip it onto a bed of freshly cooked pasta. Top with the lobster and mushrooms, and serve at once with lemon wedges to squeeze over the lobster, if liked.

Fettuccine with Shrimp and Andouille Sausage

SERVES 4

This is a moderately spicy dish, with the pepper flavor largely provided by the sausage, so be sure to taste and adjust the seasonings. This recipe uses a combination of fresh tomatoes and canned tomato sauce for speed, but you can substitute more fresh tomatoes for the sauce if you have the extra time to cook it down.

2 tbsp olive oil

2 tomatoes, seeded and chopped

8 oz onion, chopped

1 celery stalk, chopped

½ green bell pepper, chopped

1 tbsp chopped fresh jalapeño pepper

2 garlic cloves, finely chopped

8 fl oz can tomato sauce

½ cup fish broth

¾ tsp salt

¼ tsp black pepper

1 tbsp chopped fresh basil

8 oz andouille sausage, sliced

cayenne (optional)

8–12 oz dry fettuccine or other pasta

8 oz medium shrimp, shelled and deveined

In a large skillet or saucepan, heat the olive oil. Sauté the tomatoes, onion, celery, green bell pepper, jalapeño, and garlic until the vegetables are limp, about 5 minutes. Add the tomato sauce, fish broth, salt, pepper, basil, and sausage and cook until tomato and liquids are reduced, forming a thick, rich broth, 10–15 minutes. Taste and adjust seasonings. If you want it spicier, this is the time to add cayenne in large pinches, until you reach the right heat.

While the sauce is simmering, cook the fettuccine in a large pot of boiling water. Drain and toss with a little olive oil to keep it from sticking.

Add the shrimp to the sauce and cook just until they are opaque and tightly curled, 2–3 minutes. Serve the sauce over the fettuccine.

Seafood Darioles

SERVES 4

3 oz Pasta Dough (page 9), rolled out and cut into small squares

butter for greasing

⅔ cup cheese sauce

4 oz plaice fillet, skinned and chopped

4 oz peeled cooked shrimp, thawed if frozen, chopped

1 tbsp chopped fresh parrsley

2 tbsp snipped chives

salt and ground black pepper

1 egg, beaten

2 hard-cooked eggs

⅔ cup mayonnaise

3 tbsp light cream

1 tbsp chopped dill

dill or parsley and chives, to garnish

Cook the pasta in boiling salted water for 3 minutes, then drain. Set the oven at 350°F. Butter four dariole molds and line their bases with nonstick bakers' parchment. Stand the molds on a baking sheet.

Mix the pasta with the sauce. Add the fish, shrimp, parsley, chives, seasoning, and beaten egg. Stir the mixture to make sure the ingredients are well combined, then divide it between the molds. Cover with nonstick bakers' parchment and bake for 30 minutes.

Meanwhile, finely chop the hard-cooked eggs and mix them with the mayonnaise. Add seasoning to taste, then stir in the cream and dill. Slide a fine knife blade around the inside of each mold, then invert them on individual plates. Remove the nonstick bakers' parchment and spoon a little of the egg sauce beside each mold; offer the rest of the sauce separately. Garnish with herbs and serve at once.

Seafood Lasagne

SERVES 6

12 oz fresh lasagne verdi

2 tbsp olive oil

2 tbsp butter

1 onion, finely chopped

1 bay leaf

⅓ cup all-purpose flour

1¼ cups dry white wine

1¼ cups fish broth

4 oz button mushrooms, sliced

salt and ground black pepper

1½ lb white fish fillet, skinned
    and cut into chunks

8 oz peeled cooked shrimp,
    thawed if frozen

1 lb mussels, cooked and shelled

2 tbsp chopped fresh parsley

1 cup béchamel sauce

½ cup grated Cheddar cheese

Cut the pasta into large squares (about 5 inches) or rectangular sheets. Lower the pieces of pasta one at a time into a large saucepan of boiling salted water. Bring back to a boil and cook for 3 minutes. Drain and rinse under cold water. Lay the pasta on double-thick paper towels.

Set the oven at 350°F. Heat the oil and butter in a saucepan and add the onion and bay leaf. Cook for 10 minutes, until the onion is softened slightly, then stir in the flour. Slowly pour in the wine and broth and bring to a boil, stirring all the time. Add the mushrooms and seasoning, then simmer for 10 minutes. Remove from the heat before stirring in the fish, shrimp, mussels, and parsley. Layer this fish sauce and the lasagne in a large ovenproof dish, ending with a layer of lasagne. Pour the béchamel sauce evenly over the pasta, then sprinkle the cheese on top. Bake for 40-50 minutes, until golden-brown and bubbling hot.

Salmon and Pasta Timbales

SERVES 4

2 oz Pasta Dough (page 9)
flavored with turmeric

salt and ground black pepper

7 oz can salmon

1 cup fresh white bread crumbs

1 tbsp finely chopped scallion

3 basil sprigs, finely shredded, or
1 tbsp parsley

2 oz ricotta cheese, strained

1 egg, separated

basil or parsley sprigs and
halved lemon slices, to garnish

Roll out the pasta very thinly. Take a ramekin dish and cut a paper pattern of the base or find a round cutter to fit. Grease and base-line 4 ramekins with nonstick bakers' parchment. Cut 12 circles of pasta, then cook them in boiling salted water for 3 minutes. Drain the circles and place a circle of pasta in the bottom of each ramekin. Lay the remaining pasta out on paper towels. Set the oven at 350°F.

Drain the salmon, remove any skin and bone, then mash it. Mix with the bread crumbs, scallion, basil or parsley, and ricotta cheese. Add seasoning and beat in the egg yolk. Whisk the egg white until stiff, then fold it into the salmon mixture. Divide the mixture roughly in half, then spoon one portion into the dishes, dividing it equally between them and spreading it neatly. Top each with a circle of pasta, then divide the remaining mixture between the dishes. Finally, top each with a circle of pasta. Stand on a baking sheet, cover with foil, and bake for 25-30 minutes, or until the salmon mixture is set. It will also have risen.

Allow to stand for 2 minutes, then slide a knife around the inside of each ramekin. Invert the timbales on individual plates. Remove the nonstick bakers' parchment. Serve garnished with basil or parsley and lemon.

Chicken Supreme

SERVES 4

his sauce is an old favorite, that goes well with almost any type of pasta. Serve it with a bowl of tagliatelle verdi and a side salad for an informal party, or toss the sauce with pasta shapes for a weekday meal. As the sauce itself is pale, it looks particularly good if ladled over multicolored pasta shapes. The amount of sauce can be increased to serve a crowd, and it freezes well before the cream is added.

1 tbsp oil

2 tbsp butter

1 small onion, chopped

3 boneless chicken breasts, skinned and diced

⅓ cup all-purpose flour

⅔ cup dry white wine

2 cups chicken broth

1 bouquet garni

12 oz small button mushrooms

salt and ground black pepper

1¼ cups light cream

2 tbsp chopped fresh parsley

Heat the oil and butter in a flameproof casserole. Add the onion, and cook, stirring occasionally, for 10 minutes.

Add the chicken, and brown the pieces lightly all over. Stir in the flour; then cook for 2 minutes before slowly pouring in the wine and broth. Add the bouquet garni, bring the sauce to a boil, and reduce the heat so that it is just simmering.

Stir the mushrooms into the sauce (which is very thick at this stage), and add salt and pepper to taste. Cover the casserole tightly, and cook the sauce gently for 20 minutes. The liquid that the mushrooms yield during cooking will thin the sauce slightly.

Stir the cream into the sauce, and heat it through gently; then add the parsley, and discard the bouquet garni before serving the sauce.

Brandied Chicken Livers

¼ cup butter

1 onion, finely chopped

2 garlic cloves, chopped

3 cups roughly chopped chicken livers

4 tbsp brandy

1¼ cups sour cream

4 tbsp chopped fresh parsley

Melt the butter in a skillet. Add the onion and garlic, and cook, stirring, for about 15 minutes, or until the onion has softened, but not browned.

Add the chicken livers, and cook, stirring gently and occasionally, for about 15 minutes, or until the livers have cooked.

Pour in the brandy, and immediately ignite it. When the flames have died, stir in the sour cream, and salt and pepper to taste. Heat through without boiling, and taste for seasoning. Stir in the parsley before serving the sauce on freshly cooked pasta.

Tagliatelle with Meatballs

SERVES 4

These tiny meatballs would be ideal to serve with any of the long ribbon pastas. They would also work equally well with farfalle or fusilli.

FOR THE SAUCE

1 small onion, peeled and finely chopped

1–2 garlic cloves, minced

1 cup lean ground lamb

salt and ground black pepper

1 tbsp grated lemon zest

½ cup fresh white bread crumbs

1 tbsp chopped fresh marjoram

1 tbsp pine nuts, toasted and chopped

1 medium egg, beaten

1–2 tbsp olive oil

1¼ cups puréed tomatoes

⅔ cup red wine

few sprigs of marjoram

TO SERVE

1 lb fresh tagliatelle

freshly grated Parmigiano Reggiano cheese

marjoram sprig

Place the onion, garlic, lamb, seasoning, lemon zest, bread crumbs, chopped marjoram, and pine nuts in a bowl and mix well. Bind together with the egg. Dampen your hands, then form the mixture into tiny balls, each about the size of a cherry.

Heat the olive oil in a pan and brown the meatballs on all sides. Remove from the pan and wipe the pan clean. Add the puréed tomatoes, red wine, and marjoram sprigs to the pan and bring to a boil. Boil for 5 minutes, reduce the heat, and add the meatballs. Cover with a lid and simmer gently for 5–8 minutes or until the meatballs are cooked.

Meanwhile, cook the tagliatelle in plenty of boiling salted water for 1–2 minutes or until "al dente." Drain and place on a warm serving platter. Discard the marjoram sprigs from the sauce, then spoon the sauce and meatballs over the tagliatelle. Serve with the grated cheese and garnish with a marjoram sprig.

Piquant Diced Lamb

*F*resh chilies bring this lamb mixture to life. It is delicious with substantial pasta shapes, such as long mafaldine or pappardelle, or chunky rigatoni, cicatelli di San Severo, or lumache.

5 cups diced, lean, boneless lamb

1–2 fresh green chilies, seeded and chopped

2 garlic cloves, minced

salt and ground black pepper

grated zest and juice of 1 orange

1 tbsp chopped fresh oregano

1 tbsp ground coriander

2 tbsp olive oil

1 large onion, chopped

1 red bell pepper, seeded and diced

2 tbsp all-purpose flour

2½ cups lamb or chicken broth

12 oz dry pasta shells

Mix the lamb with the chilies, garlic, plenty of salt and pepper, the orange zest, oregano, and coriander. Cover and let marinate for at least 2–3 hours or overnight.

Heat the oil in a flameproof casserole, and brown the meat. Then add the onion and bell pepper, and cook, stirring, for 5 minutes.

Stir in the flour; then pour in the broth and orange juice. Bring just to a boil, then reduce the heat, and cover the pan. Simmer the sauce very gently for 1 hour. Taste for seasoning before serving with freshly cooked pasta.

Chicken and Ham Lasagne

SERVES 6-8

*T*his is easy and delicious! Turkey may be used instead of chicken – a great way of using up a Thanksgiving roast. Add any leftover stuffing to the sauce too.

12 oz fresh lasagne verdi

2 cups béchamel sauce

1½ cups diced cooked chicken

1½ cups diced cooked ham

4 oz button mushrooms, chopped

6 scallions, chopped

2 tbsp chopped fresh parsley

1 tbsp chopped fresh sage

salt and ground black pepper

¾ cup finely crumbled Monterey Jack or Colby cheese

paprika

½ cup fresh white bread crumbs

COOK'S TIP

A mixture of crushed potato chips and a few finely chopped salted peanuts added to the bread crumbs makes a good topping.

● Cook the lasagne. Butter a 12–15 × 8-in ovenproof dish and set the oven at 350°F.

● Set aside a third of the béchamel sauce. Mix the chicken, ham, mushrooms, scallions, parsley, and sage with the rest of the sauce. Taste for seasoning, then layer this sauce in the dish with the lasagne, ending with a layer of lasagne on top. Stir the cheese into the reserved sauce (it doesn't matter if the sauce is too cool for it to melt), then spread it over the top of the pasta. Sprinkle with a little paprika and top with the bread crumbs.

● Bake for 40–50 minutes, until the topping is crisp and golden and the lasagne layers are bubbling hot.

Chicken and Ham Lasagne ▶

Classic Lasagne Al Forno

SERVES 6-8

12 oz Pasta Dough (page 9) or fresh lasagne

salt and ground black pepper

butter for greasing

1 quantity Bolognese Sauce (page 38)

1½ cups béchamel sauce

¼ cup freshly grated Parmesan cheese

● Cut the rolled-out pasta into large squares (about 5 inches) or rectangular sheets. Lower the pieces of pasta one at a time into a large saucepan of boiling salted water. Bring back to a boil and cook for 3 minutes. Drain and rinse under cold water. Lay the pasta on double-thick paper towels.

● Set the oven at 350°F. Butter a large oblong oven-proof dish (about 12–15 × 8 in). Ladle a little of the Bolognese sauce into the dish and spread it out. Dot with a little of the béchamel sauce, then add a layer of pasta. Continue layering the meat, a little béchamel and pasta, ending with pasta. Do not include much béchamel between the layers as you need most of it to cover the top of the lasagne. Sprinkle the Parmesan over the top and bake the lasagne for 45-50 minutes, until golden-brown and bubbling hot.

Beef and Mushroom Cannelloni

SERVES 4

This recipe uses porcini and chanterelle mushrooms, but if you prefer, you can use regular mushrooms.

1 cup milk

½ small onion, peeled

small piece carrot, peeled

1 celery stalk, trimmed

2–3 whole cloves

few black peppercorns

1–2 bay leaves

few parsley stalks

2 tbsp butter or margarine

¼ cup all-purpose flour

salt

½ oz dried porcini

8 oz lean ground beef

1 onion, peeled and finely chopped

2 garlic cloves, minced

¾ cup finely chopped chanterelle mushrooms

⅔ cup red wine

2 tbsp tomato paste

ground black pepper

12 fresh lasagne sheets

¾ cup sliced mozzarella cheese

Preheat the oven to 375°F, 10 minutes before baking the cannelloni. Pour the milk into a small saucepan and add the onion, carrot, celery, cloves, peppercorns, bay leaves, and parsley stalks. Slowly bring the sauce to just below boiling point then remove from the heat, cover, and leave to infuse for at least 15 minutes. Strain, reserving the milk.

Melt the butter or margarine in a small pan and stir in the flour. Cook over a gentle heat for 2 minutes then draw off the heat and gradually stir in the reserved milk. Return pan to the heat and cook, stirring until smooth, thick, and glossy. Season with the salt. Cover with a sheet of dampened waxed paper and reserve.

Soak the porcini in warm water for 20 minutes. Drain, reserving the liquor, and chop the porcini. Sauté the beef in a skillet until browned, stirring frequently to help to break up any lumps. Add the onion, garlic, porcini, and chanterelles, and continue to sauté for 5 minutes or until the onion is softened.

Pour in the wine, bring to a boil, and simmer for 5 minutes. Blend the tomato paste with the reserved porcini soaking water and 2 tablespoons of water. Stir into the beef mixture with black pepper to taste. Cook for 5 more minutes. Remove from the heat and cool.

Bring a large pan of water to a boil, add 1 tablespoon of salt, then drop in four lasagne sheets, one at a time. Cook for 2–3 minutes, ensuring that they do not stick together. Drain, lay them on clean dish towels, and pat dry. Repeat with the remaining lasagne sheets.

Use the prepared beef mixture to fill the pasta sheets and roll up. Place in the base of an ovenproof dish. Top with the prepared sauce and dot with the cheese slices. Bake the cannelloni in the oven for 25 minutes or until golden and bubbly. Serve immediately.

Beef Stew with Pasta

SERVES 4

This recipe is based on the Corsican Stufatu, but a few extra ingredients make it a hearty and filling dish.

FOR THE SAUCE

2 tbsp olive oil

1 large onion, peeled and chopped

2–3 garlic cloves, minced

1 lb chuck steak, trimmed and diced

2 tbsp seasoned flour

⅔ cup red wine

2 cups beef broth

salt and ground black pepper

2 tbsp chopped fresh oregano

4–6 baby carrots, trimmed

2 cups leeks, blanched and sliced

TO SERVE

10 oz fresh fusilli

fresh grated Parmesan cheese

chopped fresh oregano

Preheat the oven to 350°F, 10 minutes before cooking the stew. Heat the oil in a large pan and sauté the onion and garlic for 5 minutes or until softened but not browned.

Toss the meat in the seasoned flour, then add to the pan and brown, stirring frequently. Sprinkle in any remaining flour and cook for 2 minutes. Gradually stir in the wine and broth. Bring to a boil, stirring, then remove from the heat and stir in seasoning to taste and the oregano. Pour into a casserole dish, cover with a lid, and cook for 1½ hours.

Cut the carrots in half if large. Cook in boiling water for 3 minutes, drain, and add to the stew with the leeks. Continue to cook for 30 minutes or until the meat is tender.

Meanwhile, cook the fusilli in plenty of boiling salted water for 1–2 minutes or until "al dente." Drain and stir into the stew. Sprinkle with the grated Parmesan and oregano and serve.

Beef Stew with Pasta ▶

Brandelle with Porcini and Anchovies

SERVES 4

As this is based on the famous pesto sauce, treat it in exactly the same way. Store in the refrigerator in a screw top jar. Dispel any air bubbles and cover with a thin layer of olive oil. Consume within 24 hours.

FOR THE SAUCE

½ oz dried porcini mushrooms

6–8 tbsp olive oil

2 firm tomatoes, peeled, seeded, and chopped

½ cup pine nuts

4 garlic cloves

small bunch basil leaves

4 anchovy fillets, soaked in milk for 30 minutes, chopped

TO SERVE

1 lb fresh brandelle

freshly shaved Parmigiano Reggiano cheese

Soak the porcini in warm water for about 20 minutes. Drain, reserving the soaking liquor, and chop the porcini. Heat 2 tablespoons of the oil in a pan and gently sauté the porcini for 2 minutes. Strain the soaking liquid, then add to the porcini and cook until the liquid has almost evaporated. Add the tomatoes and heat for 1 minute.

Place the mushroom mixture with the pine nuts, garlic, basil leaves, and anchovies in a food processor. Blend for 1 minute. With the motor still running, gradually pour in the remaining oil until a thick paste is formed.

Meanwhile, cook the brandelle in plenty of boiling salted water for 1–2 minutes or until "al dente." Drain and return to the pan. Add the mushroom paste and toss lightly until the pasta is coated. Serve immediately sprinkled with the shaved Parmigiano Reggiano.

Farfalle with Turkey and Porcini

SERVES 4

Turkey is traditionally reserved for special occasions, which seems a great shame. As turkey is so low in fat, we really should be eating more of it.

FOR THE SAUCE

1 oz dried porcini mushrooms

1 red bell pepper, seeded

1 green bell pepper, seeded

3 tbsp olive oil

2 garlic cloves, thinly sliced

8 oz turkey breast meat, trimmed and thinly sliced

1 cup button mushrooms, wiped and sliced

6 tbsp dry white wine

salt and ground black pepper

2 tbsp chopped fresh flat leaf parsley

TO SERVE

1 lb fresh farfalle

freshly shaved Parmigiano Reggiano cheese

Soak the porcini in warm water for about 20 minutes. Drain, chop finely, and reserve.

Preheat the broiler to high, then charbroil the bell peppers for 10 minutes or until the skins have blistered. Remove from the heat; place in a plastic bag until cool. Skin and cut into thin strips.

Heat the oil in a pan and sauté the garlic and turkey for 5 minutes or until the turkey is sealed. Add the chopped porcini and button mushrooms and continue to sauté for 3 more minutes.

Add the pepper strips and wine to the pan and simmer for 5 minutes. Stir in the seasoning to taste and chopped parsley. Cover with a lid and remove from the heat while cooking the fresh farfalle.

Cook the farfalle in plenty of boiling salted water for 1–2 minutes or until "al dente." Drain and place on a warm serving plate. Top with the reserved turkey mixture and serve sprinkled with the grated cheese.

Pasta Lamb Bake

SERVES 4

This dish can be made ahead of time and cooked later. If doing this, make the sauce slightly thinner as, while it sits, the pasta will soak up more of the sauce than if you cook it immediately.

FOR THE SAUCE

8 oz lean lamb

2 tbsp olive oil

1 onion, peeled and chopped

2 garlic cloves, minced

8 sun-dried tomatoes, chopped

1 red bell pepper, seeded and chopped

⅔ cup red wine

1¼ cups puréed tomatoes

1 tbsp chopped fresh oregano

salt and ground black pepper

TO SERVE

8 oz fresh farfalle

¾ cup grated mozzarella cheese

Preheat the oven to 375°F, 10 minutes before baking the pasta dish. Trim the lamb and dice.

Heat the oil in a skillet and sauté the onion, garlic, sun-dried tomatoes, and red bell pepper for 5 minutes or until softened. Add the lamb and sauté for a further 3 minutes or until sealed. Add the red wine, puréed tomatoes, and oregano with seasoning to taste. Simmer for 5 minutes, then remove from the heat.

Meanwhile, cook the farfalle in plenty of boiling salted water for 1 minute or until amost "al dente." Drain and return to the pan. Add the lamb and sauce and toss lightly.

Spoon the mixture into an ovenproof dish and top with the grated mozzarella cheese. Bake the pasta dish in the preheated oven for 20 minutes or until the cheese has melted and is golden and bubbly.

Salmon-stuffed Shells

SERVES 4

Look out for very large pasta shells in good delis or Italian grocery stores. If you cannot find them, then substitute large lumache.

9 oz salmon fillet, skinned

⅔ cup water

⅔ cup dry white wine

2 tbsp butter

1 small onion, finely chopped

¼ cup all-purpose flour

3 cups sliced small button mushrooms

⅔ cup light cream

6 tbsp freshly grated Parmesan cheese

salt and ground black pepper

¾ cup ricotta cheese

1 cup fresh bread crumbs

2 tbsp chopped fresh parsley

2 tbsp snipped chives

12–16 large pasta shells

sprigs of herbs, to garnish

Lay the salmon in a saucepan. Add the water and wine. Heat until just simmering, then remove the pan from the heat, and let sit for 15 minutes. Drain and flake the fish, reserving the liquid, but discarding any bones.

Preheat the oven to 375°F.

Melt the butter in a small saucepan. Add the onion, and cook for 10 minutes, stirring, until it has softened. Stir in the flour; then add the cooking liquor from the salmon and the mushrooms. Bring to a boil, stirring, and simmer gently for 3 minutes. Mix in the cream, 2 tablespoons of the Parmesan, and salt and pepper to taste. Pour the mushrooms and the sauce into an ovenproof gratin dish.

Mix the salmon with the ricotta, bread crumbs, parsley, chives, and salt and pepper to taste.

Cook the pasta shells in boiling salted water for about 12 minutes, or until tender. Drain well, and rinse under cold water; then drain again.

Fill the shells with the salmon mixture. Arrange them on top of the sauce, and sprinkle the remaining Parmesan over them. Bake in the preheated oven for about 20 minutes, or until they are hot, and have browned. Serve at once, garnished with sprigs of herbs.

Cauliflower and Salami Cannelloni

SERVES 4–6

10 oz cauliflower, divided into small florets

salt and ground black pepper

1 cup cream cheese

6 tbsp freshly grated Parmesan cheese

1 cup fresh white bread crumbs

1 egg, beaten

a little butter, for greasing

12 cannelloni tubes

1 cup shredded salami

2½ cups puréed tomatoes

Cook the cauliflower in boiling salted water for 6 minutes; then drain well. Leave the cauliflower for 10 minutes to cool a little; then mix it with the cream cheese, 2 tablespoons of the Parmesan, the bread crumbs, egg, and salt and pepper to taste.

Preheat the oven to 350°F, and grease an ovenproof dish with a little butter.

Cook the cannelloni in plenty of boiling salted water for 5 minutes, or until just tender. Drain and rinse under cold water, opening the tubes as you do so. Put the cauliflower mixture into a large piping bag fitted with a plain tip, and fill the cannelloni tubes. Place them in the prepared dish.

Sprinkle the salami over the cannelloni; then spoon the puréed tomatoes over. Sprinkle with the remaining Parmesan, and bake in the preheated oven for 25–30 minutes, or until the cheese has browned, and the sauce is bubbling. Serve at once.

Turkey, Tomato, and Basil Lasagne

SERVES 4

*U*use finely chopped turkey breast, or if preferred, chopped or ground chicken breast to make this tasty lasagne.

2 tbsp olive oil

1 large onion, peeled and finely chopped

2–3 garlic cloves, minced

12 oz ground turkey

2 × 14 oz cans chopped tomatoes

salt and ground black pepper

2 tbsp chopped fresh basil

6–8 fresh lasagne verdi sheets

2 cups zucchini, peeled, sliced lengthwise, and blanched

½ cup grated mozzarella cheese

fresh basil sprigs, to garnish

● Preheat the oven to 375°F, 10 minutes before baking the lasagne. Heat the oil in a large pan and sauté the onion and garlic for 5 minutes or until the onion is softened. Add the ground turkey and continue to sauté for a further 5 minutes or until sealed.

● Add the contents of the cans of tomatoes, bring to a boil, then reduce the heat and simmer for 10 minutes or until a thick consistency is formed. Season to taste and stir in the basil.

● Bring a large pan of water to a boil, add 1 tablespoon salt, then drop in four lasagne sheets, one at a time. Cook for 2-3 minutes, ensuring that they do not stick together. Drain, lay them on clean dish towels, and pat dry. Repeat with the remaining lasagne sheets.

● Place about a third of the sauce in the base of an ovenproof dish and cover with a layer of blanched zucchini slices, then 3–4 lasagne sheets. Repeat the layering, finishing with a layer of sauce. Sprinkle with the grated cheese. Bake the lasagne in the oven for 20–25 minutes or until the cheese is golden. Serve garnished with fresh basil sprigs.

Turkey, Tomato, and Basil Lasagne ▶

Ravioli with Mixed Mushrooms

SERVES 4

*A*good flavored tomato sauce is an ideal choice to serve with this ravioli, with a final sprinkling of freshly grated Parmesan cheese to serve.

3 tbsp butter

2 small onions, peeled and finely chopped

2 cups finely chopped mixed mushrooms

½ cup ricotta cheese

salt and ground black pepper

12 oz Pasta Dough (page 9)

1¼ cups puréed tomatoes

2 tbsp chopped fresh basil

freshly grated Parmigiano Reggiano cheese

● For the filling, heat 2 tablespoons butter in a small pan and gently sauté one onion for 5 minutes. Add the mushrooms and sauté for a further 5 minutes, stirring frequently. Remove from the heat and let cool.

● Beat the ricotta until smooth. Mix in the cooled mushrooms with seasoning to taste. Roll out the pasta dough and proceed to make the ravioli as described on page 146.

● For the sauce, melt the remaining butter in a pan and sauté the remaining onion for 5 minutes. Add the puréed tomatoes and simmer for 10 minutes. Season to taste and add the basil.

● Cook the ravioli in plenty of boiling salted water for 4–5 minutes or until "al dente" and drain. Return to the pan. Add the sauce and toss the cooked ravioli lightly until coated. Serve with the grated cheese.

Stuffed Lumache

*L*umache ("snails") come in a variety of sizes, and the very large ones are intended for filling with a stuffing. Here, they are nestled together on a bed of vegetables before being browned in the oven.

FOR THE LUMACHE

2 tbsp butter

1 onion, finely chopped

1⅓ cups finely chopped mushrooms

1 cup bread crumbs

salt and ground black pepper

1 tbsp chopped fresh oregano

1 cup ricotta cheese

1 bunch of watercress, leaves only, finely chopped

freshly grated nutmeg

16 large lumache

1¼ cups béchamel sauce

4 tbsp freshly grated Parmesan cheese

FOR THE VEGETABLE BASE

2 tbsp olive oil

1 large onion, halved and thinly sliced

1 garlic clove, minced

1 green bell pepper, seeded, halved, and thinly sliced

1 red bell pepper, seeded, halved, and thinly sliced

2 medium zucchini, thinly sliced

6 tomatoes, peeled, seeded, and quartered

First, prepare the stuffing for the lumache. Melt the butter in a saucepan. Add the onion, and cook, stirring, for 5 minutes. Then add the mushrooms, and continue to cook, stirring occasionally, for a further 10 minutes. Mix in the bread crumbs, salt and pepper to taste, and oregano. Then add the ricotta cheese and watercress. Season with a little grated nutmeg to taste, and set aside.

Preheat the oven to 400°F.

Cook the lumache in plenty of boiling salted water for about 12 minutes, or until tender. Drain well, rinse under cold water, and drain again so they do not close up.

Meanwhile, prepare the béchamel sauce.

Next prepare the vegetable base. Heat the oil in a skillet. Add the onion, garlic, and bell peppers. Cook, stirring, for 15 minutes, or until the onion has softened. Stir in the zucchini, and cook for 2 minutes; then add the tomatoes with salt and pepper to taste. Cook for 2–3 minutes, to soften the tomatoes; then spoon the mixture into an ovenproof dish or four individual dishes.

Fill the lumache with the mushroom mixture, and arrange them on the vegetable base. Spoon a little béchamel sauce over the top of each stuffed lumache, and sprinkle with a little Parmesan. Bake for about 15 minutes, or until the tops have browned.

Bacon and Pine Nut Triangles

SERVES 4–6

First, make the pasta dough, and set it aside to rest.

Heat the olive oil in a small saucepan. Add the bacon and onion; then cook, stirring, for 8–10 minutes. Remove the pan from the heat, and stir in the pine nuts, olives, oregano, and salt and pepper to taste. Set aside to cool.

Roll out half the pasta dough to form a 12-inch square. Cut the dough into 2-inch wide strips; then cut these across into 2-inch squares. Work with a third of the squares at a time, keeping the remainder loosely covered with plastic wrap to prevent the pasta drying out.

Brush the squares with beaten egg. Place a tiny mound of stuffing in the middle of a square (you need less than half a teaspoon – cutlery spoon, that is, not a measure – for each square). Then fold one corner of the pasta diagonally over the filling, and pinch the edges together to seal the mixture in a triangular-shaped pasta. Repeat with the remaining rolled squares, using about half the filling. Then roll the remaining dough out, and repeat the process with the remaining filling.

Prepare the serving ingredients before cooking the pasta. Mix the tomatoes with the basil, and salt and pepper to taste. Make a white wine sauce.

Cook the pasta in boiling salted water for 3–4 minutes. Drain the pasta well; then mix it with the sauce. Spoon the mixture into one large, warmed serving bowl or individual dishes. Top with the tomatoes and basil, and garnish with sprigs of basil, if using. Serve at once, offering freshly grated Parmesan cheese with the pasta.

FOR THE BACON AND PINE NUT TRIANGLES

6 oz Pasta Dough (page 9)

1 tbsp olive oil

½ cup finely chopped, lean rindless bacon

1 small onion, finely chopped

1 tbsp chopped fresh oregano

⅓ cup ground or very finely chopped pine nuts

6 black olives, pitted and chopped

1 tbsp chopped fresh oregano

salt and ground black pepper

1 egg, beaten

TO SERVE

8 ripe tomatoes, peeled, seeded, and roughly chopped

4 sprigs of basil, shredded

1¼ cups white wine sauce

sprigs of basil, to garnish

freshly grated Parmesan cheese

Turkey Cannelloni with Lemon Sauce

This is a good way in which to transform the leftovers of a roast turkey into a tempting meal. Instead of using bought tubes, try making fresh pasta, as here. Alternatively, for results of a similar standard, buy fresh lasagne, and use it to roll around the filling. The prepared cannelloni, coated in sauce, may be frozen for up to 3 months.

6 oz Pasta Dough (page 9)

a little butter, for greasing

1 cup béchamel sauce

4 cups finely chopped or ground cooked turkey

1⅓ cups chopped button mushrooms

2 cups fresh white bread crumbs

3 tbsp snipped chives

1 tbsp chopped fresh tarragon

2 tbsp chopped fresh parsley

salt and ground black pepper

grated zest of 1 lemon

½ cup grated mild Cheddar cheese

Make the pasta dough, and divide it in half. Roll out one half to form a square that is slightly larger than 12 inches. Trim the edges, and cut the pasta into nine 4-inch squares. Repeat with the remaining pasta dough; then cook the squares in plenty of boiling salted water for 3 minutes. Drain well, rinse under cold water, and lay out on a clean dish cloth.

Preheat the oven to 350°F, and grease an ovenproof dish with a little butter.

Make the béchamel sauce.

Mix the turkey with the mushrooms, half the bread crumbs, the chives, tarragon, parsley, and salt and pepper to taste. Stir in a little of the sauce – just enough to bind the ingredients into a firm mixture. Divide the mixture in half. Roughly mold half the mixture into a cylinder shape on a plate, and mark it into nine equal portions.

Cut off a portion of stuffing, roll it into a sausage, and place it on a piece of pasta; then roll up the pasta to form cannelloni. Place in the prepared ovenproof dish. Repeat this process with the remaining sheets of pasta and portions of stuffing.

Stir the lemon zest into the remaining béchamel sauce, and taste it for seasoning before pouring it over the cannelloni. Mix the remaining bread crumbs with the cheese. Sprinkle this over the sauce, and bake in the oven for about 30 minutes, or until the topping is crisp, and the cannelloni have heated through.

Easy-over Ravioli

SERVES 4

This recipe is a simple version of ravioli and is designed for those of us who have hectic lives. You can try the recipe with a variety of fillings. I have used ground chicken, but it would work equally well with ground lamb, beef, or pork.

2 tbsp olive oil

1 jalapeño chili, seeded and finely chopped

6 scallions, trimmed and finely chopped

8 oz ground chicken

¼ cup ready-to-eat dried apricots, finely chopped

¼ cup toasted and chopped pine nuts

1 cup fresh white bread crumbs

1 medium egg, beaten

12 oz Pasta Dough (page 9)

Spicy Tomato Sauce (page 32)

few sprigs of flat leaf parsley

Heat 1 tablespoon oil in a pan and sauté the chili for 2 minutes. Add the scallions and sauté for 1 more minute.

Easy-over Ravioli

Add the chicken and sauté for 5 minutes or until cooked. Stir in the apricots, pine nuts, and bread crumbs, mixing well. Remove from the heat and add the egg to the mixture. Bind together. Return to the heat and cook gently for 2 minutes or until completely cooked. Keep warm.

Meanwhile, roll out the pasta dough and cut into 3-inch squares. Bring a large pan of water to a boil and add 1 tablespoon oil. Add the pasta squares, one at a time, and cook for about 3–4 minutes. Carefully remove and keep warm between clean, warm dish towels.

Reheat the tomato sauce, stirring occasionally. Place 2–3 cooked pasta squares onto warm plates. Top with a spoonful or two of the chicken mixture and cover with a further layer of pasta. Drizzle over a little tomato sauce and hand the remaining sauce separately. Garnish with flat leaf parsley sprigs.

Tortelloni with Ricotta and Herbs

SERVES 4

You can vary the herbs you use according to personal preference and availability. If liked, you can also use chopped spinach or even arugula.

1 cup ricotta cheese

½ cup finely chopped fontina cheese

4 tbsp chopped fresh mixed herbs, such as basil, sage, flat leaf parsley, and oregano

1 medium egg yolk

salt and ground black pepper

½ tsp grated nutmeg

12 oz Pasta Dough (page 9)

Butter and Tomato Sauce (page 53)

extra 2 tbsp chopped fresh herbs, to serve

freshly grated Parmigiano Reggiano cheese

For the filling, mix the cheeses with the 4 tablespoons chopped herbs, egg yolk, seasoning, and nutmeg in a bowl. Roll out the pasta to 4-inch wide strips.

Place the filling in a pastry bag and pipe small rounds onto one half of each strip. Moisten the edges and fold the dough over to completely encase the filling. Cut out into squares and proceed to form the tortelloni as described on page 114.

Cook the tortelloni in plenty of boiling salted water for 4-5 minutes or until "al dente." Drain and return to the pan.

Gently heat the sauce then pour over the cooked tortelloni. Toss lightly until coated. Serve immediately, sprinkled with extra chopped herbs and handing some grated Parmigiano Reggiano cheese separately.

Tortelloni with Parma Ham

Tortelloni take a little time and practice to make, but do persevere as they are well worth that extra bit of effort and are far superior to store-bought ones. To begin with, use a simple sauce as used here, then as you get more proficient you can try different sauce and filling combinations.

1–2 tsp butter

2 small onions, peeled and finely chopped

½ cup finely chopped mushrooms

1 cup ricotta cheese

½ cup grated Gruyère cheese

4 oz Parma ham, trimmed and finely shredded

12 oz Pasta Dough (page 9)

1 tsp olive oil

4 scallions, trimmed and finely chopped

14 oz can chopped tomatoes

salt and ground black pepper

2 tbsp chopped fresh flat leaf parsley

freshly grated Parmesan cheese

For the filling, melt the butter in a small pan and gently sauté one onion for 3 minutes. Add the mushrooms and continue to sauté for a further 3 minutes or until the mushrooms are lightly cooked. Drain and reserve.

Beat the ricotta cheese until creamy. Beat in the Gruyère cheese, the drained mushrooms, and ham. Mix together. Make the dough and roll out into long, thin sheets about 4 inches wide.

Place the filling in a large pastry bag and pipe small rounds of the filling onto one half of the dough. Brush the dough with a little water and fold over to completely encase the filling.

Cut into squares using a fluted cookie cutter, making sure each square contains filling. Moisten the edges and fold each square in half to form a triangle, pinching the edges together. Pull the two corners together, wrapping them round the tip of your finger. Pinch the corners together on the seam. Repeat until all the triangles have been formed. Cook the tortelloni in plenty of salted boiling water for 4–5 minutes. Drain and transfer to a serving dish.

While cooking the tortelloni, make the sauce. Heat the oil and gently sauté the other onion and scallions for 2 minutes. Add the contents of the can of tomatoes and simmer for 5 minutes. Add seasoning to taste and the chopped parsley. Pour over the cooked tortelloni and serve with grated Parmesan cheese.

Tortelloni with Parma Ham ▶

Rich Pork and Beef Stuffing

This is a popular filling for pasta as the combination of pork and beef, enriched with chicken livers, gives pasta an excellent flavor.

1 tbsp olive oil

1 small onion, finely chopped

2 garlic cloves, minced

scant ¼ cup finely chopped chicken livers

1 tsp ground coriander

1 tsp chopped fresh marjoram

2 tbsp chopped fresh parsley

¾ cup lean ground pork

¾ cup lean ground steak

½ cup fresh white bread crumbs

2 tbsp brandy

salt and ground black pepper

Heat the olive oil in a small saucepan. Add the onion and garlic. Cook, stirring, for 2–3 minutes. Stir in the chicken livers, and cook for about a minute, or until just set. Remove the pan from the heat.

Stir in the coriander, marjoram, and parsley. Mix the pork and steak in a bowl, and stir in the onion and chicken liver mixture. Pound the ingredients until thoroughly combined. Then pound in the bread crumbs and brandy, and season well.

Vegetarian Pasta

Smoked Mozzarella with Arugula and Watercress

Pasta and Ratatouille

Goat Cheese with Grapes and Bows

Orecchiette with Herbs

Brandelle Genoese

Lentil and Pumpkin Lasagne

Garlic Cheese with Sun-dried Tomatoes

Spicy Okra and Mango

Mushroom Ravioli

Macaroni with Peppers and Basil

Verdi Vegetables with Vermicelli

Fusilli with Wild Mushrooms

Patty Pan and Avocado Topping

Whole Wheat Lasagne with Mediterranean Vegetables

Tagliatelle with Garbanzo Beans and Basil

Thin Spaghetti with Garlic, Oil, and Chilies

Creamy Eggplant Sauce

Fresh Spinach and Scallion Cream

Tomato Spaghetti with Mushrooms

Beet and Cheese Ravioli

Creamy Mushroom Pasta Pie

Mushroom Cannelloni

Cannelloni with Greens and Walnuts

Tagliolini with Seven Fresh Herbs

Tagliatelle with Baby Artichokes and Pine Nuts

Lasagne Verdi with Mushrooms and Ragù Sauce

Fresh Ravioli with Spinach and Ricotta Stuffing

Golden Rutabaga Sauce

Walnut Tortellini Tossed with Cucumber and Stilton

Feta Circles with Walnut Oil and Olives

Tagliatelle with Lentil Sauce

Pinwheel Pasta Bake

Pasta with Ricotta Cheese, Black Olives, and Capers

Mushroom Stroganoff with Pasta

Deep-fried Mushroom Pasta Pockets

Tagliatelle Neapolitan

Gratin of Mushroom Cappelletti

Smoked Mozzarella with Arugula and Watercress

SERVES 2

The piquant combination of arugula and watercress combines well with lightly smoked mozzarella in this dressing. Toss it with freshly cooked pasta shapes, such as spirals, elbows, rigatoni, penne, or lumache.

2 tbsp olive oil

1 garlic clove, chopped

½ red bell pepper, seeded and diced

4 black olives, thinly sliced

1 bunch of watercress, leaves only, roughly chopped

6 arugula leaves, shredded

1¼ cups diced smoked mozzarella cheese

salt and ground black pepper

Heat the oil in a small saucepan. Add the garlic, red bell pepper, and olives. Cook for 2 minutes, then add the watercress and arugula, and stir until the leaves are just limp.

Remove the pan from the heat, and stir in the mozzarella with salt and pepper to taste. Toss into freshly cooked pasta, and serve at once.

Pasta and Ratatouille

*R*atatouille is a classic Mediterranean dish; combine it with pasta and you have an all-time favorite. Canned tomatoes are used in this recipe but if you prefer you can use 1½ lb fresh peeled tomatoes and an extra tablespoon of tomato paste.

FOR THE SAUCE

1 medium eggplant, trimmed and sliced

salt

4 tbsp olive oil

1 large onion, peeled and thinly sliced

2–4 garlic cloves, chopped

1½ cups sliced zucchini

2 × 14 oz cans chopped tomatoes

1 tbsp tomato paste

6 tbsp red wine

ground black pepper

1 tbsp chopped fresh oregano

1 tbsp chopped fresh flat leaf parsley

¾ cup button mushrooms, wiped and halved

TO SERVE

10 oz fresh orecchiette

¾ cup sliced mozzarella cheese

Layer the eggplant in a colander, sprinkling between each layer with salt. Let sit 30 minutes. Drain, rinse well in cold water, and pat dry.

Heat the oil in a large pan and sauté the eggplant, onion, garlic, and zucchini for 5–8 minutes or until softened. (You may need to add a little more olive oil as the eggplant will soak it up.)

Add the tomatoes. Blend the tomato paste with the wine and stir into the pan with the black pepper, oregano, parsley, and mushrooms.

Bring to a boil, reduce the heat, cover with a lid, and simmer for 15 minutes or until the vegetables are tender but still retain a bite.

Meanwhile, cook the orecchiette in plenty of boiling salted water for 1–2 minutes or until "al dente." Drain and place in the base of an ovenproof gratin dish.

Pour over the prepared sauce and top with the sliced mozzarella cheese. Place under a medium hot broiler and cook for 5–8 minutes or until the cheese has melted and is golden.

Goat Cheese with Grapes and Bows

This will serve six as a first course. Otherwise, hungry diners may find the portions slightly small for a hearty main meal, but it is ideal for an average appetite and lunch. The flat shape of bows is ideal for this sauce, but you can use any other pasta shapes, if you like.

3 tbsp olive oil

2 garlic cloves, minced

1 onion, halved and thinly sliced

12 oz farfalle or other pasta shapes

16 black olives, pitted and thickly sliced

2 cups halved, seedless green grapes

¾ cup soft goat cheese

Heat the oil in a saucepan. Add the garlic and onion, and cook, stirring, for 10 minutes, or until the onion has softened but not browned. Meanwhile, cook the pasta in plenty of boiling salted water according to the instructions on the package.

Stir the olives and grapes into the onion, and cook for 2–3 minutes, until really hot. Quickly stir in the goat cheese, then remove the pan from the heat, and toss the sauce with hot, freshly drained pasta. Serve at once.

Orecchiette with Herbs

SERVES 4

*Y*ou can vary the herbs that you use according to availability and personal taste. The flavor will be better if you finely chop the herbs rather than blending them to a paste in a food processor.

FOR THE SAUCE

4 tbsp butter

2 garlic cloves, finely chopped

6 tbsp chopped fresh mixed herbs, such as basil, oregano, flat leaf parsley, chives, rosemary, and sage

grated zest and juice of 1 lemon

¼ cup toasted pine nuts

1 tbsp extra virgin olive oil

TO SERVE

1 lb fresh orecchiette

freshly shaved Parmigiano Reggiano cheese, to serve

● Melt the butter in a pan and sauté the garlic for 3 minutes. Add the herbs and lemon zest and juice, and continue to sauté for 2 minutes. Stir in the toasted pine nuts.

● Meanwhile, cook the orecchiette in plenty of boiling salted water for 1–2 minutes or until "al dente." Drain, reserving 2 tablespoons of the cooking liquor.

● Return the pasta to the pan with the cooking liquor and add the herb sauce and olive oil. Toss lightly and serve immediately with the freshly shaved Parmigiano Reggiano cheese.

Orecchiette with Herbs ▶

Brandelle Genoese

SERVES 4

*T*his sauce will work as well with any of the prepared homemade unfilled pastas as with ravioli or tortelloni.

FOR THE SAUCE

4 tbsp olive oil

1 large onion, peeled and chopped

2 garlic cloves, finely chopped

2½ cups puréed tomatoes

1 tbsp roughly torn fresh basil

salt and ground black pepper

2 medium eggs, beaten

TO SERVE

1 lb fresh brandelle

½ cup freshly grated Parmesan cheese

● Heat the oil in a large pan and sauté the onion and garlic for 8 minutes or until very soft. Pour in the puréed tomatoes and bring to a boil. Reduce the heat and simmer for 10 minutes. Add the basil leaves and seasoning to taste.

● Meanwhile, cook the brandelle in plenty of boiling salted water for 1–2 minutes or until "al dente." Drain.

● Gently reheat the sauce and, without allowing the sauce to boil, whisk in the eggs. Cook gently, whisking throughout until the sauce thickens. Add the pasta and Parmesan cheese, toss lightly, and serve immediately.

Lentil and Pumpkin Lasagne

SERVES 6

Pumpkin and lentils make a satisfying alternative to the traditional meat filling for lasagne. Use homemade or pre-cooked lasagne for this dish.

1 large onion, finely chopped

2 tbsp olive oil

1 zucchini, diced

1 green bell pepper, seeded and diced

1–2 garlic cloves, minced

1 lb pumpkin purée, fresh or canned

¾ cup red lentils

14 oz can chopped tomatoes

3 cups well-flavored vegetable broth

salt and ground black pepper

2 tbsp chopped fresh mixed herbs

fresh whole wheat lasagne made with 1 cup fine whole wheat flour and 1 large egg, or 6 large sheets whole wheat lasagne

1½ cups ricotta cheese

1½ cups sour cream

1 cup grated Cheddar cheese, loosely packed

Cook the onion in the oil until softened but not browned, then stir in the zucchini and bell pepper and cook for another 2 minutes. Add the garlic, pumpkin purée, lentils, and tomatoes and stir well. Add the broth, herbs, and seasonings, then bring the sauce to a boil. Simmer for 20–25 minutes, until the lentils are soft and the sauce has thickened.

Preheat the oven to 400°F. Prepare the pasta by mixing together the flour and egg, then process it through a pasta machine into six thin strips of lasagne. Bring a large pan of water to a boil and cook the lasagne quickly, 2 or 3 sheets at a time, for 1 to 2 minutes, until it floats to the top of the pan. Drain.

Place half the lentil mixture in the bottom of a suitable buttered ovenproof dish and top with half the pasta. Repeat the layers. Mix the ricotta and sour cream together and season with salt and pepper. Add half the cheese, then spread the mixture over the lasagne, topping it with the remaining cheese.

Bake the lasagne in the preheated oven for 30–40 minutes, until the topping is set and brown.

Garlic Cheese with Sun-dried Tomatoes

SERVES 4

8 sun-dried tomatoes

generous ¾ cup full-bodied red wine

1 small onion, finely chopped

2 tbsp chopped fresh oregano

2 bay leaves

salt and ground black pepper

4 tbsp olive oil

8 oz garlic-flavored Teifi cheese, cut into cubes

2 pickled walnuts, chopped

4 tbsp chopped fresh parsley

COOK'S TIP

Teifi cheese is a firm, moist cheese rather like Gouda in texture. It is readily available from delicatessens, both plain and with a variety of flavoring ingredients added, including garlic. Gouda may be substituted, in which case 3 chopped garlic cloves should be added to the tomato and wine mixture. Alternatively, try Gapron or Gaperon, the strong French, dome-shaped peppered cheese that is heavily laced with garlic.

Use a pair of kitchen scissors to snip the sun-dried tomatoes into small pieces. Put them in a small saucepan with the wine, onion, oregano, bay leaves, and salt and pepper to taste. Heat gently until simmering. Then cover the pan, and cook for 5 minutes. Remove from the heat, and let sit for 2 hours.

Add the olive oil, cheese, and walnuts to the tomato mixture, stir well, and let marinate overnight. To serve, strain the liquid from the cheese mixture into a large saucepan. Bring to a boil, and boil hard for 3 minutes, whisking occasionally. Pour this hot dressing over freshly cooked pasta. Add the strained cheese and tomato mixture and the parsley. Toss well and serve at once with pasta.

Spicy Okra and Mango

SERVES 4

Serve this mixture with fresh pasta shapes, or the dried types, which tend to be a bit thicker when cooked, such as gli strozzapreti, cicatelli di San Severo, rigatoni, or lumache.

8 oz small, young okra

4 tsp ground coriander

1 large firm mango

3 tbsp olive oil

1 large onion, chopped

1 large red bell pepper, seeded, halved lengthwise and sliced

2 garlic cloves, minced

2 green chilies, seeded and chopped

4 tsp chopped fresh oregano

salt and ground black pepper

1 lime, cut into wedges, to serve

The okra must be small, firm, bright in color and unblemished. Old fibrous or large okra will not cook successfully. Trim the stalk ends and points off the pods, then slice them thinly, and put in a bowl. Add the coriander, and toss well.

The mango should be just ripe, but still firm (fruit that is soft or too sweet will not complement the okra). Peel the mango; then slice the flesh off the large, flat central pit. Cut the slices into small pieces.

Heat the oil in a saucepan. Add the onion, bell pepper, garlic, chilies, and oregano; then cook, stirring occasionally, for 10 minutes. Stir in the okra, and cook over a fairly high heat for about 3–5 minutes, until the okra slices are slightly browned in part, and just tender. Stir in the mango, taste for seasoning, and serve. Toss the okra mixture with the pasta; then arrange lime wedges around the edge of the dish so that their juice may be squeezed over to taste.

Mushroom Ravioli

*O*nce you have tasted fresh, homemade ravioli, you will never buy it ready-made again.

8 oz Pasta Dough (page 9)

dash of olive oil

chopped, fresh parsley, to garnish

freshly grated Parmesan cheese,
   to serve

FOR THE MUSHROOM SAUCE

3 tbsp butter

2 cups sliced mushrooms

⅓ cup all-purpose flour

2½ cups milk

FOR THE FILLING

2 tbsp olive oil

1 garlic clove, minced

3 tbsp chopped fresh thyme

½ lb button mushrooms, finely
   chopped

1 cup fine, fresh white bread
   crumbs

salt and ground black pepper

Keep the fresh pasta dough covered in plastic wrap at rom temperature. Make the mushroom sauce. Melt the butter and cook the mushrooms until their liquid has evaporated. Stir in the flour, reduce the heat and slowly add the milk, stirring, until the sauce boils. Reduce the heat, and simmer for 3 minutes. Season to taste.

To make the filling, heat the oil in a large skillet and add the garlic and fresh thyme. Cook for 1–2 minutes, then stir in the mushrooms and fry for 3–5 minutes. Stir in the bread crumbs, and season to taste with salt and ground black pepper. Remove from the heat and allow to cool completely.

Make the ravioli following the instructions on page 146.

To cook the ravioli, bring a large saucepan of water to a boil and add the ravioli with a dash of olive oil. Cook for about 6 minutes, stirring occasionally, until tender. Drain.

Meanwhile, reheat the mushroom sauce. Serve the Mushroom Ravioli with the mushroom sauce, sprinkled with chopped parsley and grated Parmesan cheese.

Macaroni with Peppers and Basil

SERVES 4

When using chili peppers take care as their heat level can be deceptive. Remove the seeds as well as the membrane that the seeds are attached to. As a general guide, remember the smaller the chili the hotter the heat level.

FOR THE SAUCE

2 red bell peppers, seeded

2 yellow bell peppers, seeded

2 green bell peppers, seeded

1–3 jalapeño chilies, seeded

4 tbsp olive oil

I large onion, peeled and finely sliced

3 smoked or regular garlic cloves, finely sliced

2 cups puréed tomatoes

salt and ground black pepper

few sprigs of opal basil

TO SERVE

1 lb fresh macaroni

sprigs of opal basil

freshly grated Romano cheese

Heat the broiler to high then charbroil the bell peppers and chili peppers for 10 minutes or until the skins have blistered. Remove from the heat and place in a plastic bag until cool. Peel and cut into thin strips.

Heat the oil in a large pan and sauté the onion and garlic for 5 minutes or until softened. Add the peppers with the puréed tomatoes and bring to a boil. Cover with a lid, reduce the heat, and simmer for 5–8 minutes or until the sauce has thickened. Add the seasoning to taste and the basil sprigs.

Meanwhile, cook the macaroni in plenty of boiling salted water for 1–2 minutes or until "al dente." Drain and return to the pan. Add the prepared sauce and toss lightly. Serve immediately garnished with the opal basil sprigs and handing the grated cheese separately.

◀ *Macaroni with Peppers and Basil*

Verdi Vegetables with Vermicelli

SERVES 4-6

A lovely summer recipe to be eaten warm or cold, with chunks of crusty French bread.

12 oz dried vermicelli (long, thin spaghetti)

dash of olive oil

1 tbsp butter

1½ cups snow peas, sliced lengthwise

1 cup zucchini, shredded lengthwise

¼ cup pimiento-stuffed olives, sliced

salt and freshly ground black pepper

2 tbsp chopped fresh parsley

2 tbsp chopped fresh mint

squeeze of fresh lime juice

fresh herbs

lime slices

Bring a large saucepan of water to the boil and add the vermicelli with a dash of olive oil. Cook for about 5 minutes, stirring occasionally, until tender. Drain and set aside.

Melt the butter in a large skillet and sauté the sliced snow peas and the zucchini for about 5 minutes, stirring occasionally.,

Add the remaining ingredients except the lime juice to the vegetable mixture and cook for a further 5 minutes, stirring occasionally. Mix in the vermicelli and cook for 2–3 minutes, until heated through. Squeeze the fresh lime juice over the mixture and serve, garnished with fresh herbs and lime slices.

Fusilli with Wild Mushrooms

SERVES 4

Wild mushrooms, such as porcini are increasingly available and are the special ingredient in this dish. Dried porcini can be found in Italian delicatessens; they need to be soaked in water for 30 minutes before using in the recipe.

¾ lb dried long fusilli (twists)

dash of olive oil plus ¼ cup

1 garlic clove, minced

2 tbsp chopped fresh thyme

generous ¼ lb shiitake
  mushrooms, sliced

generous ¼ lb oyster mushrooms

½ oz dried porcini, soaked,
  drained, and sliced

salt and ground black pepper

freshly grated Parmesan cheese,
  to serve

Bring a large saucepan of water to a boil, and add the fusilli with a dash of olive oil. Cook for about 10 minutes, stirring occasionally, until tender. Drain and set aside, covered.

Heat the olive oil in a large skillet, and add the garlic and fresh thyme. Cook for 1–2 minutes, then stir in all the mushrooms and the season to taste with salt and ground black pepper.

Fry the mushroom mixture over high heat for 3–4 minutes to brown slightly, then turn the mixture into the saucepan containing the fusilli. Toss together briefly, then serve with a little freshly grated Parmesan cheese.

Patty Pan and Avocado Topping

SERVES 4–6

Small, yellow patty pan squash are complemented by the avocado in this sautéed mixture, which makes a colorful first course, or light lunch dish. Halve the quantities if the mixture is served as a topping for a first-course portion of pasta. Fresh pasta shapes are the best base for this topping.

¼ cup butter	salt and ground black pepper
2 onions, sliced	4 avocados
1 carrot, halved and thinly sliced	juice of ½ lemon
1 sprig of tarragon	8 large sprigs of dill, chopped
1 lb patty pan squash, halved horizontally	

Melt the butter in a large saucepan. Add the onions, carrot, and tarragon. Stir well, cover, and cook for about 15 minutes, or until the onions have softened.

Stir in the patty pan, salt and pepper to taste, and cover the pan; then continue to cook for a further 15 minutes, stirring once or twice, until the squash are tender but not too soft.

Halve the avocados, remove their pits, and cut them into quarters lengthwise. Peel each segment of avocado and slice it crosswise. Sprinkle with the lemon juice. Stir the avocado into the patty pan mixture, add the dill, and mix well. Then taste for seasoning before serving. Toss the vegetables into a large bowl of pasta, or spoon them on top of individual dishes of pasta.

Whole Wheat Lasagne with Mediterranean Vegetables

SERVES 4

With the greater emphasis on healthy eating, more people are adopting the Mediterranean way of eating. With their vast array of sun-ripened vegetables, delicious pastas, breads, and rich unctuous oils, it is easy to see why. Try this recipe, which captures all the richness of the ingredients.

3 tbsp olive oil

1 onion, peeled and chopped

3 garlic cloves, minced

6 sun-dried tomatoes, chopped

2 cups chopped eggplant

1 yellow bell pepper, seeded and chopped

1 red bell pepper, seeded and chopped

2 cups chopped zucchini

2 cups puréed tomatoes

⅔ cup red wine

salt and ground black pepper

1 tbsp chopped fresh oregano

6–8 fresh whole wheat lasagne sheets

4 firm tomatoes, sliced

½ cup grated mozzarella cheese

extra chopped fresh oregano

Preheat the oven to 375°F, 10 minutes before baking the lasagne. Heat the oil in a skillet and sauté the onion, garlic, and sun-dried tomatoes for 5 minutes. Add the eggplant, yellow and red peppers, and zucchini, and continue to sauté for 3 more minutes.

Stir in the puréed tomatoes, wine, seasoning to taste, and the oregano. Bring to a boil, reduce the heat, and simmer for 15 minutes or until the vegetables are almost cooked.

Bring a large pan of water to a boil, add 1 tablespoon salt, then drop in four lasagne sheets, one at a time. Cook for 2–3 minutes, ensuring that they do not stick together. Drain, lay them on clean dish towels, and pat dry. Repeat with the remaining lasagne sheets.

Place a layer of the vegetable sauce in the base of an ovenproof dish and top with half the lasagne sheets. Cover with the remaining sauce and then the lasagne sheets.

Arrange the tomato slices on top and sprinkle with the grated cheese. Bake in the oven for 25 minutes or until the cheese is golden and brown. Serve sprinkled with chopped oregano.

Tagliatelle with Garbanzo Beans and Basil

SERVES 4

 asta and garbanzo beans with aromatic fresh basil make a wonderful combination of flavors.

4 tbsp olive oil

1 garlic clove, minced

6 tbsp snipped chives

4 sage leaves, chopped

salt and ground black pepper

2 × 14 oz cans garbanzo beans, drained

1 lb tagliatelle verdi

6 basil sprigs

Heat the olive oil, garlic, chives, sage, salt and ground black pepper with the garbanzo beans in a large saucepan for about 3 minutes. The idea is to heat the ingredients rather than to cook them.

Add the drained pasta and toss well. Leave the pan over the lowest heat setting while you use scissors to shred the basil sprigs over the pasta, discarding any tough stalk ends.

Mix lightly and serve.

Thin Spaghetti with Garlic, Oil, and Chilies

SERVES 4

1 lb fine spaghetti

salt to taste

1¼ cups olive oil

8 garlic cloves, minced

4 chilies, seeded and chopped

Plunge the pasta into about 8 cups of boiling water. Season to taste and add a splash of olive oil.

Mix the remaining ingredients together.

When the pasta is cooked "al dente" drain it and toss in the dressing. Serve immediately.

Creamy Eggplant Sauce

Serve this sauce with shells, twists, bows, rigatoni, or other short shapes. Pasta flavored with vegetables also makes a colorful tempting base. Beet-, spinach-, and mushroom-flavored shapes make a colorful mixture.

1 lb eggplants	4 tbsp dry white vermouth or white wine
salt and ground black pepper	
5 tbsp olive oil	1½ cups light cream
4 garlic cloves, minced	4 tbsp freshly grated Parmesan cheese
1 large onion, finely chopped	
½ cup finely ground walnuts	4 large sprigs of basil, shredded
	sprigs of basil, to garnish

● Trim the ends off the eggplants, then dice them quite small, and layer them in a colander, sprinkling each layer with salt. Place over a bowl, and set aside for 30 minutes. Rinse and pat dry on paper towels.

● Heat the oil in a large saucepan, and cook the garlic and onion for 10 minutes. Then add the eggplant, and stir so that the pieces are evenly coated in oil. Cook, stirring often, until the eggplant is tender (about 15 minutes, depending on the size of the pan and heat).

● Stir in the walnuts, then add the vermouth or wine, and heat, stirring, for a few minutes. Stir in the cream and Parmesan cheese, and heat gently, stirring all the time. Do not boil the sauce.

● Remove the pan from the heat, and taste the sauce for seasoning. Stir in the basil, then ladle the sauce over freshly cooked pasta, and serve garnished with sprigs of basil.

Fresh Spinach and Scallion Cream

SERVES 4

Take advantage of washed, ready-to-cook baby spinach leaves to make this tempting pasta topping. If you want to make a less calorie-rich meal, then use low-fat soft cheese or fromage frais instead of mascarpone. This sauce really does go with any shape or form of pasta.

1 large red bell pepper and 6 ripe tomatoes, peeled, seeded and diced, to serve (optional)

salt and ground black pepper

2 tbsp butter

1 bunch of scallions, trimmed and chopped

12 oz young spinach leaves, washed and left very wet, stalks discarded, and torn into pieces if large

a little grated nutmeg

1 cup mascarpone

If you intend serving the pepper and tomato topping, then start by skinning the bell pepper and tomatoes. Dice the flesh of the pepper and tomatoes, and mix them together, adding a little salt. Set aside.

Melt the butter in a large saucepan. Add the scallions, and cook, stirring, for 2 minutes. Then add the spinach, packing it into the pan. Cover the pan tightly, and cook for 5 minutes. Shake the pan often to prevent the spinach sticking.

When the spinach has greatly reduced in volume, is wilted, and just tender, add salt, pepper, and nutmeg to taste. Stir in the mascarpone over a low heat. When the mascarpone has melted and warmed, spoon the mixture over the chosen, freshly cooked pasta. Add the topping, if using, and serve at once.

Tomato Spaghetti with Mushrooms

SERVES 4–6

For this dish you need to include at least one kind of dried mushroom as this will give the depth of flavor that is so typical of Italian mushroom-based dishes. Dried porcini keep well, and are an ingredient that no well-stocked kitchen should be without.

FOR THE SAUCE

½ oz dried porcini mushrooms

3 tbsp olive oil

1 red onion, peeled and cut into wedges

3–6 smoked or regular garlic cloves, thinly sliced

1½ cups mushrooms, such as oyster or chanterelle, wiped and sliced

1½ cups button mushrooms, wiped and sliced

6 tbsp red wine

2 tbsp extra virgin olive oil

salt and ground black pepper

2 tbsp chopped fresh sage

TO SERVE

1 lb fresh tomato spaghetti

fresh chopped sage leaves

Soak the porcini in warm water for about 20 minutes. Drain, reserving the soaking liquid, and chop the porcini.

Heat the oil in a pan and sauté the onion and garlic for 3 minutes. Add the chopped porcini, oyster or chanterelle, and button mushrooms. Sauté for a further 5 minutes, stirring frequently.

Strain the porcini soaking liquid into the pan and add the red wine. Bring to a boil, then simmer for 5 minutes or until the mushrooms are just cooked and the liquid has been reduced by about half. Stir in the extra virgin olive oil, seasoning to taste, and sage. Cover with lid, remove from the heat, and reserve.

Meanwhile, cook the tomato spaghetti in plenty of boiling salted water for 1–2 minutes or until "al dente." Drain and return to the pan. Add the mushrooms and sauce and toss ingredients lightly. Serve, garnished with the fresh chopped sage leaves.

Tomato Spaghetti with Mushrooms ▶

Beet and Cheese Ravioli

SERVES 4–6

Beet and cheese make an unusual and delicious combination.

1 cup ricotta cheese

½ cup grated Gruyère cheese

2 tbsp snipped fresh chives

1 medium egg yolk

salt and ground black pepper

1 lb Pasta Dough (page 9), flavored with beet juice

⅔ cup plain yogurt

freshly snipped chives, to garnish

Blend the ricotta, Gruyère cheese, chives, egg yolk, and seasoning together in a bowl until smooth. Reserve.

Roll the pasta dough out and proceed to make the ravioli as described on page 146. Once one sheet of dough has been filled, repeat until all the dough and filling has been used. Let the ravioli dry on clean dish towels for 1 hour before cooking.

Cook the ravioli in plenty of boiling salted water for 4–5 minutes or until "al dente." Drain and return to the pan. Add the yogurt and stir lightly. Sprinkle with the snipped chives and serve immediately.

Creamy Mushroom Pasta Pie

This dish can be made in advance and simply reheated before serving so that you won't be tied to the kitchen.

1 lb puff pastry, thawed if frozen	1¼ cups button mushrooms, sliced
milk, to glaze	about 12 baby corn, cut into chunks
FOR THE FILLING	⅓ cup all-purpose flour
2 cups dried, whole wheat pasta shells	⅔ cup milk
dash of olive oil	salt and ground black pepper
2 tbsp butter	¾ cup mature Cheddar cheese
1 clove of garlic, minced	chopped fresh parsley, to garnish

Preheat the oven to 400°F. Roll the pastry out into two rectangular pieces, each measuring 6 × 4 inches. Set one rectangle aside to make the base of the pastry case. Take the other piece and cut out an inner rectangle using a ruler and a sharp knife, leaving a 1-inch border to make the rim of the pastry case. Reserve the inner rectangle to make the lid and, using a sharp knife, score it to make a pattern. Brush a little milk around the edges of the base of the pastry case, and place the rim in position on top.

Place on a baking sheet with the lid alongside, and brush all the surfaces with a little milk to glaze. Bake for about 15–20 minutes, or until well-risen and golden-brown. Remove from the oven, and transfer the pastry case to a wire rack to cool. If the center of the pastry case has risen too high, gently press down to create a hollow space. Place on a serving plate.

To make the filling, bring a large saucepan of water to a boil and add the whole wheat pasta shells with a dash of olive oil. Cook for about 10 minutes, stirring occasionally, until tender. Drain well and set aside.

Melt the butter in a large saucepan, and sauté the garlic, mushrooms, and baby corn for 5–8 minutes, or until softened. Stir in the flour, and mix to form a paste. Gradually stir in the milk, a little at a time, stirring well after each addition. Bring the sauce slowly to a boil, stirring constantly to prevent lumps from forming. Season with salt and ground black pepper. Stir in the grated cheese and continue to cook for a further 2–3 minutes, until the cheese has melted.

Stir the pasta in the sauce, then spoon the sauce into the pastry case. Sprinkle with the chopped fresh parsley, then place the lid on top and serve.

Mushroom Cannelloni

SERVES 4

*C*annelloni is a time-consuming dish to prepare, but it is always worth the effort. Cook more cannelloni pasta than is required to allow for any split ones.

8 dried cannelloni tubes

dash of olive oil

butter, for greasing

1 quantity Mushroom Sauce (page 125)

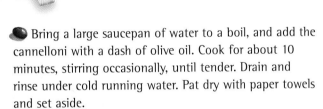

FOR THE FILLING

2 tbsp olive oil

1 clove of garlic, minced

1 onion, finely chopped

1 tbsp chopped fresh thyme

½ lb button mushrooms, finely chopped

½ cup fine, fresh bread crumbs

salt and ground black pepper

Bring a large saucepan of water to a boil, and add the cannelloni with a dash of olive oil. Cook for about 10 minutes, stirring occasionally, until tender. Drain and rinse under cold running water. Pat dry with paper towels and set aside.

To make the filling, heat the oil in a large skillet and sauté the garlic, onion, and thyme for about 3 minutes, or until the onion has softened.

Add the chopped mushrooms to the onion mixture and continue to cook for about 10 minutes, stirring frequently. Add the bread crumbs, and season with salt and freshly ground black pepper. Stir well.

Preheat the oven to 400°F. Butter the inside of an ovenproof casserole dish. Using a teaspoon, stuff each cannelloni with the filling, then lay it in the dish.

Pour the mushroom sauce evenly over the cannelloni, then bake for about 30 minutes, until heated through and golden on top.

Cannelloni with Greens and Walnuts

SERVES 4

$\mathscr{S}$erve with a simple, crisp, fresh salad to complement the rich, cheesy sauce and walnut filling. Fresh spinach is a good alternative for this recipe.

12 dried cannelloni tubes

dash of olive oil

butter, for greasing

½ cup walnuts, chopped

FOR THE FILLING

3 tbsp olive oil

1 large onion, chopped

1 clove of garlic, minced

1 lb mustard greens, shredded

7 oz can chopped tomatoes

1 tsp dried oregano

3 tbsp chopped, fresh basil

½ lb ricotta cheese

1 cup fresh whole wheat bread crumbs

½ cup walnuts

good pinch of freshly grated nutmeg

salt and ground black pepper

FOR THE CHEESE SAUCE

2 tbsp butter

¼ cup all-purpose flour

1¼ cups milk

⅔ cup grated fontina cheese

COOK'S TIP

Sheets of fresh lasagne can be used instead of dried cannelloni. Make up 6 ounces pasta dough, and roll out to ¼ inch thick. Cut into 4 × 6 inch rectangles, and spoon some of the filling along the short end of the sheet of pasta. Roll it up into a neat tube, and place in the dish with the sealed end underneath.

● Bring a large saucepan of water to a boil, and add the cannelloni with a dash of olive oil. Cook for about 10 minutes, stirring occasionally, until tender. Drain and rinse under cold running water. Drain again, then pat dry with paper towels and set aside.

● To make the filling, heat the olive oil in a large skillet and sauté the onion and garlic for 2–3 minutes, until the onion has softened. Add the mustard greens, tomatoes, and oregano. Continue to cook for about 5 minutes, stirring frequently, until the liquid has completely evaporated. Remove from the heat and let cool.

● Place the mustard greens mixture in a food processor or blender, and add the basil, ricotta cheese, bread crumbs, walnuts, and nutmeg. Purée until smooth, then season with salt and ground black pepper.

● To make the sauce, melt the butter in a saucepan. Stir in the flour and cook for 1 minute. Gradually stir in the milk, and heat until bubbling and thickened. Stir in the grated fontina cheese.

● Preheat the oven to 375°F. Butter the inside of a shallow, ovenproof dish. Using a teaspoon, stuff each cannelloni with the filling, then lay it in the dish.

● Pour the cheese sauce evenly over the cannelloni. Sprinkle with walnuts and bake for about 30 minutes, until bubbling and golden.

Tagliolini with Seven Fresh Herbs

SERVES 4

This Tuscan dish, with Renaissance flavors, combines seven wild herbs with tagliolini, a very thin spaghetti.

4 cups fresh mixed herbs such as chives, mint, tarragon, chervil, basil, marjoram, and parsley

sea salt and ground black pepper

¼ cup extra virgin olive oil

4 ripe plum tomatoes, peeled and finely chopped, or a can of plum tomatoes, drained, chopped, and drained again

1 lb fresh or dried tagliolini (fresh are preferable)

Chop all the herbs finely and mash them in a pestle and mortar with some salt and freshly ground black pepper. Stir in the olive oil. Cook gently for 5 minutes.

Add the chopped tomatoes, cover and simmer for a further 10 minutes. Check the seasoning.

Cook the tagliolini in plenty of boiling salted water for 3 minutes – do not overcook them. Drain them quickly and then toss them into the sauce. Serve immediately, sprinkled with ground black pepper.

Taglioline with Seven Fresh Herbs ▶

Tagliatelle with Baby Artichokes and Pine Nuts

SERVES 4

In spring and autumn, tightly packed purple artichokes on their long stems appear in the markets. Their tender inner leaves are dipped into unfiltered olive oil and eaten raw, or gently sautéed for thick omelettes, or eaten with fresh tagliatelle.

8 baby artichokes

a little lemon juice

½ cup pine nuts

extra virgin olive oil

4 garlic cloves, finely chopped

small handful of fresh parsley, finely chopped

sea salt and ground black pepper

few drops of truffle oil

1 lb fresh or dried tagliatelle

grated pecorino stagionato (mature sheep-milk cheese), or Parmesan cheese, to serve

To prepare the artichokes, remove the stalks and tough outer leaves, cut the artichokes into quarters and, with a small knife, remove any hairy choke in the center. Sprinkle with lemon juice to prevent discoloring.

Boil the artichokes in salted water for 6–7 minutes. Meanwhile, brown the pine nuts in a heavy skillet.

Drain the artichokes and pat them dry. Sauté them in olive oil, with the garlic and parsley, for a few minutes, or until they are very tender.

Purée half the artichokes and stir in the pine nuts and seasoning. Stir in the remaining artichokes and drizzle over a few drops of truffle oil. Keep the sauce warm.

Cook the pasta in plenty of boiling salted water for 6–7 minutes or until it is "al dente." Drain the pasta and mix it into the sauce. Serve immediately, dredged with the grated pecorino or Parmesan.

Saffron Fusille with Peas and Chèvre

SERVES 4

There are many different chèvres. Some are very salty and sharp while others are much milder and less salty. If you have not eaten chèvre before, choose one that is mild before you sample the sharper varieties.

FFOR THE SAUCE

4 tbsp olive oil

3–4 garlic cloves, peeled and sliced

1 large onion, peeled and sliced

½ cup dry white wine

2 cups snow peas, trimmed and halved

8 oz herb-crushed chèvre, diced

fresh flat leaf parsley sprigs

TO SERVE

1 lb fresh saffron fusille

Heat the oil in a pan and sauté the garlic and onion for 5 minutes. Add the white wine, bring to a boil, and simmer for 3 minutes.

Blanch the snow peas in a pan of boiling water for 1 minute. Drain and refresh in cold water. Add to the pan with the diced herb-crushed chèvre. Heat through very gently for 3 minutes, stirring occasionally.

Meanwhile, cook the saffron fusille in plenty of salted boiling water for 1–2 minutes or until "al dente." Drain and return to the pan. Add the snow peas and chèvre mixture with the parsley. Toss lightly, then serve.

Lasagne Verdi with Mushroom Sauce

SERVES 4

This is a dish that is ideal for freezing, so when you have plenty of time, make this, then freeze it ready for use at a later date. Use any mix of mushrooms you like. You can sprinkle the yogurt topping with some grated mozzarella cheese.

3 tbsp olive oil

4 cups sliced mixed mushrooms

Double quantity Quick Tomato Sauce (page 46)

6–8 fresh lasagne verdi sheets

2 medium eggs

⅔ cup thick, unflavored yogurt

Preheat the oven to 375°F, 10 minutes before baking the lasagne. Heat the oil in a pan and gently sauté the mushrooms for 5 minutes, stirring occasionally, until softened. Remove from the heat and drain. Warm the tomato sauce if made previously and stir well.

Bring a large pan of water to a boil, add 1 tablespoon salt, then drop in four lasagne sheets, one at a time. Cook for 2–3 minutes, ensuring that they do not stick together. Drain and lay them on clean dish towels and pat dry. Repeat with the remaining lasagne sheets.

Place a layer of the tomato sauce in the base of an ovenproof dish and cover with 3–4 sheets of lasagne. Cover the lasagne with half the cooked mushrooms and top with the remaining tomato sauce. Cover with remaining lasagne sheets, then the rest of the mushrooms.

Beat the eggs with the yogurt and pour over the mushrooms. Cook the lasagne in the oven for 30 minutes or until golden.

Fresh Ravioli with Spinach and Ricotta Stuffing

SERVES 4

*W*ild sage gives a perfumed finish to this delicious dish.

FOR THE PASTA

8 oz all-purpose flour

2 eggs

a little warm water

2 tbsp extra virgin olive oil

large pinch of freshly grated nutmeg

sea salt and ground black pepper

FOR THE FILLING

8 oz spinach, cooked, well drained, and finely chopped

1 cup ricotta cheese

TO DRESS THE RAVIOLI

4 tbsp butter

few fresh sage leaves

1 cup Parmesan cheese, grated

Sift the flour onto a clean surface and make a high-walled well in the middle. Crack the eggs into the well and start to beat them in with your fingers, gradually incorporating the flour from the inside of the well. Add warm water, a spoonful at a time, until you have a soft, but not sticky dough.

Knead gently for a few minutes. Cover loosely and leave to rest in a cool place for half an hour.

Meanwhile, mix together all the ingredients for the ravioli filling.

Roll out the dough lightly and quickly to about ⅛ inch thickness. Cut into rectangles approximately 2 × 4 inches.

Place a heaped teaspoonful of filling on half of each piece of dough and fold over the other half to make a sandwich. Seal the edges of the ravioli with wet fingers.

Cook for 4–5 minutes in plenty of boiling salted water.

Melt the butter with the sage leaves. As soon as the ravioli are cooked, remove them from the water with a perforated metal spoon, dress with the butter and sage and serve immediately, dredged with freshly grated, Parmesan and black pepper.

Golden Rutabaga Sauce

SERVES 4

This is a simple and tasty dish. Toss shells, elbow macaroni, or other small shapes with the sauce to make a satisfying lunch dish.

1 lb rutabaga (½ a large rutabaga)

salt and ground black pepper

2 tbsp butter

1 small onion, finely chopped

FOR THE CHEESE SAUCE

3 tbsp butter

⅓ cup all-purpose flour

2½ cups milk

1 cup grated Cheddar cheese

Peel the rutabaga, and cut it into thick slices; then cut these into cubes. Cook in boiling salted water for 10–15 minutes or until tender.

Melt the butter in a saucepan, add the onion, and cook, stirring occasionally, for about 10 minutes, or until softened.

Drain and mash the cooked rutabaga; then press it through a fine strainer into the cooked onion. Mix well. Make the cheese sauce. Melt the butter. Stir in the flour, reduce the heat and slowly add the milk, stirring. Continue stirring until the sauce boils. Reduce the heat to low and simmer for 3 minutes. Add seasoning with the cheese. Stir over a low heat until the cheese melts. Gradually stir the cheese sauce into the rutabaga. Reheat the sauce if necessary, then pour over the cooked pasta, and serve.

Walnut Tortellini Tossed with Cucumber and Stilton

SERVES 4–6

6 oz Pasta Dough (page 9)

1 egg, beaten

1½ cups crumbled blue Stilton cheese

sprigs of tarragon, to garnish

FOR THE WALNUT STUFFING

¾ cup walnuts

¼ cup fresh whole wheat bread crumbs

2 tbsp finely chopped onion

2 tsp chopped fresh tarragon

salt and ground black pepper

5 tsp light cream

FOR THE DRESSING

2 tbsp olive oil

¼ cup butter

½ English cucumber, thinly peeled and diced

4 tbsp snipped chives

salt and ground black pepper

4 tbsp dry white vermouth or dry white wine

Make the pasta as given on page 9. Make the walnut stuffing. Grind the walnuts in a food processor. Mix them with the bread crumbs, onion, tarragon, and seasoning. Stir in the cream to bind the mixture together.

Cut the pasta dough in half. Roll out one portion to form a 12-inch square. Cut the dough into 2-inch wide strips. Then cut these across in the opposite direction to make 2-inch squares.

Work on about a quarter of the squares at a time, keeping the others covered loosely with plastic wrap to prevent the pasta drying out. Brush the squares with egg, and place a little of the filling in the middle – just less than ½ teaspoon (not a measuring spoon, but a cutlery teaspoon) of filling is sufficient for each square. Fold the pasta diagonally over the filling, and pinch the edges together to make a triangle; then curl the long side around a finger tip, and pinch the points together to shape each tortellini (see page 114). Repeat using the remaining pasta to make a total of 72 tortellini.

Once the tortellini are shaped, prepare the dressing. Heat the olive oil and butter together. The cucumber should be so finely peeled that only the very outer layer of skin is removed, leaving the outside of the vegetable quite green. Add the cucumber to the butter and oil, and cook, stirring, for 5 minutes. Stir in the chives, salt and pepper to taste, and vermouth or wine. Heat until the mixture is just simmering, then cover the pan, and leave it over the lowest heat until the pasta is ready.

Cook the tortellini in boiling salted water for 3–5 minutes. Drain well, and transfer to a heated serving dish. If you have to cook the pasta in batches, then spoon a little liquid from the cucumber over the first batch, and keep it covered and hot until successive batches are cooked.

Toss the cucumber and its liquid, and the Stilton with the cooked tortellini, and serve at once. Garnishing the tortellini with sprigs of tarragon indicates the flavor of the walnut stuffing.

A SALAD-STYLE STARTER

Prepare a half quantity of the tortellini, and serve them on a generous base of chicory and watercress salad with a little arugula if available. Then spoon over the cucumber and stilton dressing, and serve at once. The hot tortellini is delicious with the cold salad.

Feta Circles with Walnut Oil and Olives

SERVES 4

Ingredients

6 oz Pasta Dough (page 9)

5 oz feta cheese

1 egg, beaten

salt and ground black pepper

2 tbsp sunflower oil

2 tbsp butter

6 scallions, finely chopped

12 black olives, pitted and thinly sliced

3 tbsp walnut oil

2 tbsp chopped parsley

First, make the Pasta Dough.

Cut the cheese into ¼-inch cubes.

Roll out half the pasta dough to form a 12-inch square. Stamp out forty 1½-inch circles, dipping the cutter in flour occasionally to prevent it sticking to the dough.

Place cubes of cheese on 20 of the circles. Brush the remaining circles with a little beaten egg. Then sandwich the cheese between the pasta circles, pinching their edges together neatly. Repeat with the remaining dough and cheese.

Cook the pasta circles in plenty of boiling salted water for 3 minutes.

Meanwhile, heat the sunflower oil and butter, add the scallions and olives, and stir over low heat for 2–3 minutes to cook the onions lightly.

Drain the cooked pasta, and turn it into a warmed serving dish. Stir the walnut oil and parsley into the scallion and olive mixture, and pour this dressing over the pasta, scraping every last drop from the pan. Toss well, and serve at once.

DIFFERENT CHEESE FILLINGS

Feta cheese may be replaced with a full-flavored alternative, such as a blue cheese (Maytag Blue, Dolcelatte, Gorgonzola, Stilton or Danish blue), or a garlic-flavored cheese. Many of the flavored cheeses made in Vermont also go well, provided the herbs or spices are fairly powerful.

ALTERNATIVE DRESSINGS AND SAUCES

- *Toss the pasta with tomato sauce in place of the oil.*
- *Try garlic butter or lemon butter with the hot pasta.*
- *For a quick sauce, stir strained plain yogurt and chopped fresh herbs into the hot pasta.*
- *Olive paste or pesto would make a quick dressing for the feta circles.*

Tagliatelle with Lentil Sauce

SERVES 4

*T*his simple recipe is quick to make and ideal for lunch or supper.

¾ lb dried tagliatelle

dash of olive oil

2 tbsp butter

FOR THE SAUCE:

2 tbsp olive oil

2 garlic cloves, minced

1 large onion, very finely chopped

1 generous cup red lentils, washed and drained

3 tbsp tomato paste

salt and ground black pepper

2½ cups boiling water

sprigs of fresh rosemary, to garnish

freshly grated Parmesan cheese, to serve

Bring a large saucepan of water to the boil, and add the tagliatelle with a dash of olive oil. Cook for about 10 minutes, stirring occasionally, until tender. Drain, and return to the saucepan. Add the butter and stir. Cover and set aside, to keep warm.

To make the lentil sauce, heat the olive oil in a large saucepan and sauté the garlic and onion for about 5 minutes, stirring occasionally, until softened. Add the lentils, tomato paste, salt and ground black pepper, and stir in the boiling water. Bring to a boil, then simmer for about 20 minutes, stirring occasionally, until the lentils have softened.

Reheat the tagliatelle gently for 2–3 minutes, if necessary, then serve with the lentil sauce. Scatter a few sprigs of fresh rosemary over the top, and serve with freshly grated Parmesan cheese.

Pinwheel Pasta Bake

SERVES 4–6

This simple, unpretentious dish is perfect for a family supper, and makes a good recipe for the freezer. When thawed, reheat, covered, in a medium-hot oven.

1½ lb dried rotelle (pinwheels)

dash of olive oil

2 tbsp sunflower oil

1 garlic clove, minced

½ lb mushrooms, quartered

¼ lb zucchini, chopped

3 tbsp chopped fresh parsley

⅔ cup vegetable broth

2¼ cups grated mature Cheddar cheese

Bring a large saucepan of water to the boil, and add the rotelle with a dash of olive oil. Cook for about 10 minutes, stirring occasionally, until tender. Drain, and set aside.

Heat the sunflower oil in a large skillet, and sauté the garlic for 2 minutes. Add the mushrooms and zucchini, and cook, covered, for 5 minutes, or until softened.

Stir the chopped parsley and vegetable broth into the mushroom mixture, and continue to cook, covered, for a further 10 minutes. Add the rotelle, and stir in the grated cheese.

Preheat the oven to 400°F. Transfer the pasta mixture to a deep casserole dish, and bake for about 20 minutes. Serve with warm, crusty bread.

Pinwheel Pasta Bake ▶

Pasta with Ricotta Cheese, Black Olives, and Capers

SERVES 4

This pasta dish is extremely quick to prepare. The succulent black olives and the capers complement the mild flavor of the ricotta.

1 lb rigatoni pasta

a few tbsp extra virgin olive oil

½ cup loose ricotta

1 cup pitted black olives

salt and ground black pepper

½ cup capers, washed, drained, and chopped

Cook the pasta in plenty of boiling salted water for 10 minutes or until it is "al dente." Drain. Return the pasta to the pan and stir in 2 tablespoons of olive oil and the ricotta and black olives. Season with salt and plenty of ground black pepper.

Turn out into bowls and scatter over the chopped capers.

Mushroom Stroganoff with Pasta

This rich dinner-party dish is delicious served with a glass of chilled dry white wine.

¼ cup butter

2 garlic cloves, minced

1 onion, sliced into thin wedges

1½ lb mixed mushrooms (oyster, maron, cup, etc), left whole or cut in half

3 level tbsp all-purpose flour

⅔ cup vegetable broth

3 tbsp dry white wine

salt and ground black pepper

⅓ cup heavy cream

3 tbsp chopped fresh thyme

2 tbsp paprika

1½ lb cooked tagliatelle, tossed in butter, to serve

● Melt the butter in a large saucepan, and sauté the garlic and onion for about 7 minutes, until the onion has browned slightly.

● Add the mushrooms and cook for 2 minutes, then stir in the flour. Cook for 30 seconds, then gradually stir in the vegetable broth, then the wine. Bring the sauce to a boil, and season with salt and ground black pepper. Stir in the cream, fresh thyme, and paprika. Cook for a further 2 minutes, then serve with hot, buttered tagliatelle.

Mushroom Stroganoff with Pasta ▶

Deep-fried Mushroom Pasta Pockets

Serve this dish as an appetizer with a small dish of garlic mayonnaise (see Cook's Tip) for dipping.

½ lb fresh lasagne sheets

1 egg, beaten

sunflower oil, for deep frying

FOR THE FILLING

½ lb cream cheese with herbs and garlic

1½ cups button mushrooms

COOK'S TIP

To make garlic mayonnaise, mix 4 garlic cloves, minced, with 1¼ cups mayonnaise. Chill for 30 minutes before serving.

● Lay the fresh lasagne sheets out on the work surface, and stamp out rounds using a 3-inch cutter.

● Place the cream cheese and the mushrooms in a food processor, and blend to form a coarse texture.

● Spoon some of the mushroom mixture onto one half of each pasta round. Brush a little of the beaten egg around the edges of the rounds, then fold in half to encase the filling, sealing firmly with your fingers. Lay the mushroom pockets out on baking sheets, and chill in the refrigerator for 30 minutes.

● Heat the oil for deep frying, and fry the mushroom pockets in batches for about 3 minutes, until crisp and golden. Remove from the oil and drain on paper towels. Place on a baking sheet, and keep warm in a low oven until all the batches are cooked. Serve with garlic mayonnaise for dipping.

Tagliatelle Neapolitan

SERVES 4

Yellow tomatoes make this dish look particularly attractive, though red ones taste just as good. If you can't find fresh tagliatelle, use the dried egg version.

1 lb fresh, multicolored tagliatelle

dash of olive oil, plus 2 tbsp

2 garlic cloves, minced

1 onion, chopped

3 tbsp chopped fresh basil or oregano

1 lb yellow and red tomatoes, skinned, seeded, and chopped

8 oz carton strained tomatoes

salt and ground black pepper

fresh basil, to garnish

freshly grated Parmesan cheese, to serve

Bring a large saucepan of water to the boil, and add the tagliatelle with a dash of olive oil. Cook for about 5 minutes, stirring occasionally, until tender. Drain and set aside, covered.

Heat the remaining oil in a large skillet, and sauté the garlic, onion, and basil or oregano for about 3 minutes, or until the onion has softened.

Add the chopped tomato flesh and strained tomatoes, and season with salt and ground black pepper. Stir and cook for about 10 minutes, until thickened and bubbling. Serve with the tagliatelle. Garnish with fresh basil and sprinkle with freshly grated Parmesan cheese.

Gratin of Mushroom Cappelletti

SERVES 4–6

Cappelletti are also sometimes referred to as ravioli, and they can be square or circular. If you would prefer to make these square, then simply follow the instructions for ravioli on page 146.

6 oz Pasta Dough (page 9)	FOR THE MUSHROOM STUFFING
1 egg, beaten	2 tbsp butter
2–4 tbsp melted butter	1/3 cup finely chopped onion
2 cups tomato sauce	1½ cups finely chopped mushrooms
3–4 tbsp chopped fresh parsley	1 cup whole wheat bread crumbs
1 tbsp chopped fresh oregano (optional)	salt and ground black pepper
1¼ cups finely diced mozzarella cheese	1 tbsp tomato ketchup
1 cup fresh white bread crumbs	
4 tbsp freshly grated Parmesan cheese	

Roll out half the pasta dough to form a 12-inch square. Stamp out 40 1½-inch circles, dipping the cutter in flour occasionally to prevent it sticking.

Make the mushroom stuffing. Melt the butter and cook the onion for 2 minutes. Add the mushrooms and cook for 5 minutes more. Remove the pan from the heat and add the bread crumbs, seasoning, and the ketchup.

Preheat the oven to 400°F. Use half the mushroom stuffing, placing a little on 20 of the circles. Brush the remaining circles with a little beaten egg. Then sandwich the stuffing between the pasta circles, pinching their edges together neatly. Repeat with the remaining dough and stuffing.

Cook the mushroom cappelletti in plenty of boiling salted water for 3 minutes. Brush a shallow, ovenproof dish, or individual dishes, with a little of the butter. Drain the cappelletti; then transfer it to the dish, or divide among individual dishes. Spoon the tomato sauce over the pasta to cover.

Mix the parsley and oregano (you will probably need the larger quantity of parsley if you are using individual dishes), and sprinkle these herbs over the sauce. Top with the mozzarella cheese. Mix the bread crumbs and Parmesan, and sprinkle this over the top. Trickle the remaining butter over the bread crumbs and cheese; then bake the gratin in the preheated oven for 25–30 minutes, or until the mozzarella has melted, and the topping is crisp and golden. Serve at once.

Pasta Around the World

Won Ton Soup · Kopytka with Kabanos

Crispy Won Tons · Mushroom Uska

Chicken Won Tons with Vegetables · Yosenabe

Rice Sticks with Vegetables · Spätzle

Shrimp and Pork Dim Sum · Cabbage Soup with Spätzle

Mushroom Dim Sum · Uszka

Glossy Dumplings · Kreplach

Crispy Chicken Chow Mein · Beef in Oyster Sauce with Rice Sticks

Chinese Mustard Greens with Fusilli · Noodles with Japanese Fish Cake and Vegetables

Shrimp Chow Mein

· Hiyamugi

Pork Chow Mein

Won Ton Soup

SERVES 4

8 oz ground pork

4 scallions, finely chopped

2 button mushrooms, finely chopped

2 tbsp soy sauce

1 tsp sesame oil

1 package won ton skins

1 egg, beaten

cornstarch, for dusting

FOR THE SOUP

1 tbsp oil

1 boneless chicken breast, skinned and diced

2 leeks, sliced

3¾ cups good chicken broth

4 tbsp dry sherry

salt and ground black pepper

Mix the pork, scallions, mushrooms, soy sauce, and sesame oil.

To fill the won tons, take a skin. Shape a little meat into a ball and place it in the middle of the dough square. Brush the meat with egg, then fold the dough around it and pinch it together to seal in the meat. Leave the corners of the dough hanging free. Fill all the won tons in the same way and place them on a platter or board dusted with cornstarch.

For the soup, heat the oil in a saucepan. Add the chicken and leeks, and cook, stirring often, for 20 minutes, until the leek is softened and the chicken is just cooked. Pour in the broth and bring to a boil. Cover and simmer for 20 minutes. Stir in the sherry and seasoning to taste. Add the won tons to the soup, bring back to a boil and reduce the heat slightly so that it does not boil fiercely. Cook for 5 minutes. Test a won ton to make sure the filling is cooked, then ladle the soup and won tons into bowls. Serve at once.

Crispy Won Tons

These won tons are made in the same way as the ones which are cooked in soup; however, they are deep-fried until crisp and served with a sweet and sour sauce. Offer them as a first course for a Chinese meal or serve them with plain boiled rice and a dish of stir-fried vegetables to make a delicious main course.

won tons as for Won Ton Soup (page 161)	1 carrot, cut into fine 1-inch strips
oil for deep frying	4 tbsp tomato ketchup
	4 tbsp soy sauce
FOR THE SAUCE	1 tbsp superfine sugar
2 tbsp oil	2 tbsp cider vinegar
1 tsp sesame oil	⅔ cup dry sherry
1 onion, halved and thinly sliced	1 tsp cornstarch
1 green bell pepper, halved, seeded, and thinly sliced	2 canned pineapple rings, cut in small pieces

Make the won tons as on page 161. Set them aside until the sauce is ready. Heat the oil and sesame oil in a saucepan. Add the onion, green bell pepper, and carrot and cook for 5 minutes. Stir in the tomato ketchup, soy sauce, sugar, cider vinegar, and sherry. Bring to a boil, reduce the heat, and simmer for 3 minutes. Meanwhile, blend the cornstarch with 2 tablespoons cold water, then stir it into the sauce and bring to a boil, stirring all the time. Simmer for 2 minutes, then add the pineapple and set aside over low heat.

Heat the oil for deep frying to 375°F. Deep-fry the won tons a few at a time, until they are crisp and golden. Drain them on paper towels. Place the won tons on a large flat dish or platter and spoon the sauce over them. Serve and eat at once.

Chicken Won Tons with Vegetables

MAKES ABOUT 25 – SERVES 4

These are thicker than authentic won tons. This makes them easier to handle and quicker to fill – and they taste terrific! The dim sum and vegetables make an ample complete meal; if they are served with a selection of other Chinese-style dishes, then they will yield far more portions.

4 boneless chicken breasts, skinned

¼ tsp five-spice powder

8 scallions, chopped

1 tsp sesame oil

5 tbsp soy sauce

1 garlic clove, minced

1 package won ton skins

1 egg, beaten

3 tbsp oil

2 celery stalks, cut into fine 1-inch strips

1 red bell pepper, quartered, seeded, and cut in thin strips

½ medium head Chinese leaves, shredded

3 tbsp dry sherry

Cut the chicken into 50 small pieces. Place them in a basin and add the five-spice powder, 2 tablespoons of the scallions, sesame oil, 2 tablespoons of the soy sauce, and the garlic. Mix well, cover, and leave to marinate for 30 minutes.

Brush a won ton skin with beaten egg. Place a piece of chicken in the middle of it, then fold the dough around the chicken and pinch it together well. Continue filling the squares, placing them on a platter dusted with cornstarch as they are ready.

Grease a large covered dish with oil and set it to warm. Bring a large saucepan of water to a boil, then cook the won tons in batches, allowing 5 minutes after the water has come back to a boil. Drain, transfer to the dish, and keep hot.

Stir-fry the vegetables while the won tons are cooking. Heat the oil in a large skillet. Add the celery and bell pepper, and cook, stirring, for 5 minutes. Add the remaining scallions and cook for a further 2 minutes. Then add the Chinese leaves and cook for 3–5 minutes. Pour in the remaining soy sauce and sherry, and stir for 1 minute. Arrange the vegetables and won tons together on a platter and serve at once.

Rice Sticks with Vegetables

Egg noodles may be used instead of the rice sticks. Serve this as a light lunch dish or offer it with a simple main course, such as crisp roast duck or deep-fried pork in batter.

8 oz whole baby corn	6 oz bean sprouts
2 tbsp oil	4 tbsp soy sauce
1 red bell pepper, seeded, quartered lengthwise, and thinly sliced	2 tbsp dry sherry
	12 oz ribbon rice sticks
6 scallions, shredded diagonally	4 tbsp cashew nuts, roasted
8 oz Chinese leaves, shredded	2 tbsp sesame seeds, roasted

Blanch the baby corn in boiling water for 2 minutes, then drain. Have a large pan of boiling water ready for cooking the rice sticks. Heat the oil in a wok or large saucepan. Add the bell pepper and scallions, and stir-fry for 3 minutes. Add the Chinese leaves and cook for 2 minutes before stirring in the bean sprouts. Pour in the soy sauce and sherry at the same time.

Add the rice sticks to the boiling water. Bring back to a boil and cook for 1 minute, then drain at once. By the time the rice sticks are ready, all the vegetables will be cooked. Place the rice sticks in a serving dish or platter. Top with the vegetables and sprinkle with the cashew nuts and sesame seeds. Serve at once.

PASTA AROUND THE WORLD   165

Shrimp and Pork Dim Sum

MAKES 25

8 oz peeled cooked shrimp, finely chopped

4 oz ground pork

2 scallions, finely chopped

1 tsp sesame oil

1 garlic clove, minced

2 tsp soy sauce

1 package won ton skins

1 egg, beaten

soy sauce, to serve

The shrimp may be finely chopped in the food processor or blender. Mix them with the pork, scallions, sesame oil, garlic, and soy sauce. Pound the mixture well so that all the ingredients bind together. Wet your hands and shape the mixture into 25 small balls.

Brush a won ton skin with a little beaten egg. Hold the dough on the palm of your hand and place a shrimp ball on it. Flatten the shrimp ball slightly and bring the dough up and around it, leaving the top of the mixture uncovered. Brush the dough with a little extra egg, if necessary, so that the folds cling to the side of the mixture. Shape the remaining dim sum in the same way – they should have flattened bases and the dough should be wrinkled around their sides.

Place the dim sum on a greased shallow dish which will fit in a steamer, then steam them over rapidly boiling water for 15 minutes, or until the shrimp mixture is cooked. While the dim sum are cooking, prepare small dishes of soy sauce. Serve the dim sum freshly cooked: they may be dipped into the soy sauce before eating.

Mushroom Dim Sum

MAKES ABOUT 50 – SERVES 4

These are an excellent vegetarian alternative to the usual dim sum filled with pork or shrimp.

4 large Chinese dried mushrooms

4 Chinese leaves

½ × 7 oz can water chestnuts, drained and chopped

4 scallions, chopped

1 cup finely chopped button mushrooms

1 garlic clove, minced

2 tbsp cornstarch

salt

1 egg, beaten

1 package won ton skins

FOR THE SAUCE

1 tbsp oil

1 tbsp sesame oil

2 scallions, chopped

1 tbsp peeled and finely shredded fresh ginger

1 celery stalk, cut into fine 1-inch strips

1 carrot, cut into fine 1-inch strips

sherry (see method)

2 tbsp cornstarch

2 tbsp soy sauce

COOK'S TIP

The dim sum cook very well by steaming but this does require a lot of steamer space. Several layers of bamboo steamer, placed on a wok, are ideal and the dim sum should be placed in greased shallow dishes or on plates. If the plates are not greased the dim sum will stick

Place the dried mushrooms in a mug or very small bowl. Add just enough boiling water to cover them, then put a small saucer over them and weight it down to keep the mushrooms submerged. Leave to stand for 20 minutes. Blanch the Chinese leaves in boiling water for 30 seconds, so they are just limp. Drain and squeeze all the water from them, then chop them finely.

Drain the mushrooms, reserving the soaking liquid in a measuring cup and squeezing the water from the mushrooms. Discard any woody stalks, then chop the mushroom caps and mix them with the Chinese leaves. Add the water chestnuts, scallions, button mushrooms, and garlic. Stir in the cornstarch and salt to taste. Add a little beaten egg to bind the mixture, so that it clumps easily.

Prepare a large platter for the dim sum and dust it with cornstarch. Brush a won ton skin with beaten egg, then place a little of the mushroom mixture on it. Gather the dough up around the filling to make a small bundle. Press the dough together at the top to seal in the filling. Fill all the squares of dough in the same way. Place the dim sum on the floured platter and cover loosely with plastic wrap while you fill the remainder.

For the sauce, heat the oil and sesame oil together in a small saucepan. Add the scallions, ginger, celery, and carrot. Stir-fry for 2 minutes. Measure the soaking liquid from the mushrooms and add enough sherry to make it up to 1¼ cups. Blend the cornstarch to a smooth, thin paste with a little of the liquid, then stir in the rest of the liquid. Pour this into the pan, add the soy sauce and bring to a boil, stirring. Reduce the heat and taste for seasoning. Leave to simmer very gently.

Bring a large saucepan of salted water to a boil. Add the dim sum, bring back to a boil, and cook for 5 minutes. Do not boil the water rapidly. Drain well and place in a warmed serving dish. Ladle the sauce over the dim sum and serve.

Glossy Dumplings

MAKES 24

Traditionally, dumplings of this type are served with a selection of other dim sum for a light lunch or mid-afternoon snack. Serve China or Jasmine tea with the dim sum.

2 Chinese dried mushrooms

6 oz lean ground pork

1 tbsp finely chopped fresh ginger

1 garlic clove, minced

1 tsp sesame oil

2 tbsp finely chopped water chestnuts or celery stalks

2 scallions, finely chopped

2 tbsp soy sauce

pinch of five-spice powder

scallion curls, to garnish

FOR THE DOUGH

1 cup hard flour

2 tbsp leaf lard or white vegetable shortening

TO SERVE

1 garlic clove, finely chopped

1 tsp finely chopped fresh ginger

1 tbsp finely chopped scallion

1 tbsp dry sherry

about 1 cup soy sauce

COOK'S TIP

To make scallion curls, trim the roots and some of the green of scallions. Cut the green part and some of the white onion into fine shreds, leaving them all attached at the root end. Place in a bowl of iced water and leave for at least 30 minutes while the shredded scallion curls. Drain well just before using

Place the dried mushrooms in a cup. Add just enough boiling water to cover them, then put a small saucer over them and weight it down to keep the mushrooms submerged. Leave to stand for 20 minutes. Mix the pork, ginger, garlic, sesame oil, water chestnuts or celery, scallions, soy sauce, and five-spice powder. Drain the mushrooms, discard any woody stalks, then chop the caps finely. Add them to the pork and mix the ingredients.

To make the dough, place the flour in a basin. Measure 2 tablespoons boiling water and stir in the lard. When the lard has melted, pour the mixture into the flour and stir well to form a soft dough. Sprinkle a little cornstarch onto the work surface and knead the dough lightly, then roll it into a sausage and mark it into 24 pieces. Cut off a piece of dough to shape, then loosely cover the rest of the roll with plastic wrap.

Knead the dough briefly into a smooth ball, then flatten it into a circle measuring about 2–2½ inches across. Place a little of the meat mixture in the middle, then fold the dough over it to make a tiny dumpling in the shape of a turnover. Pinch and flute the edges to seal in the filling. Grease a shallow dish or plate and place the dumpling on it. Flatten and fill the remaining dough in the same way. Steam the dumplings over boiling water for 15 minutes, until very glossy and cooked through. Test one dumpling to make sure the filling is cooked.

While the dumplings are cooking, prepare the dipping sauces: place the garlic, ginger, scallion, and sherry in four separate dishes and top up with the soy sauce. Serve the dim sum freshly cooked, garnished with scallion curls.

Crispy Chicken Chow Mein

Chow mein is a Chinese dish consisting of egg noodles mixed with other ingredients. An interesting combination of textures results from frying the noodles before topping them with sauce.

4 Chinese dried mushrooms

3 boneless chicken breasts, skinned

2 tbsp cornstarch

salt

12 oz Chinese egg noodles

4 tbsp oil

1 tbsp sesame oil

1 oz fresh ginger, peeled and cut into short thin strips

4 celery stalks, cut into thin, 1-inch strips

1 bunch of scallions, shredded diagonally

4 tbsp soy sauce

⅔ cup chicken broth

4 tbsp dry sherry

Place the dried mushrooms in a mug or small bowl. Add just enough boiling water to cover them, then put a small saucer over them and weight it down to keep the mushrooms submerged. Leave to stand for 20 minutes. Drain the mushrooms, reserving the liquid, then discard any woody stems and slice the caps.

Cut the chicken into thin slices, then into fine strips. Place in a bowl or plastic bag and coat with the cornstarch, adding a little salt. Cook the noodles in a large plan of boiling salted water for 3 minutes. Drain well, then place the noodles in a large skillet and lightly pat them into a flat cake; set aside.

Heat half the oil and the sesame oil in a wok or large saucepan. Add the chicken and stir-fry until the strips are lightly browned. Add the ginger, celery, scallions, and cook for a further 3 minutes. Stir in the mushrooms and add the reserved soaking liquid from the dried mushrooms. Pour in the soy sauce, sherry, and broth and bring to a boil, stirring all the time. Leave to simmer while you cook the noodles.

Slide the noodles from the skillet onto a plate. Heat the remaining oil in the skillet, then slide the noodles into it. Cook until crisp and golden underneath. Use a large fish slice to turn the cake of noodles over. Alternatively, slide the noodle cake out onto a plate, then invert it back into the skillet. Cook the second side until crisp and golden.

Slide the noodles out onto a large platter, then pour the chicken mixture over the top. Serve at once. Diners break off portions of noodles with chopsticks or a spoon and fork, taking some of the chicken mixture with the portion. The noodles soon soften in the sauce, so they must be eaten promptly.

Chinese Mustard Greens with Fusilli

SERVES 4-6

This quick-to-prepare, nutritious dish is perfect for a light lunch when entertaining friends.

3½ cups dried fusilli (small twists)

dash of olive oil

3 tbsp sesame oil

3 garlic cloves, minced

2 carrots, peeled and cut into ribbons

8 scallions, stalks removed and leaves shredded

5–6 tbsp dark soy sauce

3 tbsp toasted sesame seeds

COOK'S TIP

To cut the carrots into wafer-thin ribbons, peel away the outside skin using a vegetable peeler, then continue peeling the carrot.

Bring a large saucepan of water to the boil, and add the fusilli with a dash of olive oil. Cook for about 10 minutes, stirring occasionally, until the pasta is tender. Drain thoroughly, and set aside.

Heat the sesame oil in a wok or large skillet, and add the garlic. Stir-fry for 30 seconds, then add the carrot ribbons. Continue to cook for 3–4 minutes, then add the shredded scallions. Cook for 2–3 minutes, stirring continuously.

Stir in the soy sauce, sesame seeds, and the fusilli. Cook for a further 2 minutes, and serve immediately.

Shrimp Chow Mein

SERVES 4

This is simple and delicious. The recipe uses fresh shrimp that are added with the bean sprouts; but frozen shrimp may be used, although they should be added as soon as the onion has softened. The drawback with frozen shrimp is that they reduce the pan temperature.

3 sheets (8 oz) thread egg noodles

1 large onion, chopped

2 tbsp sunflower or peanut oil

1 tsp Chinese five-spice powder

1 cup zucchini, cut into matchsticks

1 cup carrot, cut into matchsticks

1 green bell pepper, seeded and cut into fine strips

1 red chili, seeded and finely chopped (optional)

2 garlic cloves, finely sliced

2 cups peeled shrimp

2 large handfuls bean sprouts

¼ cup sherry

¼ cup soy sauce

½ cup water

Soak the noodles in boiling water until needed, stirring them occasionally to separate the strands. Cook the onion in the oil in a large skillet until softened but not browned. Stir in the five-spice powder and cook for a further 1 minute.

Add the zucchini, carrots, bell pepper, chili, and garlic, then stir-fry for 3–4 minutes. Drain the noodles, then add them to the skillet with the shrimp and bean sprouts. Mix the sherry, soy sauce, and water together, then pour the mixture into the pan. Cook for 2–3 minutes, tossing the vegetables and noodles together in the sauce. Serve piping hot, with extra soy sauce.

Shrimp Chow Mein ▶

Pork Chow Mein

SERVES 4

Here is another way of presenting chow mein. This time, I have used Chinese five-spice powder which, even in small quantities, gives a very strong flavor.

1 lb lean boneless pork, cut into very thin 2-inch squares

2 tsp sesame oil

1 garlic clove

2 tbsp soy sauce

6 tbsp dry sherry

pinch of five-spice powder

2 tbsp cornstarch

12 oz fresh Chinese egg noodles

2 tbsp oil

1 onion, halved and thinly sliced

1 green bell pepper, seeded, quartered lengthwise and thinly sliced

7 oz can bamboo shoots, drained and sliced

⅔ cup chicken broth

Place the pork in a bowl. Add the oil, garlic, soy sauce, and 2 tablespoons of the sherry. Mix in the five-spice, cover and leave to marinate for 2 hours.

Remove the pork from the marinade and reserve the liquid. Place the meat in a plastic bag, add the cornstarch and shake the bag, holding it closed, to coat the meat evenly. Cook the noodles in boiling salted water for 3 minutes, then drain them, rinse under cold water, and set aside.

Heat the oil in a wok or large skillet. Add the pork and stir-fry over fairly high heat until the pieces are evenly and lightly browned. Stir in the onion and bell pepper and continue to stir-fry for 5 minutes, until the pork is well cooked and the vegetables are softened very slightly. Stir in the bamboo shoots.

Mix the remaining sherry and broth into the reserved marinade, then pour this over the meat mixture. Bring to a boil, stirring, then add the noodles to the pan and mix well until heated through. Serve at once.

Kopytka with Kabanos

SERVES 4

Kopytka is the Polish equivalent of potato gnocchi.

FOR THE POTATO GNOCCHI

1 lb potatoes, cooked, mashed, and strained

2 tbsp butter

1½ cups bread flour

1 tsp salt

1 egg

freshly grated nutmeg

FOR THE SAUCE

2 tbsp olive oil

2 onions, halved and thinly sliced

1 garlic clove, minced

1 tbsp caraway seeds

4 kabanos (about 8 oz), sliced

1 lb sauerkraut, drained and shredded

salt and ground black pepper

⅔ cup sour cream

paprika

Make the gnocchi. Mix all the ingredients together. Knead lightly until smooth. Shape the dough into a thick sausage. Cut off small pieces, 1 inch long, and indent each piece with a fork.

Heat the oil in a large frying pan. Add the onions, garlic, and caraway and cook for 20 minutes. Add the kabanos and sauerkraut, then cook, stirring often, for another 20 minutes.

Cook the gnocchi. Drop the gnocchi into boiling water, bring back to a boil and cook for 4–5 minutes. Drain well. Add the gnocchi to the kabanos and sauerkraut. Mix well, season to taste, and serve at once. Top each portion with sour cream and sprinkle with paprika.

Kopytka with Kabanos ▶

Mushroom Uszka

SERVES 4

These little Polish dumplings are the same shape as tortellini. The traditional Polish filling of dried mushrooms makes the most delicious pasta.

1 cup hard flour

salt and ground black pepper

1 egg

2 dried mushrooms (Polish or Italian)

½ cup fresh white bread crumbs

2 tbsp butter

1 small onion, finely chopped

Place the flour in a bowl with ½ teaspoon salt. Make a well in the middle, then add the egg and 1 tablespoon water. Mix to form a firm dough, using a spoon at first, then knead it by hand until smooth. Cover the dough in plastic wrap.

Simmer the mushrooms in water to cover for 5 minutes, then drain. Boil the cooking liquor until it is reduced to 2 tablespoons and set it aside. Chop the mushrooms and mix them with the bread crumbs. Melt the butter in a small saucepan, add the onion and cook, stirring, for 5 minutes. Mix the cooked onion with the mushroom mixture, the reserved liquor, and seasoning to taste.

On a lightly floured surface, roll out the dough into a 12½-inch square. Cut it horizontally into 7 strips, then cut vertically to divide each strip into 7 squares. Place a little filling on each square and brush the edges of the dough with beaten egg. Fold the squares of dough in half to make triangular dumplings, sealing the edges carefully to enclose the filling. Wrap the long side of each triangle around the tip of your finger and pinch their corners together.

Bring a large saucepan of salted water to a boil. Add the uszka and bring the water back to a boil. Cook for 3 minutes. Drain and serve at once.

Yosenabe

This is the Japanese equivalent of a firepot meal, an oriental fondu, where diners select and cook their own food at the table by adding it to a pot of gently simmering broth. "Nabe" is the collective term for dishes cooked at the table, and this example is a seafood meal, where a selection of any fish and shellfish would be prepared. I have included a limited selection of seafood with broad appeal, but you may extend this according to your own tastes and availability.

FOR THE YOSENABE

2 pints chicken broth

2 pints Japanese-style broth

2 carrots, cut into carrot flowers

6 oz harusame or somen or rice
 vermicelli

1 cup firm bean curd

1 bunch of scallions

1 cup button mushrooms

16 large, uncooked shrimp, just
 defrosted if frozen

16 fresh scallops

1 lb fine-flavored thick fish fillet
 (for example grey mullet,
 monkfish, bream, hake or sea
 bass)

16 cooked, shelled mussels

FOR THE CONDIMENTS AND DIPPING SAUCE

1 white radish (daikon or mooli)

½ cucumber

1 tbsp Japanese rice vinegar

wasabi (Japanese green
 mustard)

6 tbsp sake

1 cup Japanese soy sauce

1 tsp sugar

1 tbsp lemon juice

First, prepare the Yosenabe.

Heat the Japanese-style broth until it is just simmering, then add the carrot flowers and cook for 5 minutes. Use a slotted spoon to remove them from the pan and drain well. Add the harusame, somen or fine rice noodles to the simmering broth and cook according to the instructions on the packet or remove from the heat and leave to stand in the broth for about 15 minutes, until tender. Drain the noodles over a bowl, reserving the broth.

Cut the bean curd into neat, diamond-shaped pieces. Trim the scallions and cut them into 1½–2-inch lengths. Use a fine-pointed knife to cut evenly spaced narrow strips out of the tops of the mushrooms, working from the center and curving out down the side of each mushroom cap.

Uncooked shrimp are sold with shells on or peeled. If the shrimp are whole, then remove their heads and peel them. Remove the dark vein that runs down the back of the prawn with the tip of a sharp knife. Slice the scallops in half or into three slices if they are large. Skin the fish fillet and cut the fish into neat chunks, discarding any stray bones.

Arrange all the prepared ingredients on a serving platter, cutting the noodles up slightly (alternatively, they may be divided between individual plates, which can make the cooking process easier and ensures that everyone gets their fair share of the ingredients).

Next, prepare the condiments and dipping sauce. Coarsely grate the radish and cucumber, keeping them separate. Drain the cucumber well in a sieve, then mix it with the rice vinegar. Arrange small piles of the radish and cucumber on small plates.

Mix the wasabi with a little water to make a smooth, green paste. This mustard-like horseradish mixture is extremely hot and taken in very small quantities, so warn unwary guests!

Heat the sake, soy sauce, sugar and lemon juice together in a saucepan until the sugar has dissolved. Boil the mixture, then remove it from the heat. Allow the dipping sauce to cool before pouring it into small dishes.

To serve the Yosenabe, heat the chicken broth and Japanese broth together until boiling, then place the pan on a spirit burner to keep the stock only just simmering. Provide plates and chopsticks, then invite diners to cook pieces of food in the simmering stock. The cooked food is then dipped in the dipping sauce or a little wasabi is eaten with it (especially the fish). The radish and cucumber are also eaten in small amounts to complement the hot ingredients.

Spätzle

This is an example of a pasta-dumpling cross from Eastern European culinary traditions. The secret of making a successful batter lies in having everything ready beforehand, and using the correct amount of each ingredient. Spätzle may be treated as gnocchi, and served with butter or olive oil or other simple dressings, such as sour cream and chives or dill. However, they are also the ideal accompaniment for rich meat or game sauces and good in substantial meat and vegetable hotpots or soups.

FOR THE SPÄTZLE	TO SERVE
2 cups all-purpose flour	¼ cup melted butter
½ tsp salt	
4 eggs, beaten	
about 3 tbsp water	

To make the spätzle, first, mix the flour and salt in a bowl, making a well in the middle. Add the eggs; then gradually work in the flour, and beat hard until the batter is very thick and smooth. Add the water gradually, so that you can beat the batter without difficulty. However, the mixture should be thick, elastic, and quite "stringy" in texture, not freely pouring.

Prepare a large saucepan of boiling salted water, and have a slotted spoon ready. Pour the melted butter for serving into a warmed dish, and keep this hot ready to receive the cooked spätzle. Rinse a small cutting board under cold running water, and wet a large, flat-bladed kitchen knife in the same way. Drop a large pat of the batter on the board. Regulate the heat under the pan of water so that the water is just boiling.

Use a cutting and sliding action to scrape thin, short lengths of the batter sideways into the pan of boiling water. Rinse the knife under running cold water every three or four cuts to prevent the batter sticking to it. The water must be boiling, otherwise the spätzle will stick to the bottom of the pan. Cook the batter in batches. Once the spätzle have been in the pan for about 30 seconds, gently ease them off the bottom with the slotted spoon.

Boil the spätzle for 2–3 minutes, until they are swollen and firm. Drain them well, and place them in the hot butter, toss them in it, and keep hot until all the batter has been cooked. Serve piping hot.

178 PASTA AROUND THE WORLD

Cabbage Soup with Spätzle

SERVES 6

¼ cup butter

1 large onion, halved and thinly sliced

2 garlic cloves, finely chopped

2 large carrots, halved and sliced

2 celery stalks, sliced

1 bay leaf

1 lb lean bacon, for boiling in one piece

8 cups water

½ quantity Spätzle (page 178)

6 cups shredded cabbage

salt and ground black pepper

6 tbsp chopped fresh parsley

Melt the butter in a large saucepan. Add the onion, garlic, carrots, celery, and bay leaf. Cook, stirring, for 5 minutes. Place the piece of bacon in the pan, and pour in the water. Bring slowly to a boil, and, as the water boils, skim off and discard any scum that rises to the surface. Reduce the heat, if necessary, to keep the water just simmering; then cover the pan, and cook for 45 minutes.

Meanwhile, make the spätzle batter, and cook as given on page 178. Drain them, and set aside.

Remove the meat from the pan, and dice it, discarding any fat. Return the meat to the soup, and add the cabbage. Taste for seasoning, stir in salt and pepper, and bring back to a boil; then reduce the heat, and cover the pan. Simmer for 15 minutes. Add the spätzle and parsley, and cook for a further 5 minutes; then serve piping hot.

Uszka

SERVES 4-6

To be completely authentic, these Polish dumplings would need to be made slightly smaller than here, but they are a bit easier to make this size. They are a classic accompaniment for bortsch (beetroot soup) and, if you want to serve them in soup, cut the pasta into seven strips, then across into 49 squares and make tiny, filled pasta appropriate to soup.

DRIED MUSHROOMS
Polish dried wild mushrooms are threaded on long strings, and hung to dry. You will find the authentic ingredients hanging in Polish delis; however, dried porcini or ceps may be substituted. Do not use Chinese dried mushrooms (shiitake) as they have a quite different, strong flavor.

6 oz Pasta Dough (page 9)	1½ cups fresh white bread crumbs
5 large dried mushrooms (see note)	salt and ground black pepper
2 tbsp butter	1 egg, beaten
1 onion, very finely chopped	⅓ cup butter, to serve

First, make the pasta dough and set aside while you prepare the filling.

Put the mushrooms into a small saucepan, and add enough water to cover them. Bring to a boil, then reduce the heat, and cover the pan. Simmer the mushrooms for about 5 minutes, or until they are tender. Drain the mushrooms, reserving the liquid. Rinse the pan out; then strain the liquid back into it through a strainer lined with cheesecloth (this removes any grit that has come from the mushrooms). Boil the liquid until it has reduced to about 2 tablespoons; then set it aside.

Chop the mushrooms finely, discarding any tough stalk ends. Melt the butter in a saucepan, add the onion, and cook, stirring often, for 10 minutes. Mix the mushrooms, onion, and bread crumbs. Add salt and pepper to taste; then stir in the reduced cooking liquor.

Cut the pasta dough in half. Roll out one portion to form a 12-inch square. Cut the dough into 2 inch wide strips. Then cut these across in the opposite direction to make 2-inch squares.

Work on about a quarter of the squares at a time, keeping the others covered loosely with plastic wrap to prevent the pasta drying out. Brush the squares with beaten egg, and place a little of the filling in the middle. Fold the pasta diagonally over the filling, and pinch the edges together to make triangles; then curl the long side around a finger tip, and pinch the points together to shape each uszka. Repeat, using the remaining pasta dough, to make a total of 72.

Cook the uszka in boiling salted water for 3–4 minutes. Drain and toss with melted butter.

SERVING SUGGESTIONS

USZKA WITH CHIVES AND TARRAGON
Add 4 tablespoons snipped chives and 2 tablespoons chopped fresh tarragon to the melted butter for serving.

USZKA WITH HORSERADISH CREAM AND BEETS
Mix 2 tablespoons horseradish sauce into 1¼ cups sour cream. Add 3 tablespoons chopped fresh dill, and a little salt and pepper to taste. Toss the freshly cooked uszka with a little melted butter and the horseradish cream. Top each portion with cooked beets cut into fine matchsticks, and serve at once.

USZKA WITH BEETS AND SCALLIONS
Coarsely grate ¾ cup cooked beets and finely chop 4 scallions. Cook the vegetables together in half the melted butter. Toss the uszka in the remaining butter; then spoon the beetroot mixture on top.

CREAMY USZKA
Make a béchamel sauce and stir in 2–4 tablespoons horseradish sauce, to taste. Toss the uszka with the sauce, adding 4 tablespoons chopped dill. Serve garnished with sprigs of dill, and offer a grated mild cheese with the uszka.

Kreplach

MAKES 72

These filled pastas are based on the traditional Jewish accompaniment for soup. They can be served with a meat gravy or tomato sauce, but the following recipe is the tastiest version I know.

FOR THE KREPLACH

½ quantity Pasta Dough (page 9)

2 tbsp beef drippings

1 small onion, grated

salt and ground black pepper

1½ cups ground, lean roast beef

1 tbsp finely chopped parsley

1 tbsp good beef gravy or the juices from underneath the drippings

1 egg, beaten

TO SERVE

3½ cups strained tomatoes

First, make the pasta dough, and set it aside to rest while you make the filling.

Melt the drippings in a saucepan. Add the onion, and cook, stirring, for 5–8 minutes, or until some of the moisture has evaporated, and the onion has lost its raw taste. Remove from the heat, and stir in salt and pepper to taste. The add the beef, parsley, and gravy, which will bind the mixture. Taste for seasoning.

Cut the dough in half. Roll out one half to form a square slightly larger than 12 inches. Trim the edges; then cut the dough into 2-inch wide strips and across into 2 inch squares. Brush the squares with beaten egg. Place a little filling in the middle of each square until you have used half of the mixture; then fold one corner of the dough over to enclose the filling, forming a triangular-shaped piece of pasta. Pinch the edges of the dough together well. Repeat with the remaining dough and filling.

Cook the kreplach in boiling salted water, or add them to clear soup. Cook for about 3 minutes, until tender. Drain or serve with the soup. Strained tomatoes may be served with the kreplach if they are not cooked in soup.

Beef in Oyster Sauce with Rice Sticks

SERVES 4

1 lb rump steak or frying steak	4 tbsp water
1 tbsp cornstarch	12 oz ribbon rice sticks
1 tbsp soy sauce	2 tbsp oil
3 tbsp oyster sauce	1 bunch of scallions, chopped
4 tbsp dry sherry	½ an iceberg lettuce, shredded

Cut the beef across the grain into very thin slices (partially freezing the steak makes this easier). Mix the steak with the cornstarch. When the meat is well coated, add the soy sauce, oyster sauce, sherry, and water. Mix well and set aside to marinate for 3–4 hours.

Cook the rice sticks according to the instructions on the packet.

Meanwhile, heat the oil in a large skillet or wok. Drain the beef, reserving the marinade, and add it to the oil with the scallions. Stir-fry until the pieces of beef are lightly browned. Then add the marinade and bring to the boil, stirring all the time. Simmer for 2 more minutes.

Drain the rice sticks and transfer them to a warmed serving dish. Add the lettuce to the beef mixture and stir well. Braise the lettuce for 2 minutes, then ladle the mixture over the rice sticks and serve at once.

Noodles with Japanese Fish Cake and Vegetables

SERVES 4

Japanese fish cake bears no resemblance to the European product of the same name. Kamaboko, the Japanese name for it, is a smooth-textured loaf, sometimes with a red exterior, bought cooked and in slices. It is served as part of the celebratory New Year menu. In this recipe, the fish cake is served with vegetables and noodles.

FOR THE NOODLES	FOR THE DIPPING SAUCE
2 slices Japanese fish cake	6 tbsp Japanese soy sauce
1 carrot	2 tbsp sake
1 leek	1 tsp sugar
4 oz snow peas	⅔ cup Japanese-style broth
¼ head of Chinese leaves	pinch of wasabi
12 oz udon noodles	1 scallion, finely chopped
salt	
1¼ cups chicken broth	
12 large cooked shrimp	

First, prepare the dipping sauce. Heat the soy sauce, sake, sugar, and stock, stirring until the sugar dissolves. Bring to a boil, then remove from the heat, and let cool. Add a small pinch of wasabi, and stir in the scallion; then pour the sauce into small dishes.

Now, prepare the noodles, fish cake, and vegetables. Cut the fish cake into matchstick-sized strips. Cut the carrot and leek into matchstick-sized pieces also. Top and tail the snow peas, and shred the Chinese leaves.

Cook the noodles in boiling salted water for about 15 minutes, or following the instructions on the package, until tender. Meanwhile, bring the chicken broth to a boil. Add the carrot and leek, and simmer for 1 minute. Then add the snow peas, and cook for a further minute. Finally, add the Chinese leaves, and bring back to a boil. Add the shrimp, and remove the pan from the heat. Let sit for 2 minutes.

Drain the noodles, and divide them between four bowls. Carefully spoon the vegetables and shrimp over the noodles; then pour the broth over them. Top with the pieces of fish cake, and serve at once.

Hiyamugi

This is a Japanese dish of cold noodles. Hiyamugi are thin, white noodles of vermicelli thickness. To be authentic, ice cubes ought to be added to the noodles, and cold water is sometimes poured over them. The noodles and other ingredients are lifted from the water, and dipped into sauce before being eaten.

FOR THE NOODLES

2 eggs, beaten

1 tsp Japanese soy sauce

a little oil

12 oz hiyamugi

salt

4 scallions

8 button mushrooms

3-inch piece of English cucumber

16 cooked, peeled shrimp

FOR THE DIPPING SAUCE

1¼ cups Japanese-style broth

1–2 tbsp dried bonito fish

5 tbsp Japanese soy sauce

4 tbsp sake

1 tsp sugar

1 tsp finely shredded fresh
   ginger

First, make the dipping sauce. Heat the broth with the bonito fish until boiling, then strain it into a clean saucepan, and stir in the soy sauce, sake, and sugar. Bring to a boil, stirring; then remove from the heat. Add the ginger, and let cool.

Meanwhile, prepare the noodles. Beat the eggs with the soy sauce. Heat a coating of oil in a skillet. Pour in the egg mixture, and cook until it is beginning to set; then lift the edge of the omelet, and let the raw egg on top run onto the hot surface of the skillet. When the omelet has set, slide it onto a plate.

Cook the hiyamugi in boiling salted water for 8–10 minutes, or according to the instructions on the package, until just tender. Drain, and rinse under cold water; then let drain.

Cut the scallions finely on the diagonal. Slice the mushrooms thinly, and cut the cucumber into fine matchstick strips. Cut the omelet into small squares.

To serve the hiyamugi, divide the noodles between four dishes. Top with the prepared ingredients, and serve with the dipping sauce. If liked, the dishes of noodles can be served on a bed of crushed ice.

Sweet Pasta

Chocolate Bows with White Chocolate Sauce

Hidden Plums

Apricot Macaroni Pudding

Spiced Apricot Rounds

Summer Fruit Sauce

Chocolate Fruit Dreams

Sweet Baked Ravioli

Lokshen Pudding

Oranges with Chocolate Ribbons

Chocolate Spirals with Pistachio
and Rose Cream

Sweet Fettuccine with Maple Syrup

Farfalle with Cardamom

Orange Angel Hair with Fruits

Coconut Spaghettini

*P*asta is used in sweet dishes in many countries. It is good with fruit and many spices.

Glossary of Sweet Pastas

Plum and Blackberry Compote

Fruit Compotes for pasta
Stewed fruits may be served with noodles and plain pasta. Cherries, plums, apricots, and other full-flavored fruits should be used. There are Eastern European and Italian dishes of this type.

Fruit-filled pastas
Pasta shapes filled with whole cherries, plums, apricots, or other fruit, boiled and served with butter, sugar, and sour cream are popular in many Eastern European cuisines.

Lokshen Pudding
A Jewish pudding of noodles (tagliatelle or ribbon noodles) in which boiled noodles are baked with eggs, dried fruit, cinnamon, and sugar.

Macaroni Milk Pudding
A British pudding. Macaroni is baked in milk and sugar until the milk has been absorbed, and the pasta is tender and creamy. Vanilla, lemon zest, or a cinnamon stick may be added.

Mohn Nudeln
Austrian dessert of noodles tossed with butter, sugar, and poppy seeds.

Sussen Nudelauf
An Austrian dessert of noodles layered with apples or plums and sugar, then baked. Fried bread crumbs form a crisp topping, and sour cream is served with the pudding.

Cherry Pierozki

Polish Poppy Seed Pudding
A traditional Christmas Eve pudding. The cooked ribbon noodles are tossed with butter, sugar, and poppy seeds.

Noodles with poppy seeds is also a popular combination for sweet puddings in other Eastern European countries.

Sevyian
An Indian milk pudding with vermicelli (vermicelli being known as sev, or sevyian). The vermicelli is broken into small pieces, and simmered in milk. Green cardamoms, raisins or golden raisins, pistachio nuts, and almonds are added. Rose water is used, and cloves may be added. The sweet mixture is cooked until the milk has been absorbed, and the pasta is thick and creamy – delicious warm or cold.

Chocolate Bows with Chocolate Sauce

Sweet-flavored pastas
A popular American concept, pasta may be flavored with chocolate, fruit, or other foods, and served with sweet sauces or with butter and sugar or cream.

Chocolate Bows with White Chocolate Sauce

SERVES 4

The unusual combination of the pasta texture and sweet flavor may not be to everyone's liking but chocolate fans will approve.

6 oz Pasta Dough (page 9)	1 tsp natural vanilla extract
2 tbsp unsweetened cocoa powder	8 oz white chocolate
3 tbsp confectioners' sugar	3 tbsp light corn syrup
1 tbsp walnut oil	2 tbsp unsalted butter
	½ cup chopped walnuts

Make the pasta dough, adding the cocoa powder and confectioners' sugar to the flour before mixing in the egg and using 1 tablespoon walnut oil and the vanilla extract instead of the olive oil. Roll out the dough into a 12-inch square.

Cut the dough into 1½-inch strips, then cut them across in 1½-inch squares. Pinch the opposite corners of a square of dough together, pleating the dough in the middle of the square and pressing it firmly, to make a small bow with pointed ends. Set the bow aside on a surface dusted with confectioners' sugar. Do not cover the bows.

Before cooking the bows, prepare the white chocolate sauce. Break the chocolate into squares and place in a heatproof bowl. Add the light corn syrup and butter, then stand the bowl over a small saucepan of barely simmering water. Stir until the chocolate melts and the sauce is smooth. Turn the heat off and set the pan and bowl aside.

Cook the bows in just-boiling water for 3 minutes. Meanwhile, pour some chocolate sauce on warmed plates. Drain the bows, then arrange them on the sauce. Sprinkle with nuts and serve at once.

Hidden Plums

SERVES 4

Fruit dumplings of this type, encased in a dough made of potato and boiled as for ravioli, are typical of Eastern European cooking. Keep the main course simple and light when serving these for dessert as they are quite filling.

1 lb potatoes

½ cup hard plain flour

1 egg

12 firm plums

3 oz white almond paste

¼ cup unsalted butter

confectioners' sugar for dredging

1¼ cups sour cream

● Boil the potatoes in their skins for 20 minutes, or until tender. Drain and peel them, then press them through a fine strainer. Mix in the flour. Make sure the mixture is not too hot for the egg before mixing it in to make a dough. Knead the dough together, then cut it into 12 equal portions. Keep the dough covered when you are not working with it.

● Slit the plums down one side and remove their pits. (If the pits do not come out easily you will have to halve the plums, but this is less successful.) Divide the almond paste into 12 small pieces and place a little in the middle of each plum. Flatten a portion of dough, place a plum on it, then knead it around the fruit to enclose it completely. Pinch the dough to seal it thoroughly.

● Bring a large saucepan of water to a boil. Melt the unsalted butter and set it aside over very low heat to keep hot without cooking. Add the plums and cook for 3–5 minutes, drain them well, then spoon them into a heated serving dish. Pour the butter over and dredge the plums thickly with confectioners' sugar. Serve immediately, offering sour cream with the hidden plums.

Apricot Macaroni Pudding

SERVES 4-6

generous ½ cup short cut macaroni

2 tbsp butter

15-oz can apricots

1 tbsp cornstarch

½ pt evaporated milk

¼ cup sugar

1 tbsp brown sugar

● Preheat the oven to 350°F. Cook the macaroni in boiling salted water for 5 minutes, drain, and return to the saucepan.

● Butter an ovenproof dish then add the remaining butter to the macaroni. Turn half the buttered macaroni into the dish.

● Drain the can of apricots and mix the juice with the cornstarch. Arrange half the apricots on top of the macaroni.

● Heat the cornstarch and juice. Add the hot mixture to the cold evaporated milk and sugar and return the mixture to a low heat for a few minutes. Pour half the liquid over the macaroni and apricots.

● Place the remaining macaroni on top of the apricots and pour on the remaining sauce. Arrange the other apricots on top of the pudding and sprinkle with brown sugar. Bake for 35 minutes or until macaroni is cooked.

Spiced Apricot Rounds

SERVES 6

2 cups finely chopped ready-to-eat dried apricots

1 tsp ground cinnamon or allspice

2 tbsp confectioners' sugar

grated zest and juice of 1 orange

10 oz Pasta Dough (page 9)

1 egg, beaten

5 tbsp clear honey

½ cup flaked almonds, toasted

orange slices, to decorate

whipped cream, to serve

Mix the apricots, cinnamon or allspice, confectioners' sugar, and orange peel. Cut the dough in half and roll out one portion into a 12-inch square. Use a 2-inch round fluted cutter or a shaped cutter to stamp out pieces of dough. If you work neatly, you will get 36 shapes.

Brush a piece of dough with the beaten egg, place a little of the apricot mixture in the middle, then cover with a second piece of dough. Pinch the edges together firmly to seal in the filling. Continue until all the shapes are used, then repeat with the second portion of dough. Place the finished rounds on a plate lightly dusted with cornstarch and keep them loosely covered while you fill the other shapes.

Bring a large saucepan of water to a boil and cook the pasta in batches for 5 minutes each. Drain well. While the pasta is cooking, heat the orange juice and honey. Serve the hot pasta coated with the honey and orange juice and sprinkled with the toasted flaked almonds. Decorating individual plates with attractive pieces of sliced orange improves the appearance of the dessert. Serve with whipped cream.

Spiced Apricot Rounds ▶

Summer Fruit Sauce

SERVES 4

Serve this sauce with pasta shapes, either bought or homemade. Instead of pouring the sauce over the pasta, ladle the sauce into dishes, then top it with pasta and sprinkle with chopped nuts and confectioners' sugar.

8 oz red currants

⅓ cup superfine sugar

juice of 1 orange

8 oz strawberries, halved

8 oz raspberries

mint sprigs, to decorate

Place the red currants, sugar, and orange juice in a saucepan. Heat gently until the sugar dissolves, then bring to a boil. Cook gently for 1 minute, then remove from the heat.

Mix the strawberries and raspberries into the red currants. Add the mint sprigs, if liked, and mix lightly, then pick them out to use as a decoration when serving the sauce.

Chocolate Fruit Dreams

SERVES 6

1 quantity chocolate pasta dough (see Chocolate Bows, (page 188)

8 oz strawberries, sliced

6 tbsp maple syrup

8 oz raspberries

1¼ cups whipping cream, whipped

2–3 tbsp toasted chopped hazelnuts

Make the pasta dough, roll it into a 12-inch square and cut it into 1-inch strips. Cut the strips at an angle to make diamond shapes (rather like cutting almond paste leaves when decorating a cake). Cook the pasta in boiling water for 3 minutes, then drain it well.

In a bowl, mix the sliced strawberries with the maple syrup. Add the drained pasta and mix lightly. Mix the raspberries with the pasta and strawberries, taking care to keep them whole. Divide the fruit and pasta between 6 dishes. Top with generous swirls of cream, then sprinkle with toasted chopped hazelnuts. Serve at once.

Sweet Baked Ravioli

SERVES 6-8

FOR THE PASTA

1¼ lb flour

4 oz butter

4 oz sugar

4 eggs

1 tbsp fresh yeast

¼ pint milk

FOR THE FILLING

14 oz chestnuts

4 oz bitter cocoa

2 oz sugar

4 oz chopped almonds

4 oz amaretti biscuits, crumbled

7 oz orange marmalade

For the pasta, mix together the flour, butter, sugar, 3 eggs, and the yeast dissolved in tepid milk. Knead the dough for 20 minutes and wrap in a tea towel. Leave to rise for an hour.

For the filling, boil the chestnuts, peel, press through a sieve or blend in a liquidizer, and mix with the cocoa, sugar, almonds, amaretti, and marmalade. Combine well.

Roll out the pasta into a thin sheet and cut into circles 2 inches in diameter. Place some filling on each and close into a semicircle. Arrange on a greased baking sheet and brush with beaten egg. Bake at 350°F for 20 minutes.

Lokshen Pudding

SERVES 4

8 oz egg vermicelli

1 tsp salt

½ tsp oil

½ cup chopped candied fruit peel

½ cup almond slivers

2 oz butter

¼ tsp ground cinnamon

¼ tsp allspice

¼ cup sugar

2 eggs, beaten

⅔ cup cream

20 halved almonds, to decorate

Preheat the oven to 350°F. Cook the vermicelli in a large saucepan of boiling water to which the salt and oil have been added. Test after 2 minutes. If the vermicelli is almost cooked, drain and return to the saucepan.

Add the candied peel, almond slivers, and the butter cut into small knobs. Mix well. Sprinkle the spices over the mixture.

Mix the sugar with the beaten egg and add to the pasta mixture. Lastly stir in the cream. Turn into a buttered pie dish and bake for 10 minutes.

Remove from the oven after 10 minutes and decorate with 'almond flowers' i.e. make petals with the halved almonds. Return to the oven for a further 8–10 minutes until golden.

Oranges with Chocolate Ribbons

SERVES 4

*I*n this recipe, chocolate is combined with oranges that have been marinated in brandy, providing a simple yet exotic dessert, suitable for any dinner party or special occasion.

4 large oranges

¼ cup sugar

2–3 tbsp brandy

2–3 whole cloves

8 oz chocolate fettuccine

1 tbsp sliced toasted almonds

1 tbsp confectioners' sugar, sifted

lightly whipped heavy cream or thick, plain yogurt

Peel the oranges, taking care to remove all the bitter white pith. Slice thinly and place in a glass mixing bowl.

Dissolve the sugar with ⅔ cup water in a heavy pan over moderate heat. Once dissolved, bring to a boil and boil for 5 minutes or until a light sugar syrup is formed.

Remove from the heat and stir in the brandy and cloves. Pour over the oranges. Leave for at least 2 hours, turning the oranges occasionally in the marinade.

Cook the chocolate fettuccine in plenty of boiling water for 1–2 minutes or until "al dente," then drain. Arrange in small nests on four individual serving plates. Spoon the oranges over the pasta and sprinkle with the sliced toasted almonds and confectioners' sugar. Serve with the cream or yogurt.

Orange with Chocolate Ribbons ▶

Chocolate Spirals with Pistachio and Rose Cream

SERVES 4

*S*tirred into freshly whipped cream, rose water gives a lightly perfumed and fragrant cream which combines well with the raspberries and chocolate in this receipe.

FOR THE DESSERT

¼ cup unsalted shelled pistachio nuts

⅔ cup heavy whipping cream

1 tbsp rose water

2 cups fresh raspberries

8 oz fresh chocolate tagliatelle

rose petals, to decorate

Preheat the oven to 400°F and roast the pistachio nuts for 10 minutes. Remove from the oven, cool, and roughly chop.

Whip the cream lightly, stir in the rose water, and chill until required. Clean the raspberries, rinsing lightly, and dry on paper towels.

Cook the chocolate tagliatelle in plenty of boiling water for 1–2 minutes or until "al dente." Drain and stir in the cream. Arrange the pasta in small nests with the raspberries. Scatter with the chopped pistachios and decorate with rose petals. Serve immediately.

Sweet Fettuccine with Maple Syrup

SERVES 4

When using pasta for desserts, cook the pasta in unsalted water, then toss the cooked pasta in melted butter. Here I have used some toasted nuts to serve with the pasta and poured over maple syrup – certainly not for serious weight watchers!

FOR THE DESSERT

1 cup mixed shelled nuts, such as pecan halves, skinned hazelnuts, and blanched almonds.

4 tbsp unsalted butter

1 tsp ground cinnamon

4 tbsp maple syrup

8 oz fresh fettuccine

fresh strawberries and sprigs of mint, to decorate

Preheat the oven to 400°F and roast the nuts for 10 minutes or until golden. Remove from the oven and cool.

Melt the unsalted butter in a pan and stir in the ground cinnamon, maple syrup, and roasted mixed nuts.

Meanwhile, cook the fettuccine in plenty of boiling water for 1–2 minutes or until "al dente." Drain and return to the pan. Pour over the maple syrup and nut sauce and toss lightly. Serve immediately decorated with the strawberries, cut into fans, and mint sprigs.

◀ *Sweet Fettuccine with Maple Syrup*

Farfalle with Cardamom

SERVES 4

Vanilla-flavored superfine sugar is easily prepared. Simply place 1-2 vanilla beans in a screw top jar, fill with superfine sugar, and leave for 2 weeks. Keep topping up the sugar after use; then it can be used for months.

2½ cups skim milk

1 medium egg

¼ cup vanilla-flavored superfine sugar

6 cardamom pods, split

8 oz fresh farfalle, dried

2 tbsp butter

Preheat the oven to 325°F and lightly butter an ovenproof dish. Warm the skim milk. Beat the egg with the vanilla-flavored superfine sugar, then gradually beat in the warmed milk. Add the cardamom pods.

Place the farfalle in the buttered ovenproof dish and pour over the milk mixture. Dot with small pieces of butter. Bake in the oven for about 45 minutes or until the pasta is cooked, stirring occasionally. Remove the cardamom pods and serve warm.

Orange Angel Hair with Fruits

SERVES 4

*I*f preferred you can use an unflavored pasta for this dish; alternatively, try using a chocolate pasta. When making flavored pastas, it is an excellent idea to make double the quantity and store half of it for later use.

4 oz orange angel hair pasta

1 medium egg

2 tbsp liquid honey, or to taste

½ tsp ground cinnamon

3 tbsp butter, melted

⅓ cup raisins

½ cup chopped candied cherries

½ cup candied angelica or other candied fruits, chopped

1–2 tsp confectioners' sugar, sifted

● Preheat the oven to 400°F and lightly butter an ovenproof dish. Cook the angel hair pasta in plenty of boiling water for 1 minute or until "al dente." Drain, rinse under hot water, and thoroughly drain.

● Beat the egg with the honey and cinnamon. Stir in the drained pasta and melted butter. Mix the raisins, cherries, and angelica together.

● Spoon half the pasta mixture into the base of the buttered dish and cover with the raisin mixture. Top with the remaining pasta mixture. Bake in the oven for 25 minutes. Serve warm sprinkled with confectioners' sugar.

Orange Angel Hair with Fruits ▶

Coconut Spaghettini

SERVES 4

*T*his recipe is based on a traditional Indian dessert, normally served at the end of the Ramadan fast. It is delicately flavored with rose water and cardamom.

2½ cups milk

2 green cardamom pods, split

1 tbsp rose water

3 oz fresh spaghettini

4 tbsp liquid honey

1⅓ cups shredded coconut

¼ cup sliced almonds

⅓ cup ready-to-eat dried apricots, finely chopped

● Place the milk and cardamom pods in a pan and bring to a boil. Reduce the heat and simmer very gently for 10 minutes; stir occasionally. Take care that the mixture does not burn.

● Add the rose water and spaghettini to the milk and stir for a few minutes. Simmer for about 8 minutes, then add the honey. Increase the heat and boil for 2 minutes, then again reduce the heat to a simmer.

● Stir in the coconut, almonds, and apricots, and continue to simmer for 20 minutes, stirring occasionally until the mixture is thick and creamy. Discard the cardamom pods, stir lightly, and serve warm.

All about Risotto

"Risotto" means "little rice." It is an Italian dish that can be flavored with meat, poultry, fish, vegetables, shellfish, and game and served as a main course. Risotto is cooked in a large shallow pan in broth, or a mixture of broth and wine, and flavored with the ingredients described. It may also be simply flavored with cheese or saffron and served as a side dish. The most famous example is risotto Milanese which is traditionally served with *Osso Buco*. If risotto is served as a main course, the remainder of the meal should be light. This also applies if serving risotto as an appetizer or dessert when a light main meal should be served as an accompaniment.

As well as being delicious, the basis of the risotto, the rice, is also nutritious. Being a complex carbohydrate, it contains starch and fiber and is digested slowly. It is also a good source of potassium and the B vitamins Niacin and Thiamin. A 2-ounce raw portion of rice also provides approximately 10% of an adult's R.D.A. of protein. Containing virtually no cholesterol or fat, the rice is ideal for those watching their fat intake. It is also

gluten free, making it easily digestible and suitable for coeliacs. The additional ingredients will raise fat and calorie counts, therefore it should not always be considered healthy, especially if creams or high fat meats are used.

Risottos are one of the most delicious of Italian dishes. The technique of cooking short-grain rice is traditional and involves stirring hot broth into the rice. A variety of ingredients are added to the basic risotto recipe to produce many combinations of color, flavor, and texture. Long gone is the myth that risottos exist as a means to use up leftover foods. As rice is so filling, a risotto makes an economical meal for a family, its versatility never allowing for boredom. Risottos are best eaten freshly cooked, but some may be frozen if their flavorings allow. In this case, do not completely cook the rice, cool it, and freeze. Defrost risotto thoroughly and reheat with additional butter or oil until completely hot right through, and creamy in texture.

In Veneto, Italy, the dish is so popular it commands its own festival or "Risotto Rendezvous."

The four-day celebration enables guests to taste a whole host of risotto recipes containing many different ingredients, and competition for the best recipe is fierce. Risotto is cooked on the streets in huge iron pans, and guests are invited to indulge at their will.

Some Essentials

To achieve the characteristic creamy consistency of risotto, there are a few points to consider. The first and most important of these is the type of rice used. Long-grain rices will not give the desired result. To achieve the required texture, only authentic risotto rices should be used for these recipes. This is not a problem as the most common risotto rice, arborio rice, is widely available. There are three risotto rices that are all grown in Italy. The first of these is *Vialone nano*, a medium-grain, round rice which is grown in the Veneto area of Italy. It has a less creamy texture than the following varieties. Arborio rice is a plump, longer grained rice from Piedmont. It is able to absorb a high quantity of liquid without losing its bite, and is classed as a "superfino" rice. It gives a delicious, creamy result and is perhaps the most commonly used risotto rice outside of Italy. The final rice, *carnaroli*, is a smaller superfino grain rice than arborio and is from the Lombardy region. It too will absorb large quantities of liquid without becoming soggy.

The high starch quantity of all these grains allows them to absorb liquid more slowly, resulting in a creamy texture. It is therefore important that the rice is not washed before cooking.

The second point to consider when making risotto is the broth. If possible, use a good homemade broth, varying the flavor according to the recipe. Use fish, beef, chicken, lamb, vegetable, or pork broth. If this is not possible, aim to use a good quality prepared broth. This will add fantastic flavor to the dish as the rice absorbs it while cooking.

Thirdly, choose your pan carefully. A shallow, heavy-based pan is best, approximately 10 inches in diameter and 4 inches deep.

Cooking Risotto

The correct heat should be maintained during cooking. If the dish is cooked quickly on a high heat, the liquid will evaporate too quickly for the rice to absorb it and swell. If too low a heat is used, then slow cooking will give a soggy end result and the rice will not cook evenly. A perfect risotto is neither too runny nor too dry, but tender, creamy, and holding together.

The actual cooking method is simple, but requires constant attention. Here are a few tips to consider for the perfect risotto.

Firstly, heat the broth or broth and wine, if using a mixture, to boiling point. Reduce the heat to maintain a gentle simmer throughout the cooking time. Adding hot liquid makes the rice grains swell, but keeps them firm. It also ensures the continuous cooking of the rice. If cold liquid is added the rice will take longer to cook and the required texture will not be obtained.

Whilst the liquid is being heated, onion, garlic, and other flavorings are cooked in butter or butter and oil, in a large shallow pan. It is important not to let the onion brown, as the dish will be too sweet and the color will be incorrect. The rice is then stirred into the onion and cooked while stirring, for 2 minutes until coated in butter and oil.

A small quantity of hot broth is then added and cooked, stirring until it has been absorbed by the rice. After this initial addition, the hot liquid continues to be added in small quantities, allowing for absorption in between. During this period the risotto requires constant stirring. It should take approximately 20 minutes for the dish to cook after the initial addition of broth.

The liquid quantities and timings of the recipes given in this book are approximate guidelines. Some dishes may require more or less liquid and a longer or shorter cooking time, according to the pan used, the type of rice, and the flavoring ingredients. Should the risotto become dry, hot water should be added to top up the liquid.

The risotto is ready to eat when a creamy texture has been achieved and the rice is firm to the bite, but tender. It should be neither chalky nor soggy.

Serving Risotto

Ideally the risotto should "rest" for a few minutes before serving in warm shallow bowls or plates. It is usually simply eaten with a fork and is often served with freshly grated Parmesan or Romano cheeses stirred in, and of course a glass of Italian wine.

The recipes in the following section demonstrate the versatility of this delicious dish, covering a whole range of dishes using meat, poultry, fish and shellfish, vegetables, and game. There are even some sweet recipes, that will make a perfect finale to a meal.

Vegetarian Risotto

Milanese	Green Risotto
Chili Bean Risotto	Olive, Caper, and Tomato Risotto
Four Cheese Risotto	Yellow Risotto
Green Vegetable Risotto	Mediterranean Vegetable Risotto
Cheese and Sun-dried Tomato Risotto	Risotto Primavera
Spinach, Nutmeg, Raisin, and Pine nut Risotto	Risotto Bianco
	Risotto with Squash
Oriental Vegetable Risotto	
	Spinach and Blue Cheese Risotto
Tuscan Bean Risotto	
	Saffron, Bell Pepper, and Marsala Risotto
Minestrone	
	Fragrant Herb Risotto
Fennel and Orange Risotto	
	Buttery Pumpkin and Hazelnut Risotto
Walnut, Garlic, and Thyme Risotto	
	Pilav-style Risotto
Pumpkin and Blue Cheese Risotto	
	Risotto with Vermicelli
Mixed Onion Risotto	
	Tomato and Red Onion Risotto
Olive Risotto	
	Orange, Sage, and Mushroom Risotto
Asparagus Risotto	
	Lemon and Shallot Risotto
Red Risotto	

Milanese

SERVES 4

Risotto alla Milanese is an Italian classic. Golden yellow in color and aromatic in flavor, this dish can be served as an accompaniment or as a supper with crusty bread and salad.

5 cups vegetable broth

⅓ cup butter

1 medium onion, finely chopped

1 garlic clove, minced

2 cups arborio rice

a large pinch of saffron

salt and white pepper

1 cup freshly grated Parmesan cheese

Pour the broth into a saucepan and bring to a boil. Reduce the heat to a gentle simmer.

Meanwhile, melt ¼ cup butter in a large saucepan and gently fry the onion and garlic for 2–3 minutes until softened but not browned. Stir in the rice and cook, stirring, for 2 minutes, until well coated in butter.

Add a ladleful of broth and cook gently, stirring, until absorbed. Continue adding the broth ladle-by-ladle to the rice until half the broth is used and the rice becomes creamy. Sprinkle in the saffron and seasoning.

Add the remaining broth until the risotto becomes thick, but not sticky. This will take about 25 minutes and shouldn't be hurried. Just before serving, carefully stir in the remaining butter and the Parmesan cheese. Serve immediately.

Chili Bean Risotto

SERVES 4

*P*acked full of the flavors of Mexico, this tasty risotto makes a substantial main meal served on its own.

5 cups vegetable broth

2 tbsp vegetable oil

1 large onion, finely chopped

1 garlic clove, minced

1 green chili, seeded and finely chopped

2 green bell peppers, seeded and diced

2 cups arborio rice

1 tsp ground cumin

1 tsp ground coriander

1 tsp chili powder

salt and ground black pepper

14 oz can kidney beans, drained and rinsed

12 oz can corn, drained and rinsed

4 medium tomatoes, peeled, seeded, and chopped

Pour the broth into a saucepan and bring to a boil. Reduce the heat to a gentle simmer.

Meanwhile, heat the oil in a large saucepan and gently fry the onion, garlic, chili, and bell peppers for 4–5 minutes until softened, but not browned. Stir in the rice and cook, stirring, for 2 minutes until the rice is coated in the vegetable mixture.

Add a ladleful of broth and cook gently, stirring, until absorbed. Continue adding the broth ladle-by-ladle until half the broth is used. Stir in the spices, seasoning, and kidney beans.

Continue adding the broth until the risotto becomes thick, but not sticky. This will take about 25 minutes and shouldn't be hurried.

Stir in the corn and tomatoes. Mix well, adjust seasoning if necessary, and serve.

Chili Bean Risotto ▶

Four Cheese Risotto

SERVES 4

*T*his dish is a rich combination of cheeses in a creamy rice mixture. Serve with freshly steamed vegetables as a main meal.

5 cups vegetable broth

¼ cup butter

8 oz shallots, finely shredded

2 cups arborio rice

salt and ground black pepper

½ cup freshly grated Parmesan cheese

⅓ cup coarsely grated Red Leicester cheese

¼ cup crumbled Gorgonzola cheese

¼ cup diced mozzarella cheese

snipped fresh chives, to garnish

Pour the broth into a saucepan and bring to a boil. Reduce the heat to a gentle simmer.

Meanwhile, melt the butter and gently fry the shallots for 2–3 minutes until softened but not browned. Stir in the rice and cook, stirring, for 2 minutes, until the rice is well coated in the butter.

Add a ladleful of broth and cook gently, stirring, until absorbed. Continue adding the broth until the mixture becomes thick, creamy, and the rice is tender. This will take about 25 minutes and shouldn't be hurried. Season well.

Just before serving, stir in the Parmesan cheese and gently mix in the other cheeses. Sprinkle with chives and serve immediately before the cheeses melt.

Green Vegetable Risotto

SERVES 4

This dish makes an excellent accompaniment to meat or fish dishes, and can also be served as a vegetarian main meal.

8 oz small broccoli florets

4 oz fine asparagus spears

8 oz savoy cabbage, shredded

5 cups vegetable broth (see method)

¼ cup garlic and herb butter

4 cups trimmed and shredded leeks

2 cups arborio rice

salt and ground black pepper

4 tbsp chopped fresh parsley

Bring a saucepan of water to a boil and cook the broccoli for 3–4 minutes until just tender; cook the asparagus and cabbage for 1 minute until just tender. Drain the vegetables and set aside. Reserve the cooking water and use to make up the broth.

Pour the broth into a saucepan and bring to a boil. Reduce the heat to a gentle simmer.

Meanwhile, melt the garlic and herb butter in a large saucepan and gently fry the leeks for 2–3 minutes until softened but not browned. Stir in the rice and cook, stirring, for 2 minutes until the rice is well coated in the leek mixture.

Add a ladleful of broth and cook gently over moderate heat, stirring, until absorbed. Season well. Continue adding the broth until the risotto becomes thick, but not sticky, and the rice is tender. This will take about 25 minutes.

Stir in the cooked vegetables and chopped parsley, and heat through for 2–3 minutes until hot. Serve immediately.

Spinach, Nutmeg, Raisin, and Pine Nut Risotto

SERVES 4

Spinach and nutmeg is a classic combination that is ideal served as an accompaniment to a rich meat casserole.

2 lb young spinach leaves, trimmed

5 cups vegetable broth

¼ cup butter

1 medium onion, finely chopped

2 cups arborio rice

1 tsp grated nutmeg

⅓ cup seedless raisins

½ cup toasted pine nuts

salt and ground black pepper

◉ Wash the spinach leaves and place in a large saucepan while they are still wet. Cover and place over a high heat for 4–5 minutes until wilted. There will be sufficient water on the spinach from washing to steam

◀ *Spinach, Nutmeg, Raisin, and Pine Nut Risotto*

the leaves. Drain well, reserving any cooking liquid, and roughly chop. Set aside.

◉ Pour the broth into a saucepan and bring to a boil. Reduce the heat to a gentle simmer.

◉ Meanwhile, melt the butter in a large saucepan and gently fry the onion for 2–3 minutes until softened but not browned. Stir in the rice and cook, stirring, for 2 minutes until the rice is well coated in the onion mixture.

◉ Add the spinach cooking water and cook gently, stirring, until absorbed. Add the broth ladle-by-ladle until the liquid is absorbed and the rice thickens and becomes creamy and tender. Keep the heat moderate. This will take about 25 minutes.

◉ Mix in the nutmeg, cooked spinach, raisins, and pine nuts. Season well and serve.

Cheese and Sun-dried Tomato Risotto

SERVES 4

This is an extra rich risotto with the delicious intense taste of sun-dried tomatoes that can be served as a side dish or as a simple supper.

½ cup sun-dried tomatoes, soaked as directed

5 cups vegetable broth

¼ cup butter

1 medium onion, finely chopped

2 cups arborio rice

1 tsp dried mixed herbs

salt and ground black pepper

¾ cup freshly grated Romano cheese

1 oz piece Romano cheese

flat leaf parsley, to garnish

◉ Drain the tomatoes, reserving the liquid, and slice into thin strips. Set aside.

◉ Pour the broth into a saucepan and bring to a boil. Reduce the heat to a gentle simmer.

◉ Meanwhile, melt the butter in a large saucepan and gently fry the onion and tomato for 2–3 minutes until softened but not browned. Stir in the rice and cook, stirring, for 2 minutes, until the rice is well coated in the tomato mixture.

◉ Add the tomato soaking liquid and cook gently, stirring until absorbed. Add the herbs and seasoning. Ladle in the broth, one ladleful at a time, until the liquid is absorbed and the rice becomes thick, creamy, and tender. Keep the heat moderate. This will take about 25 minutes.

◉ Gently stir in the grated cheese and pile into a warmed serving dish. Using a vegetable peeler, shave pieces of cheese over the top and garnish with parsley to serve.

Oriental Vegetable Risotto

SERVES 4

Try serving this combination of rice and stir-fried vegetables as an accompaniment to a Chinese meal. Its delicate flavors are perfect to serve with fish or poultry.

2 tbsp vegetable oil

1 bunch scallions, trimmed and chopped

1 medium red bell pepper, seeded and sliced

1 medium yellow bell pepper, seeded and sliced

4 oz snow peas, topped and tailed

4 oz oyster mushrooms

2 oz bean sprouts

2 tbsp dark soy sauce

5 cups vegetable broth

2 garlic cloves, finely chopped

1-in piece fresh ginger, grated

2 cups arborio rice

1 tsp five-spice powder

2 tsp sesame oil

salt and white pepper

1 tbsp toasted sesame seeds

Heat 1 tablespoon oil in a wok or large skillet and stir-fry the scallions, bell peppers, and snow peas over a high heat for 2 minutes. Add the oyster mushrooms, bean sprouts, and soy sauce, and stir-fry for a further 1 minute. Set aside.

Pour the broth into a saucepan and bring to a boil. Reduce the heat to a gentle simmer.

Meanwhile, heat the remaining oil in a large saucepan and gently fry the garlic and ginger for 1–2 minutes until softened. Add the rice and cook, stirring, for 2 minutes until the rice is well coated in the mixture.

Add the broth, ladle-by-ladle, until the broth is absorbed and the rice is thick, creamy, and tender. Keep the heat moderate. This will take about 25 minutes. Stir in the five-spice powder.

Fold in the stir-fried vegetables and sesame oil. Heat gently for 1–2 minutes until hot. Taste and season. Serve sprinkled with sesame seeds.

Tuscan Bean Risotto

SERVES 4

This is a delicious combination of red beans and bell peppers, flavored with the oregano. It makes a filling main meal when served with crusty bread and a salad.

5 cups vegetable broth

2 tbsp olive oil

1 large onion, finely chopped

1 garlic clove, minced

2 red bell peppers, seeded and chopped

1 tsp dried oregano

2 cups arborio rice

4 tbsp extra-dry white vermouth

14 oz can kidney beans, drained and rinsed

4 medium tomatoes, peeled, seeded, and chopped

salt and ground black pepper

chopped fresh oregano, to garnish

Pour the broth into a saucepan and bring to a boil. Reduce the heat to a gentle simmer.

Meanwhile, heat the oil in a large saucepan and gently fry the onion, garlic, bell peppers and dried oregano for 2–3 minutes until just softened but not browned. Add the rice and cook, stirring, for 2 minutes until well coated in the vegetable mixture.

Add the broth ladle-by-ladle, until it is all absorbed and the rice is thick, creamy, and tender. Keep the heat moderate. This will take about 25 minutes.

Stir in the vermouth, beans, and tomatoes. Season well. Heat through for 3–4 minutes, stirring occasionally, until hot. Serve garnished with the chopped fresh oregano.

Minestrone

*F*or a filling meal on a cold day, this hearty risotto is the perfect comfort food.

¾ cup topped, tailed, and halved green beans

2 cups shredded green cabbage

5 cups vegetable broth (see method)

¼ cup butter

1 large onion, finely chopped

1 garlic clove, minced

2 carrots, peeled and diced

2 celery stalks, trimmed and diced

2 cups arborio rice

14 oz can flageolet or cannellini beans, rinsed and drained

7 oz can chopped tomatoes

salt and ground black pepper

1 tbsp chopped fresh parsley

Parmesan shavings, to garnish

● Bring a saucepan of water to a boil and cook the green beans for 3–4 minutes until tender; cook the cabbage for 2–3 minutes until tender. Drain the vegetables and set aside. Reserve the cooking water and use to make up the stock.

● Pour the broth into a saucepan and bring to a boil. Reduce the heat to a gentle simmer.

● Meanwhile, melt the butter in a large saucepan and gently fry the onion, garlic, carrot, and celery for 2–3 minutes until softened but not browned. Add the rice and cook, stirring, for 2 minutes until the rice is well coated in the vegetable mixture.

● Add a ladleful of broth and cook gently, stirring until absorbed. Continue adding the broth until it is all absorbed and the rice becomes thick, creamy, and tender. This will take about 25 minutes and shouldn't be hurried.

● Stir in the cooked vegetables, beans, and tomatoes, and season well. Heat through, stirring occasionally, for 3–4 minutes until hot. Serve sprinkled with parsley and Parmesan shavings.

Fennel and Orange Risotto

SERVES 4

*T*his light and fragrant risotto would make an interesting starter or supper.

5 cups vegetable broth

2 bulbs fennel

2 tbsp butter

1 tbsp olive oil

2 celery stalks, trimmed and chopped

2 medium leeks, trimmed and shredded

2 cups arborio rice

3 medium oranges

salt and ground black pepper

Pour the broth into a saucepan and bring to a boil. Reduce the heat to a gentle simmer.

Meanwhile, trim the fennel, reserving the fronds, and cut into thin slices. Melt the butter with the oil in a large saucepan and gently fry the fennel, celery, and leeks for 3–4 minutes until just softened. Add the rice and cook, stirring, for a further 2 minutes until well mixed.

Add a ladleful of broth and cook gently, stirring, until absorbed. Continue ladling the broth into the rice until the rice becomes creamy, thick, and tender. This will take about 25 minutes and shouldn't be hurried.

Remove the zest and extract the juice from 1 orange and mix into the rice. Carefully slice off the peel and pith from the remaining oranges, and holding the fruit over the saucepan, slice out the orange sections and add to the rice, along with any juice that falls. Gently mix into the rice, season well and serve garnished with the reserved fennel fronds.

Fennel and Orange Risotto ▶

Walnut, Garlic, and Thyme Risotto

SERVES 4

*W*alnuts and their oil enrich this risotto that can be served simply with a light salad.

5 cups vegetable broth

2 tbsp butter

1 tbsp olive oil

4 garlic cloves, minced

½ cup very finely chopped walnuts

2 tbsp chopped fresh thyme or 2 tsp dried

2 cups arborio rice

salt and ground black pepper

1 tbsp walnut oil

½ cup walnut pieces

sprig of fresh thyme, to garnish

Pour the broth into a saucepan and bring to a boil. Reduce the heat to a gentle simmer.

Meanwhile, melt the butter with the oil in a large saucepan and gently fry the garlic, chopped walnuts, and thyme for 2 minutes. Stir in the rice and cook, stirring, for a further 2 minutes until the rice is well coated in the walnut mixture.

Add the broth, ladle-by-ladle, until all the liquid is absorbed and the rice is thick, creamy, and tender. Keep the heat moderate. This will take about 25 minutes and shouldn't be hurried.

Adjust the seasoning. Stir in the walnut oil. Serve the risotto sprinkled with the walnut pieces and garnish with thyme.

Pumpkin and Blue Cheese Risotto

SERVES 4

Pumpkin has an earthy taste and absorbs the flavors from other ingredients during cooking. In this risotto it combines with blue cheese to make a very rich dish.

5 cups vegetable broth

¼ cup butter

1 medium onion, finely chopped

1 lb pumpkin flesh, diced

2 cups arborio rice

salt and ground black pepper

½ cup crumbled blue cheese, such as Gorgonzola, Stilton or Danish blue

2 tbsp chopped fresh parsley

Pour the broth into a saucepan and bring to a boil. Reduce the heat to a gentle simmer.

Meanwhile, melt the butter in a large saucepan and gently fry the onion for 2–3 minutes until softened but not browned. Add the pumpkin and continue to cook, stirring, for 6–7 minutes until just beginning to soften.

Stir in the rice and cook, stirring, for 2 minutes until the rice is well coated in the pumpkin mixture. Add the broth, ladle-by-ladle, until all the liquid is absorbed and the rice is thick, creamy, and tender. Keep the heat moderate. This will take about 25 minutes.

Season well and gently stir in the blue cheese. Serve sprinkled with chopped parsley.

Mixed Onion Risotto

This dish makes a tasty accompaniment to roast meats or roasted vegetables.

5 cups vegetable broth	1 tbsp lemon juice
¼ cup butter	2 tsp superfine sugar
1 tbsp vegetable oil	2 cups arborio rice
8 oz shallots, halved	⅔ cup dry white wine
2 medium onions, finely sliced	salt and ground black pepper
2 medium red onions, finely chopped	4 tbsp snipped fresh chives

Pour the broth into a saucepan and bring to a boil. Reduce the heat to a gentle simmer.

Meanwhile, melt the butter with the oil in a large saucepan and fry the shallots and onions with the lemon juice and sugar for 8–10 minutes until richly golden and caramelized. Stir in the rice and cook, stirring, for a further 2 minutes until well mixed.

Add the wine and cook gently, stirring, until absorbed. Add the broth, ladle-by-ladle, until all the liquid is absorbed and the rice is thick, creamy, and tender. Keep the heat moderate. This will take about 25 minutes and shouldn't be hurried. Season well. Stir in the chives and serve.

Olive Risotto

SERVES 4

A mouth-watering combination of rice and olives makes this risotto an unusual side dish, or the perfect supper for an olive lover.

5 cups vegetable broth

3 tbsp extra virgin olive oil

8 oz shallots, finely sliced

2 garlic cloves, minced

2 cups arborio rice

½ cup pitted green olives

½ cup pimiento-stuffed green olives

¾ cup pitted black olives

salt and ground black pepper

2 tbsp freshly shredded basil

Pour the broth into a saucepan and bring to a boil. Reduce the heat to a gentle simmer.

Meanwhile, heat 2 tablespoons oil in a large skillet and gently fry the shallots and garlic for 2–3 minutes until softened but not browned. Add the rice and cook, stirring, for 2 minutes until well coated in the shallot mixture.

Add a ladleful of broth and cook gently, stirring, until absorbed. Continue ladling the stock into the rice until all the liquid has been absorbed and the rice becomes thick, creamy, and tender.

Stir in the olives and adjust the seasoning. Serve the risotto sprinkled with the basil and drizzled with the remaining oil.

Asparagus Risotto

SERVES 4

Lightly cooked asparagus is added to this simple risotto. It can be served on its own as a substantial starter, side dish, or supper.

8 oz asparagus spears

5 cups vegetable broth (see method)

1 tbsp olive oil

1 medium onion, finely chopped

2 cups arborio rice

4 tbsp extra dry vermouth

4 tbsp heavy cream

salt and ground black pepper

½ cup freshly grated Parmesan cheese (optional)

Cut off the very woody ends from the asparagus. Cut the spears into 2-inch lengths. Bring a small saucepan of water to a boil and cook the asparagus for 4–5 minutes until just cooked. Drain and set aside. Reserve the cooking liquid and use to make up the broth.

Pour the broth into a saucepan and bring to a boil. Reduce the heat to a gentle simmer.

Meanwhile, heat the oil in a large saucepan and gently fry the onion for 2–3 minutes until softened but not browned. Add the rice and cook, stirring, for 2 minutes.

Add a ladleful of broth and cook gently, stirring, until absorbed. Continue ladling in the broth until all the liquid has been absorbed and the rice is thick, creamy, and tender. Keep the heat moderate. This will take about 25 minutes.

Stir in the vermouth and cream. Gently mix in the cooked asparagus and season. Serve sprinkled with Parmesan, if using.

Red Risotto

SERVES 4

The vibrant color of this dish is due to fresh beet. Spoon over sour cream to serve and accompany with crusty bread and freshly steamed green vegetables for a stunning supper dish.

5 cups vegetable broth

2 tbsp butter

1 tbsp olive oil

2 medium red onions, thinly sliced

4 medium fresh raw beet, peeled and very thinly sliced in strips or coarsely grated

2 cups coarsely grated carrot

2 cups arborio rice

⅔ cup red wine

salt and ground black pepper

4 tbsp sour cream

snipped fresh chives, to garnish

Pour the broth into a saucepan and bring to a boil. Reduce the heat to a gentle simmer.

Meanwhile, melt the butter with the oil in a large saucepan and gently fry the onions, beet, and carrot for 10 minutes until just beginning to soften. Add the rice and cook, stirring, for 2 minutes until well coated in the vegetable mixture.

Add the red wine and cook gently, stirring, until absorbed. Ladle in the broth gradually over a moderate heat until all the liquid is absorbed and the rice is thick, creamy, and tender. This will take about 25 minutes.

Add seasoning to taste. Serve immediately topped with sour cream and sprinkled with chopped chives.

Red Risotto ▶

Green Risotto

SERVES 4

This fresh tasting dish is the perfect accompaniment to fish and chicken dishes

5 cups vegetable broth

2 tbsp vegetable oil

1 large onion, finely chopped

2 green bell peppers, seeded and chopped

2 cups arborio rice

⅔ cup dry white wine

2 cups frozen peas

2 tsp ground coriander

salt and ground black pepper

4 tbsp chopped fresh cilantro

2 scallions, finely chopped

Pour the broth into a saucepan and bring to a boil. Reduce the heat to a gentle simmer.

Meanwhile, heat the oil in a large saucepan and gently fry the onion and bell peppers for 3–4 minutes until just softened but not browned. Add the rice and cook, stirring, for 2 minutes until well coated in the pepper mixture.

Add the wine and cook gently, stirring, until absorbed. Ladle in the broth gradually, until half the liquid is absorbed. Mix in the frozen peas. Continue ladling in the broth until the rice becomes thick, creamy, and tender. The heat should be moderate. This will take about 25 minutes. Stir in the ground coriander and seasoning. Mix in the cilantro and serve sprinkled with the scallions.

Olive, Caper, and Tomato Risotto

SERVES 4

The traditional combination of ingredients in this dish gives a thoroughly Italian flavor to this risotto.

3¾ cups vegetable broth

2 tbsp olive oil

1 large onion, finely chopped

1 garlic clove, minced

2 cups arborio rice

1 tsp dried mixed herbs

⅔ cup red wine

14 oz can chopped tomatoes

salt and ground black pepper

1 cup pitted black olives

2 tbsp capers

Romano cheese shavings, to garnish

◄ *Olive, Caper, and Tomato Risotto*

Pour the broth into a saucepan and bring to a boil. Reduce the heat to a gentle simmer.

Meanwhile, heat the oil in a large saucepan and gently fry the onion and garlic for 2–3 minutes until softened but not browned. Add the rice and herbs and cook, stirring, for 2 minutes until well coated in the onion mixture.

Add the wine and chopped tomatoes and cook gently, stirring, until absorbed. Ladle in the broth gradually and cook until all the liquid is absorbed and the rice is thick, creamy, and tender.

Season well and stir in the olives and capers. Serve topped with shavings of Romano cheese and sprinkled with black pepper.

Yellow Risotto

SERVES 4

The sunny colors in this dish will brighten up any meal. For maximum impact, serve the risotto with contrasting colored salads.

5 cups vegetable broth

2 tbsp butter

1 tbsp vegetable oil

1 large onion, finely chopped

1 yellow bell pepper, seeded and chopped

8 oz pumpkin flesh, diced

2 cups arborio rice

large pinch of saffron

salt and white pepper

12 oz can corn, drained

halved grilled yellow tomatoes, to garnish

Pour the broth into a saucepan and bring to a boil. Reduce the heat to a gentle simmer.

Meanwhile, melt the butter with the oil in a large saucepan and gently fry the onion, pepper, and pumpkin for 4–5 minutes until just softened. Add the rice and cook, stirring, for 2 minutes until the rice is well coated in the vegetable mixture.

Add a ladleful of broth and cook gently, stirring until absorbed. Continue ladling in the broth until half of it is used. Sprinkle in the saffron and seasoning. Mix in the corn.

Continue adding the broth until all the liquid is absorbed and the rice is thick, creamy, and tender. Keep the heat moderate. This will take about 25 minutes. Garnish and serve.

Mediterranean Vegetable Risotto

SERVES 4

This risotto makes a stunning main course. Serve simply with herb or cheese bread.

1 medium eggplant	5 cups vegetable broth
2 medium zucchini	1 medium onion, finely chopped
1 red bell pepper	2 cups arborio rice
2 medium tomatoes	⅔ cup dry white wine
1 red onion	salt and ground black pepper
2 garlic cloves	⅓ cup diced halloumi or feta cheese
6 tbsp olive oil	
2 tbsp chopped fresh rosemary or 2 tsp dried	fresh rosemary, to garnish

First prepare the vegetables. Trim and dice the eggplant into 1-inch pieces. Trim and slice the zucchini. Seed and dice the bell pepper into 1-inch cubes. Quarter the tomatoes. Peel and cut the red onion into eight wedges. Peel and thinly slice the garlic.

Place all the vegetables in a bowl and gently stir in 5 tablespoons olive oil and the rosemary until well mixed. Preheat the broiler to a hot setting. Pile the vegetables into the broiler pan and cook the vegetables for 8–10 minutes, turning frequently, until lightly charred and tender. Set aside.

Pour the broth into a saucepan and bring to a boil. Reduce the heat to a gentle simmer.

Meanwhile, heat the remaining oil in a large saucepan and gently fry the onion for 2–3 minutes until softened. Add the rice and cook, stirring, for 2 minutes until well coated in the onion mixture.

Add the wine and cook gently, stirring, until absorbed. Ladle in the broth gradually, until all the liquid is absorbed and the rice is thick, creamy, and tender. Keep the heat moderate. This will take about 25 minutes. Season well.

Gently mix in the prepared vegetables and heat through for 2–3 minutes until hot. Serve sprinkled with the cheese and garnished with fresh rosemary.

Risotto Primavera

selection of lightly cooked spring vegetables is stirred into this risotto. It is very much a celebration of the season when young vegetables are at their best.

6 oz asparagus	1 large onion, finely chopped
¾ cup young carrots, trimmed	2 cups arborio rice
6 oz young turnips, trimmed	salt and ground black pepper
6 oz sugar snap peas	4 oz young spinach leaves, washed and trimmed
5 cups vegetable broth (see method)	2 tbsp chopped fresh chervil
⅓ cup butter	fresh chervil, to garnish

First prepare the vegetables. Cut off the woody ends from the asparagus spears, and cut into 2-inch lengths. Depending on size, leave the carrots and turnips whole or cut in half or quarters. Top and tail the peas. Bring a saucepan of water to a boil and cook the vegetables until just tender: asparagus for 6–7 minutes; carrots and turnips for 6–7 minutes; and the peas for 3–4 minutes. Drain, reserving the cooking water, and refresh under cold water. Set aside. Reserve the cooking liquid and use to make up the vegetable broth.

Pour the broth into a saucepan and bring to a boil. Reduce the heat to a gentle simmer.

Melt ¼ cup butter in a large saucepan and gently fry the onion for 2–3 minutes until just softened but not browned. Add the rice and cook, stirring, for 2 minutes until the rice is coated in the onion mixture. Season well.

Add a ladleful of broth and cook gently, stirring, until absorbed. Continue ladling the broth into the rice until all the liquid is absorbed and the rice is thick, creamy and tender. Keep the heat moderate. This will take about 25 minutes.

Stir in the spinach, chopped chervil, and cooked vegetables and cook for 2–3 minutes until hot. Adjust seasoning and serve with remaining butter on top and garnished with chervil.

Risotto Bianco

SERVES 4

*T*his risotto is a simple combination of mushrooms and rice with just a hint of thyme and cream.

5 cups vegetable broth	2 cups arborio rice
¼ cup garlic and herb butter	salt and white pepper
1 medium onion, finely chopped	4 tbsp extra-dry vermouth
1 garlic clove, minced	4 tbsp heavy cream
3 cups sliced button mushrooms	fresh thyme, to garnish
1 tsp dried thyme	

Pour the broth into a saucepan and bring to a boil. Reduce the heat to a gentle simmer.

Meanwhile, melt the butter and gently fry the onion, garlic, mushrooms, and thyme for 3–4 minutes until softened but not browned. Add the rice and cook, stirring, for 2 minutes until well coated in the mushroom mixture. Season.

Add a ladleful of broth and cook gently, stirring, until absorbed. Continue ladling in the broth until all the liquid is absorbed and the rice is thick, creamy, and tender. Keep the heat moderate. This will take about 25 minutes.

Stir in the vermouth and cream. Garnish and serve.

Risotto with Squash

Squash combines with tomatoes in this buttery risotto. Serve this as an unusual accompaniment to a casserole, or as a delicious main meal.

3¾ cups vegetable broth

⅓ cup butter

2 medium red onions, finely chopped

2 garlic cloves, minced

1 lb butternut squash flesh, diced

2 cups arborio rice

salt and ground black pepper

⅔ cup dry white wine

14 oz can chopped tomatoes

2 tbsp chopped fresh parsley

● Pour the broth into a saucepan and bring to a boil. Reduce the heat to a gentle simmer.

● Meanwhile, melt the butter and gently fry the onion, garlic, and squash for 7–8 minutes until just softening. Add the rice and cook, stirring, for 2 minutes until well mixed. Season well.

● Add the wine and chopped tomatoes and cook gently, stirring, until absorbed. Add the broth, ladle-by-ladle, until the liquid is absorbed and the rice is thick, creamy, and tender. Keep the heat moderate. This will take about 25 minutes.

● Adjust seasoning if necessary. Serve sprinkled with chopped parsley.

Risotto with Squash ▶

Spinach and Blue Cheese Risotto

The delicate, earthy flavor of spinach combines perfectly with the richness of the Italian blue cheese, Gorgonzola. This makes a perfect supper dish.

2 lb fresh young spinach, trimmed

5 cups vegetable broth

¼ cup butter

1 bunch scallions, trimmed and finely chopped

2 cups arborio rice

salt and ground black pepper

¾ cup diced Gorgonzola cheese

2 tbsp chopped fresh chives

shredded scallion, to garnish

● Wash the spinach and place in a large saucepan while still wet. Cover and cook for 4–5 minutes until wilted. There will be sufficient water on the spinach from washing to steam the leaves. Drain well, reserving any cooking liquid, then chop.

● Pour the broth into a saucepan and bring to a boil. Reduce the heat to a gentle simmer.

● Meanwhile, melt the butter in a large saucepan and gently fry the scallions for 2–3 minutes until softened but not browned. Stir in the rice and cook, stirring, for 2 minutes until the rice is well coated in the onion mixture. Season well.

● Add the spinach cooking water and cook gently, stirring, until absorbed. Add the broth ladle-by-ladle until all the liquid is absorbed and the rice is thick, creamy, and tender. Keep the heat moderate. This will take about 25 minutes.

● Stir in the spinach, the Gorgonzola cheese and chopped chives. Adjust seasoning if necessary. Garnish and serve.

Saffron, Bell Pepper, and Marsala Risotto

SERVES 4

This colorful and fragrant risotto has the added sweetness of bell peppers and Marsala wine.

2 medium red bell peppers	2 tbsp olive oil
2 medium yellow bell peppers	1 medium onion, finely chopped
2 medium green bell peppers	2 cups arborio rice
4 tbsp Marsala wine	a large pinch of saffron
5 cups vegetable broth	salt and ground black pepper

Preheat the broiler to a hot setting. Halve and seed the bell peppers and place on the broiler rack. Cook for 7–8 minutes, turning occasionally, until the peppers are charred and softened. Carefully peel off the charred skin, then slice into thin strips. Place in a shallow bowl and mix in the Marsala wine. Set aside.

Pour the broth into a saucepan and bring to a boil. Reduce the heat to a gentle simmer.

Meanwhile, heat the oil in a large saucepan and gently fry the onion for 2–3 minutes until just softened, but not browned. Add the rice and cook, stirring, for 2 minutes until well coated in the onion mixture.

Add a ladleful of broth and cook gently, stirring, until absorbed. Continue ladling the broth into the rice until half the broth is used and the rice becomes creamy. Sprinkle in the saffron and seasoning.

Continue adding the broth until the risotto becomes thick and the rice is tender. This will take about 25 minutes and shouldn't be hurried.

Stir in the bell pepper mixture and adjust seasoning before serving.

Fragrant Herb Risotto

SERVES 4

Use any combination of your favorite herbs in this recipe. Their delicate flavors are enhanced by the addition of white wine, and make this the perfect accompaniment to a fish meal.

3¾ cups vegetable broth

2 tbsp olive oil

2 medium leeks, trimmed and shredded

2 cups arborio rice

1¼ cups dry white wine

salt and ground black pepper

2 tbsp each of chopped parsley, sage, basil, marjoram, and tarragon

2 tbsp sour cream

mixed fresh herbs, to garnish

Pour the broth into a saucepan and bring to a boil. Reduce the heat to a gentle simmer.

Meanwhile, heat the oil in a large saucepan and gently fry the leeks for 2–3 minutes until softened but not browned. Add the rice and cook, stirring, for 2 minutes until the rice is well coated in the leek mixture.

Pour in half the wine and cook gently, stirring, until absorbed. Add the remaining wine, and ladle in the broth gradually until all the liquid is absorbed and the rice is thick, creamy, and tender. Keep the heat moderate. This will take about 25 minutes.

Season. Stir in the chopped herbs and cream. Garnish and serve.

Buttery Pumpkin and Hazelnut Risotto

SERVES 4

This delicious combination of juicy pumpkin, nuts, and tangy orange makes a memorable main course dish

5 cups vegetable broth

⅓ cup butter

1 large onion, finely chopped

1 lb pumpkin flesh, diced

2 garlic cloves, minced

2 cups arborio rice

grated zest of ½ an orange

salt and ground black pepper

½ cup freshly grated Parmesan cheese

½ cup toasted chopped hazelnuts

orange zest, to garnish

Pour the broth into a saucepan and bring to a boil. Reduce the heat to a gentle simmer.

Meanwhile, melt ¼ cup butter in a large saucepan and gently fry the onion, pumpkin, and garlic for 7–8 minutes until just softened. Add the rice and cook, stirring, for 2 minutes until well mixed.

Add a ladleful of broth and cook gently, stirring, until absorbed. Continue ladling in the broth until half is used and the rice becomes creamy. Add the grated orange zest and season.

Continue adding the broth until the risotto becomes thick and the rice is tender. This will take about 25 minutes. Stir in the remaining butter and grated cheese. Serve sprinkled with the hazelnuts, and garnish with orange zest.

Pilav-style Risotto

The warm, spicy, and sweet Middle Eastern flavors in this risotto offer the perfect accompaniment to a rich meat dish.

5 cups vegetable broth	2 cups arborio rice
1 tbsp olive oil	a large pinch of saffron
2 tbsp butter	salt and ground black pepper
1 medium red onion, finely chopped	3 tbsp chopped fresh cilantro
1 tbsp lemon juice	2 tbsp toasted pine nuts
½ cup thinly sliced no-need-to-soak dried apricots	2 tbsp sliced toasted blanched almonds
1 cinnamon stick, broken	fresh cilantro, to garnish

Pour the broth into a saucepan and bring to a boil. Reduce the heat to a gentle simmer.

Meanwhile, heat the oil and butter in a large saucepan and gently fry the onion, lemon juice, apricots, and cinnamon stick for 2–3 minutes until the onion is softened but not browned. Add the rice and cook, stirring, for 2 minutes until well mixed.

Add a ladleful of broth and cook gently, stirring, until absorbed. Continue ladling the broth into the rice until half the broth is used and the rice becomes creamy. Sprinkle in the saffron and seasoning.

Continue adding the broth until the risotto becomes thick. This will take about 25 minutes and shouldn't be hurried. Discard the cinnamon stick.

Mix in the chopped cilantro and adjust the seasoning if necessary. Serve the risotto sprinkled with the toasted nuts and garnished with cilantro.

Risotto with Vermicelli

SERVES 4

An unusual dish combining rice, pasta, and cream cheese. This makes a filling meal and need only be served with a crisp salad.

4 oz tricolor vermicelli pasta or spaghetti, broken into short lengths

1 tbsp olive oil

5 cups vegetable broth

¼ cup butter

1 medium onion, finely chopped

1 garlic clove, minced

2 cups arborio rice

½ cup soft cheese with garlic and herbs

4 tbsp heavy cream

salt and ground black pepper

3 tbsp chopped fresh parsley

1 oz piece Parmesan cheese

Bring a saucepan of water to a boil and cook the pasta according to the instructions on the package. Drain well and mix with the olive oil. Set aside.

Pour the broth into a saucepan and bring to a boil. Reduce the heat to a gentle simmer.

Meanwhile, melt the butter and gently fry the onion and garlic for 2–3 minutes until just softened but not browned. Add the rice and cook, stirring, for 2 minutes until well coated in the onion butter.

Add the broth, ladle-by-ladle, until all the liquid has been absorbed, and the rice is thick, creamy, and tender. Keep the heat moderate. This will take about 25 minutes.

Carefully mix in the cooked pasta, soft cheese, cream, and seasoning. Stir in the chopped parsley. Pile into a serving dish. Using a vegetable peeler, shave off pieces of Parmesan and sprinkle over the risotto to serve.

Tomato and Red Onion Risotto

For a substantial lunch or supper, serve this flavorful dish with crusty bread and a green salad.

½ cup soaked sun-dried tomatoes	2 cups arborio rice
4 oz cherry tomatoes, halved	1 tsp dried mixed herbs
3¾ cups vegetable broth	salt and ground black pepper
¼ cup butter	⅔ cup dry white wine
2 medium red onions, finely chopped	14 oz can chopped tomatoes
2 cloves garlic, minced	1 tbsp tomato paste
1 tbsp lemon juice	1 tsp superfine sugar
	2 tbsp chopped fresh parsley

Drain the sun-dried tomatoes, reserving the liquid. Slice into thin strips. Preheat the broiler to a hot setting and cook the cherry tomatoes for 1–2 minutes until lightly charred. Set aside.

Pour the broth into a saucepan and bring to a boil. Reduce the heat to a gentle simmer.

Meanwhile, melt the butter and gently fry the onion, garlic, lemon juice, and sun-dried tomato for 2–3 minutes until just softened but not browned. Add the rice and cook, stirring, for 2 minutes until well mixed. Add the herbs and season.

Add the wine, chopped tomatoes, tomato paste, and sugar, and cook gently, stirring, until absorbed. Ladle in the broth gradually until it is all absorbed and the rice is thick, creamy, and tender. Adjust the seasoning if necessary.

Gently stir in the broiled cherry tomatoes and serve sprinkled with chopped parsley.

Orange, Sage, and Mushroom Risotto

SERVES 4

Tangy oranges and the aromatic flavor of sage enliven this mushroom risotto dish.

3¾ cups vegetable broth

¼ cup garlic and herb butter

2 tbsp olive oil

1 medium onion, finely chopped

3 cups sliced open cup mushrooms

2 large open mushrooms, sliced

2 cups arborio rice

salt and ground black pepper

1 tsp powdered sage

1¼ cups unsweetened orange juice

2 medium oranges

1 tbsp chopped fresh sage

orange zest, to garnish

◀ *Orange, Sage, and Mushroom Risotto*

Pour the broth into a saucepan and bring to a boil. Reduce the heat to a gentle simmer.

Meanwhile, melt the butter with the oil in a large saucepan and gently fry the onion and mushrooms for 3–4 minutes until just softened. Add the rice and cook, stirring, for 2 minutes until well mixed. Season and add the powdered sage.

Add the orange juice and cook gently, stirring, until absorbed. Add the broth ladle-by-ladle until it is all absorbed and the rice is thick, creamy, and tender. Keep the heat moderate. This will take about 25 minutes.

Carefully peel the oranges removing the pith at the same time. Holding the oranges over the risotto, slice out the orange sections and gently mix them into the rice. Adjust the seasoning, and mix in the chopped sage. Serve garnished with orange zest.

Lemon and Shallot Risotto

SERVES 4

In this dish golden shallots are mixed with the delicate flavors of lemon and fresh tarragon. This is the perfect risotto to serve with fish or seafood.

5 cups vegetable broth

1 tbsp olive oil

2 tbsp butter

8 oz shallots, halved

1 tbsp lemon juice

1 tsp superfine sugar

2 cups arborio rice

finely grated zest of 1 lemon

salt and ground black pepper

2 tbsp chopped fresh tarragon

4 tbsp heavy cream

½ cup freshly grated Parmesan cheese

fresh tarragon and lemon zest, to garnish

Pour the broth into a saucepan and bring to a boil. Reduce the heat to a gentle simmer.

Meanwhile, heat the oil and butter in a large saucepan and fry the shallots with the lemon juice and sugar for 6–7 minutes until golden brown and lightly caramelized. Add the rice and cook, stirring, for 2 minutes until well mixed.

Add a ladleful of broth and cook gently, stirring, until absorbed. Continue ladling the broth into the rice until half the broth is used and the rice becomes creamy. Sprinkle in the lemon zest and seasoning.

Continue adding the broth until the risotto becomes thick and the rice is tender. This will take about 25 minutes and shouldn't be hurried.

Stir in the chopped tarragon, cream, and grated Parmesan cheese. Adjust seasoning if necessary. Garnish and serve.

Risotto with Meat

Sweet-and-sour Beef Risotto · Sweet Chili and Basil Risotto

Chargrilled Pork with Mixed Bell Peppers · Persian Lamb Risotto

Ham and Bean Risotto · Risotto Bolognese

Ham and Leek Risotto · Rosemary Lamb Risotto

Ham and Mixed Mushroom Risotto · Risotto with Meatballs and Coriander

Bacon and Spinach Risotto · Mixed Meat Risotto

Beef Ragu Risotto · Beef and Broccoli Risotto

Chili Beef Risotto · Lamb and Raspberry Risotto

Fried Lamb and Fava Bean Risotto · Pork, Saffron, and Basil Risotto

Beef and Olive Risotto ·

Sweet-and-sour Beef Risotto

SERVES 4

Try a taste of the orient with this tasty risotto. Packed with tender beef, Chinese flavors, and spices, it makes a delicious meal.

5 cups beef broth

¼ cup butter

1 tbsp oil

8 oz lean beef steak, trimmed and very thinly sliced

1 medium onion, finely chopped

2 garlic cloves, minced

2 tsp fresh ginger, chopped

2 tsp five-spice powder

2 cups arborio rice

salt and ground black pepper

1 green bell pepper, quartered and sliced

1 red bell pepper, quartered and sliced

2 tbsp dark brown sugar

3 tbsp rice wine vinegar

¼ cup bean sprouts

8 oz prepared fresh pineapple

1 tbsp sesame oil

Pour the broth into a large saucepan and bring to a boil. Reduce the heat to a gentle simmer.

Meanwhile, melt the butter in a large skillet and add the oil. Gently fry the beef for 2–3 minutes. Add the onion, garlic, ginger, and five-spice powder, cook for 2 minutes, stirring, until the onion has softened and the meat browned. Stir in the rice and cook, stirring, for 2 minutes until the rice is well coated in the butter and oil.

Add a ladleful of broth to the pan and cook gently, stirring, until the broth is absorbed. Continue adding a ladleful of broth to the rice until half of the broth has been used and the rice becomes creamy. Season well and continue adding broth and stirring for a further 15 minutes.

Stir in the bell peppers, and blend the sugar and vinegar. Add to the pan, mixing well. Continue to add the remaining broth for a further 10 minutes. Stir in the bean sprouts and pineapple pieces 2–3 minutes before serving. Add the sesame oil and serve the risotto in a warm bowl.

Chargrilled Pork with Mixed Bell Peppers

SERVES 4

Tender pork is marinated in a delicious spicy marinade then broiled, adding a delicious flavor and color to this risotto.

12-oz piece lean pork fillet, halved lengthwise

2 tbsp dark soy sauce

2 tbsp red wine

1 tbsp liquid honey

1 tbsp dark brown sugar

2 garlic cloves, minced

½ tsp ground cinnamon

1 tsp sesame oil

FOR THE RISOTTO

5 cups pork or vegetable broth

¼ cup butter

1 leek, sliced

2 garlic cloves, minced

2 cups arborio rice

1 red bell pepper, seeded and chopped

1 green bell pepper, seeded and chopped

1 yellow bell pepper, seeded and chopped

2 tsp fennel seeds

Put the pork pieces in a shallow dish. Mix together the soy sauce, red wine, honey, brown sugar, garlic, cinnamon, and sesame oil. Pour the mixture over the pork, turning to coat completely. Leave for a few minutes. Meanwhile heat the broiler to medium and cook the pork for 20 minutes, turning once, brushing with the marinade until cooked through.

Meanwhile, pour the broth into a large saucepan and bring to a boil. Reduce the heat to a gentle simmer. Melt the butter in a large skillet and gently fry the leek and garlic for 2–3 minutes until the leek is softened but not brown. Stir in the rice and cook for 2–3 minutes, stirring, until well coated in butter.

Add a ladleful of broth and cook gently, stirring until the liquid has been absorbed. Continue adding a ladleful of broth until half of the broth has been used and the rice becomes creamy.

Continue adding the broth for 10 minutes. Add the bell peppers and fennel seeds, stirring well. Continue to cook, adding more broth for a further 15 minutes until the risotto is thick but not sticky.

Remove the pork from the broiler and slice. Stir into the rice and serve in a warmed bowl.

Ham and Bean Risotto

SERVES 4

The smoked ham gives a delicious flavor to this dish. Combined with the beans, wine, and fresh herbs, it is a simple but tasty dish.

3¾ cups vegetable broth

1¼ cups dry white wine

¼ cup butter

1 red onion, finely chopped

1 garlic clove, minced

1½ cups diced smoked ham

2 cups arborio rice

salt and ground black pepper

pinch of turmeric

4 oz shelled fava beans, thawed if frozen

4 oz thin green beans, trimmed

4 oz canned flageolet beans in brine, drained

½ cup freshly grated Romano cheese

1 tbsp chopped fresh sage

Pour the broth and wine into a large pan and bring to a boil. Reduce the heat to a gentle simmer.

Meanwhile, melt the butter in a large skillet and gently fry the onion, garlic, and ham for 2–3 minutes until the onion is softened but not browned. Stir in the rice and cook, stirring, for 2–3 minutes until the rice is well coated in butter.

Add a ladleful of broth to the rice, cook gently, stirring, until the liquid has been absorbed. Continue to add a ladleful of broth to the rice until half of the broth has been used and the rice becomes creamy. Season well and add the turmeric.

Continue adding broth until the risotto becomes thick but not sticky, about 25 minutes.

Meanwhile, cook the fava beans and green beans in boiling water for 5 minutes. Five minutes before the end of the risotto cooking time, add the boiled beans and canned flageolet beans. Stir in the cheese and sage and serve in a warmed bowl.

Ham and Leek Risotto

*H*am and leeks are a great combination, especially when enhanced by a grainy mustard as in this dish. One of the many flavored mustards now available could be added for variety.

5 cups vegetable or pork broth

¼ cup butter

3 large leeks, sliced

2 garlic cloves, minced

1⅓ cups ham, trimmed and cut into strips

2 cups arborio rice

1 tbsp whole grain mustard

salt and ground black pepper

8 canned artichoke hearts in brine, drained and halved

½ cup freshly grated Parmesan cheese

1 tbsp chopped fresh cilantro

● Pour the broth into a large saucepan and bring to a boil. Reduce the heat to a gentle simmer.

● Meanwhile, melt the butter in a large skillet and gently fry the leeks, garlic, and ham slices for 2–3 minutes until the leeks have softened. Stir in the rice and cook, stirring, for 2 minutes until the rice is well coated in butter.

● Add a ladleful of the broth and cook gently, stirring, until the liquid has been absorbed. Continue to add a ladleful of broth to the rice until half of the broth has been used and the rice becomes creamy. Stir in the mustard and season well.

● Continue adding the broth until the risotto becomes thick but not sticky, about 25 minutes. Stir in the artichoke hearts 2–3 minutes before the end of cooking time. Add the cheese and cilantro and serve in a warmed bowl.

Ham and Mixed Mushroom Risotto

SERVES 4

*P*orcini mushrooms, also known as ceps, are much sought after by Italians for their nutty flavor. They are readily available dried, and are simply softened in hot water and used in small quantities in many classic recipes.

¼ cup dried porcini mushrooms

3 cups vegetable broth

1¼ cups dry white wine

⅓ cup butter

1 onion, finely chopped

3 garlic cloves, minced

2¼ cups wiped and sliced chestnut mushrooms

2¼ cups baby button mushrooms, wiped

2 cups arborio rice

salt and ground black pepper

1½ cups oyster mushrooms

½ cup Parma ham, cut into strips

1 tbsp chopped fresh parsley or thyme

2 tbsp freshly grated Parmesan cheese

Soak the porcini mushrooms in warm water according to package instructions. Thinly slice and reserve soaking liquid.

Pour the broth and wine into a large saucepan and bring to a boil. Reduce the heat to a gentle simmer.

Meanwhile, melt the butter in a large skillet and gently fry the onion and garlic for 2–3 minutes until softened but not browned. Add all the mushrooms except the oyster mushrooms and cook for a further 2 minutes, stirring.

Add the rice and porcini with soaking liquid, stirring, until the liquid has been absorbed. Stir in a ladleful of broth and wine mixture. Cook gently until absorbed and continue to add a ladleful of broth until half of the broth has been used and the rice is creamy. Season well.

Continue to add the broth in small quantities until the risotto becomes thick but not sticky, about 25 minutes. Five minutes before the end of cooking time, stir in the oyster mushrooms and Parma ham strips.

Just before serving, stir in the herbs and cheese, adjust seasoning and serve in a warm bowl.

Bacon and Spinach Risotto

SERVES 4

Spinach and bacon are a classic combination. Using smoked bacon adds flavor which perfectly complements the spinach and tomatoes.

5 cups vegetable broth

¼ cup butter

1 red onion, halved and sliced

2 garlic cloves, minced

1⅓ cups smoked bacon, derinded and cut into strips

2 cups arborio rice

salt and ground black pepper

large pinch of grated nutmeg

2 tomatoes, seeded and chopped

6 oz spinach, trimmed and washed

½ cup freshly grated Romano cheese

finely pared zest of 1 lemon

Pour the broth into a large saucepan and bring to a boil. Reduce the heat to a gentle simmer.

Meanwhile, melt the butter in a large skillet and gently fry the onion, garlic, and bacon for 2–3 minutes until the onion has softened but not browned and the bacon is sealed. Stir in the rice and cook, stirring, for 2 minutes until the rice is well coated in butter.

Add a ladleful of broth to the pan and cook gently until absorbed. Continue to add the broth in small quantities until half of the broth has been used and the rice is creamy. Season well and add the nutmeg and tomatoes.

Continue to add the broth until the risotto becomes thick but not sticky, about 25 minutes.

Meanwhile, cook the spinach in a large, lidded pan for a few minutes. Stir into the risotto 2–3 minutes before serving with the cheese and lemon zest.

Beef Ragu Risotto

SERVES 4

A ragoût is a thick, spiced stew of meat, fish, or poultry that can be made with or without vegetables. This recipe combines classic flavors to make a deliciously satisfying meal.

3¾ cups beef broth

1¼ cups red wine

¼ cup butter

1 tsp oil

2 cups trimmed and cubed lean beefsteak

1 large onion, cut into eight

1 garlic clove, minced

2 cups arborio rice

salt and ground black pepper

1 carrot, halved and sliced

2 celery stalks, sliced

1 tbsp tomato paste

2 large tomatoes, seeded and chopped

1 tbsp chopped fresh oregano

◄   *Beef Ragu Risotto*

Pour the broth and wine into a saucepan and bring to a boil. Reduce the heat to a gentle simmer.

Meanwhile melt the butter in a large skillet with the oil and gently fry the beef for 3 minutes, stirring, until sealed. Add the onion and garlic and cook for 2 minutes until the onion is softened but not browned. Stir in the rice and cook, stirring, for 2 minutes until the rice is well coated in butter.

Add a ladleful of the broth and wine mixture to the rice and cook gently, stirring, until the liquid is absorbed. Continue adding small quantities of the broth mixture until half of the broth has been used and the rice is creamy. Season well and add the carrot, celery, tomato paste, and tomatoes.

Continue adding the broth mixture until the risotto becomes thick but not sticky, about 25 minutes. Sprinkle in the herbs and serve in a warm bowl with warm crusty bread.

Chili Beef Risotto

SERVES 4

This dish has a lot of heat. If you find it too much to handle, reduce the number of chilies or omit the chili powder.

3¾ cups beef broth

2 tbsp butter

1 tbsp oil

2 cups lean beefsteak, trimmed and cut into 2-in cubes

1 onion, finely chopped

2 garlic cloves, minced

1 tsp chili powder

2 cups arborio rice

2 red chilies, seeded and sliced

14 oz can chopped tomatoes

1 cup canned red kidney beans, drained

salt and ground black pepper

1 tbsp chopped fresh oregano or basil

¼ cup freshly grated mozzarella cheese

Pour the broth into a saucepan and bring to a boil. Reduce the heat to a gentle simmer.

Meanwhile, melt the butter with the oil in a large skillet. Gently cook the beef for 3–4 minutes until sealed. Add the onion, garlic, and chili powder and cook for 2–3 minutes until the onion has softened but not browned. Stir in the rice and cook for 2 minutes, stirring, until the rice is well coated in butter.

Add a ladleful of broth and cook gently, stirring, until the liquid is absorbed. Continue adding small quantities of the broth until half of the broth has been used and the rice becomes creamy. Add the chilies, tomatoes, kidney beans, and seasoning.

Continue adding the broth until the risotto becomes thick but not sticky, about 25 minutes.

Just before serving, stir in the herbs and add the mozzarella cheese. Serve in a warm bowl.

Fried Lamb and Fava Bean Risotto

SERVES 4

urmeric is used in this recipe to delicately color and flavor the rice, which complements the green color of the beans perfectly. Turmeric is a member of the ginger family and has a pungent flavor and woody aroma.

3¾ cups lamb broth

1¼ cups dry white wine

¼ cup butter

2 cups trimmed and cubed lean lamb

1 onion, finely chopped

2 garlic cloves, minced

2 cups arborio rice

juice of 1 lemon

1 tbsp brown sugar

pinch of turmeric

salt and ground black pepper

1 tsp paprika

4 oz shelled fava beans, thawed if frozen

2 tbsp freshly grated Romano cheese

Pour the broth and wine into a saucepan and bring to a boil. Reduce the heat to a gentle simmer.

Meanwhile, melt the butter in a large skillet and cook the lamb gently for 2–3 minutes, stirring, until sealed. Add the onion and garlic and cook for a further 2 minutes until the onion has softened but not browned. Stir in the rice, lemon, sugar, and turmeric and cook for 2 minutes, stirring, until the rice is well coated in butter.

Add a ladleful of the broth to the rice and cook, stirring, until the liquid has been absorbed. Continue adding small quantities of broth to the rice until half of the broth has been used and the rice is creamy. Season well and add the paprika.

Cook the fava beans in boiling water for 5 minutes and drain well. Meanwhile continue adding broth to the rice until the risotto becomes thick but not sticky, about 25 minutes. Just before serving, stir in the beans and cheese.

Beef and Olive Risotto

SERVES 4

Try to use good quality olives which have been marinated in garlic and spices to add extra flavor to this recipe.

¼ cup dried porcini mushrooms

5 cups beef broth

¼ cup butter

1 tbsp oil

2 cups lean beefsteak, trimmed and cut into thin strips

2 leeks, sliced

3 garlic cloves, minced

2 cups arborio rice

salt and ground black pepper

½ cup garlic marinated black olives, drained, pitted, and halved

½ cup marinated green olives, drained, pitted, and halved

¼ cup pimiento in oil, drained and cut into strips

¼ cup walnut halves

2 tbsp chopped fresh mixed herbs such as basil, thyme, oregano, and parsley

Soak the porcini mushrooms in warm water according to package instructions. Drain and slice. Pour the broth into a saucepan and bring to a boil. Reduce the heat to a gentle simmer.

Meanwhile, melt the butter in a large skillet with the oil and gently fry the beef strips for 2–3 minutes until sealed. Add the leeks and garlic and cook, stirring, for 2 minutes. Stir in the rice and cook for a further 2 minutes, stirring, until the rice is well coated in butter.

Add a ladleful of broth to the rice and cook, stirring until the liquid has been absorbed. Continue to add small quantities of broth to the rice until half of the broth has been used and the rice is creamy. Season well and stir in the olives, mushrooms, pimiento, and walnuts.

Continue to add the broth to the pan until the risotto is thick but not sticky, about 25 minutes. Stir in the herbs, adjust the seasoning and serve in a warm bowl with ciabatta bread.

Sweet Chili and Basil Risotto

SERVES 4

Basil has a unique flavor which is closely related to its fragrance. Its oil is volatile and is lost in cooking, therefore it should only be added at the end of a recipe for full flavor.

3¾ cups broth

¼ cup butter

1 tbsp oil

2 cups lean beefsteak, trimmed and cut into strips

2 garlic cloves, minced

2 tsp fresh ginger, chopped

1 tsp chili powder

1 tbsp dark soy sauce

1 tsp chili sauce

2 tbsp liquid honey

2 cups arborio rice

ground black pepper

2 red chilies, seeded and sliced

4 scallions, trimmed and sliced

4 tbsp chopped fresh basil

Pour the broth into a saucepan and bring to a boil. Reduce the heat to a gentle simmer.

Meanwhile, melt the butter in a large skillet with the oil and gently cook the beef for 2–3 minutes until sealed. Stir in the garlic, ginger, chili powder, soy and chili sauces, and honey. Stir in the rice and cook for 2 minutes, stirring, until the rice is well coated in butter.

Add a ladleful of broth to the rice and cook, stirring, until the liquid has been absorbed. Continue to add small quantities of broth to the rice until half of the broth has been used and the rice is creamy. Season with pepper and add the red chilies, mixing well.

Continue adding the broth until the risotto becomes thick but not sticky, about 25 minutes. Just before serving, stir in the scallions and basil. Serve in a warm bowl.

Sweet Chili and Basil Risotto ▶

Persian Lamb Risotto

SERVES 4

Cilantro, fruits, and cinnamon are classic flavorings in Persian recipes and make perfect partners for lamb. Here no-need-to-soak dried apricots are used, but soak any other dried apricots, drain, and use as the recipe describes.

3¾ cups lamb broth

1¼ cups dry white wine

¼ cup butter

2 cups trimmed and cubed lean lamb

1 red onion, halved and sliced

3 garlic cloves, minced

1 tsp fresh ginger, chopped

1 tsp ground allspice

1 tsp ground cinnamon

1 tsp ground cumin

2 cups arborio rice

ground black pepper

¼ cup chopped no-need-to-soak dried apricots

¼ cup shelled walnut halves

2 tbsp chopped fresh cilantro

Pour the broth and wine into a saucepan and bring to a boil. Reduce the heat to a gentle simmer.

Meanwhile, melt the butter in a large skillet and gently fry the lamb for 2–3 minutes until sealed. Add the onion and garlic and cook for 2 minutes until the onion is softened but not browned. Stir in the ginger, allspice, cinnamon, and cumin and cook for 1 minute, stirring.

Add the rice and cook for 2 minutes, stirring, until the rice is well coated in butter. Add a ladleful of the broth and cook, stirring, until the liquid is absorbed. Continue to add small quantities of the broth to the rice until half of the broth has been used and the rice is creamy. Season well with pepper.

Continue adding the broth until the risotto is thick but not sticky, about 25 minutes. Stir in the apricots, walnuts, and cilantro and serve in a warm bowl with hot bread.

Risotto Bolognese

SERVES 4

Usually associated with spaghetti, the sauce flavoring this risotto contains all the classic ingredients.

3¾ cups beef broth

⅔ cup red wine

¼ cup butter

1 cup ground beef

2 bacon slices, derinded and chopped

1 onion, finely chopped

2 garlic cloves, minced

2 cups arborio rice

salt and ground black pepper

2 tbsp tomato paste

7 oz can chopped tomatoes

1 carrot, diced

1 celery stalk, sliced

2 tbsp chopped fresh oregano

◀ *Risotto Bolognese*

● Pour the broth and wine into a saucepan and bring to a boil. Reduce the heat to a gentle simmer.

● Meanwhile, melt the butter in a large skillet and gently cook the ground beef and bacon for 2–3 minutes until the beef is sealed. Add the onion and garlic and cook for a further 2 minutes, stirring, until the onion has softened but not browned. Stir in the rice and cook for 2 minutes, stirring, until the rice is well coated in butter.

● Add a ladleful of broth and wine and cook gently, stirring, until the liquid has been absorbed. Continue adding broth until half of the broth has been used and the rice becomes creamy. Season well and stir in the tomato paste, tomatoes, carrot, and celery.

● Continue adding the broth until the risotto becomes thick but not sticky, about 25 minutes. Stir in the oregano and serve in a warmed bowl.

Rosemary Lamb Risotto

SERVES 4

Rosemary has a powerful flavor and should be used in moderation. Unlike other herbs it will withstand cooking and is usually used in combination with lamb.

4 cups lamb broth

⅔ cup rosé wine

¼ cup butter

1 tbsp olive oil

2 cups cubed lean lamb

1 onion, cut into eight

2 garlic cloves, sliced

2 cups arborio rice

1 yellow bell pepper, seeded and chopped

1 green bell pepper, seeded and chopped

2 rosemary sprigs

2 tsp cumin seeds, roughly crushed

salt and ground black pepper

1 tbsp tomato paste

fresh rosemary sprigs

● Pour the broth and wine into a saucepan and bring to a boil. Reduce the heat to a gentle simmer.

● Meanwhile, melt the butter in a large skillet with the olive oil and gently fry the lamb for 2–3 minutes until sealed. Add the onion and garlic and cook, stirring, for 2 minutes until the onion has softened but not browned. Stir in the rice and cook, stirring, for 2 minutes until the rice is well coated in butter.

● Add a ladleful of broth and wine mixture and cook gently, stirring, until the liquid has been absorbed. Continue to add small quantities of broth mixture until half of the liquid has been used and the rice is creamy. Add the bell peppers, rosemary, and cumin seeds and season well. Mix the tomato paste with a little of the hot broth and stir into the rice.

● Continue adding the broth mixture until the risotto becomes thick but not sticky, about 25 minutes. Just before serving, remove the rosemary sprigs from the risotto and replace with fresh rosemary. Serve in a warm bowl.

Risotto with Meatballs and Coriander

SERVES 4

The spicy meatballs are cooked separately from the main risotto in this recipe and served on top of the rice.

FOR THE MEATBALLS

1 cup ground lamb

1 onion, finely chopped

1 garlic clove, minced

1 celery stalk, finely chopped

1 tsp ground cumin

1 tsp ground coriander

2 tbsp finely chopped dried apricots

salt and ground black pepper

1 tbsp liquid honey

2 tbsp butter

1 tbsp oil

FOR THE RISOTTO

5 cups lamb broth

¼ cup butter

1 onion, finely chopped

2 garlic cloves, minced

2 cups arborio rice

salt and ground black pepper

1 tsp coriander seeds, crushed

4 tbsp chopped fresh cilantro

● Place the ground lamb, onion, garlic, celery, cumin, coriander, apricots, seasoning, and honey in a mixing bowl and bring together. Roll into eight equal-sized balls and reserve.

● Meanwhile, pour the lamb broth into a saucepan and bring to a boil. Reduce the heat to a gentle simmer.

● Melt the butter in a large skillet and gently cook the onion and garlic for 2 minutes until the onion has softened but not browned. Stir in the rice and cook for a further 2 minutes until the rice is well coated in butter.

● Add a ladleful of broth to the rice and cook, stirring, until the liquid is absorbed. Continue adding the broth in small quantities until half of the broth has been used and the rice is creamy. Season well and add the coriander seeds.

● Continue adding the broth until the risotto is thick but not sticky, about 25 minutes.

● Meanwhile, melt the butter for the meatballs in a separate pan with the oil and cook the meatballs for 10–15 minutes, turning, until browned and cooked through. Drain and reserve.

● Stir the cilantro into the risotto and spoon into a warmed serving bowl. Arrange the meatballs on top and serve.

Mixed Meat Risotto

SERVES 4

This recipe uses one of the best known Italian ingredients, prosciutto. It has a delicate flavor and is perfect with the pork and garlic flavored mortadella sausage.

3¾ cups vegetable or pork broth

1¼ cups dry white wine

¼ cup butter

1¼ cups trimmed and cubed lean pork

1 onion, finely chopped

2 garlic cloves, sliced

2 cups arborio rice

salt and ground black pepper

⅓ cup prosciutto, cut into strips

¾ cup quartered mortadella slices

12 sun-dried tomatoes in oil, drained and cut into strips

2 tbsp chopped fresh basil

2 tbsp freshly grated Parmesan cheese

◀ *Mixed Meat Risotto*

Pour the broth and wine into a pan and bring to a boil. Reduce the heat to a gentle simmer.

Meanwhile, melt the butter in a large skillet and gently cook the pork for 2 minutes until sealed. Add the onion and garlic and cook, stirring, until the onion has softened but not browned. Stir in the rice and cook for 2 minutes, stirring, until the rice is well coated in butter.

Add a ladleful of broth and cook gently until the liquid has been absorbed. Continue to add small quantities of broth until half of the broth has been used and the rice is creamy. Season well.

Continue adding the broth for 20 minutes. Stir in the prosciutto and mortadella, sun-dried tomatoes and basil. Cook for a further 5 minutes until the risotto is thick but not sticky.

Just before serving, stir in the cheese and serve in a warmed bowl.

Beef and Broccoli Risotto

SERVES 4

Beef and broccoli are widely used in Chinese cookery. In this recipe soy sauce, sherry, sugar, and fennel are used to give a subtle oriental flavor.

5 cups beef broth

¼ cup butter

2 cups lean beefsteak, trimmed and cut into thin strips

1 onion, halved and sliced

2 garlic cloves, minced

3 tbsp light soy sauce

2 tbsp dry sherry

1 tsp brown sugar

¼ cup blanched almonds

2 cups arborio rice

ground black pepper

2 tsp fennel seeds

6 oz broccoli florets

2 tbsp freshly grated Parmesan cheese

Pour the broth into a saucepan and bring to a boil. Reduce the heat to a gentle simmer.

Meanwhile, melt the butter in a large skillet and sauté the beef for 2 minutes until sealed. Add the onion and garlic and cook, stirring, for 2 minutes until the onion has softened but not browned. Stir in the soy sauce, sherry, sugar, and almonds and cook for 2 minutes. Stir in the rice and cook, stirring, for a further 2 minutes until the rice is well coated in butter.

Add a ladleful of broth and cook, stirring, until the liquid has been absorbed. Continue to add small quantities of the broth until half of the broth has been used and the rice is creamy. Season well with pepper and add the fennel seeds.

Continue adding the broth until the risotto becomes thick but not sticky, about 25 minutes. Meanwhile cook the broccoli in boiling water for 5 minutes, drain well. Stir the broccoli and cheese into the risotto and serve in a warm bowl.

Lamb and Raspberry Risotto

SERVES 4

Fruit is a perfect accompaniment to lamb as it takes away some of the fattiness associated with lamb. Raspberries add a vibrant color as well as a slightly tart flavor to the dish.

5 cups lamb broth

¼ cup butter

2 cups trimmed and cubed lean lamb

1 red onion, cut into eight

3 garlic cloves, minced

2 cups arborio rice

salt and ground black pepper

2 tbsp raspberry vinegar

2 tbsp liquid honey

2 cups shredded red cabbage

1 cup raspberries

1 tsp poppy seeds

● Pour the broth into a saucepan and bring to a boil. Reduce the heat to a gentle simmer.

● Meanwhile, melt the butter in a large skillet and gently cook the lamb for 2–3 minutes until sealed. Add the onion and garlic and cook, stirring, for 2 minutes until the onion has softened but not browned. Stir in the rice and cook for a further 2 minutes, stirring, until the rice is well coated in butter.

● Add a ladleful of the broth and cook gently, stirring until the liquid has been absorbed. Continue adding broth until half of the broth has been used and the rice is creamy. Season well and add the raspberry vinegar, honey, and red cabbage.

● Continue adding the broth to the rice until the risotto is thick but not sticky, about 25 minutes. Stir in the raspberries and poppy seeds and serve in a warm bowl.

Pork, Saffron, and Basil Risotto

SERVES 4

Saffron gives the rice in this recipe a delicate yellow color and bitter-sweet flavor. Saffron is widely used in rice dishes around the world.

5 cups pork or vegetable broth

¼ cup butter

2 cups lean pork, trimmed and cut into strips

1 onion, finely chopped

2 garlic cloves, minced

2 cups arborio rice

a large pinch of saffron

salt and ground black pepper

4 oz baby corn, sliced

4 oz green beans, trimmed

4 tbsp chopped fresh basil

1 tbsp pine nuts

2 tbsp freshly grated Romano cheese

Pour the broth into a saucepan and bring to a boil. Reduce the heat to a gentle simmer.

Meanwhile, melt the butter in a large saucepan and gently fry the pork for 2 minutes until sealed. Add the onion and garlic and cook for 2 minutes until the onion is softened but not browned. Stir in the rice and cook, stirring, for a further 2 minutes until the rice is well coated in butter.

Add a ladleful of broth and cook gently until absorbed. Continue to add small quantities of broth until half of the broth has been used and the rice is creamy. Stir in the saffron, seasoning, corn, and beans.

Continue adding broth until the risotto becomes thick but not sticky, about 25 minutes. Stir in the basil, pine nuts, and cheese, serve in a warm bowl.

Risotto with Chicken, Duck, and Turkey

Thai Coconut Risotto

Duck and Orange Risotto

Chicken and Artichoke Risotto

Smoked Chicken and Mango Risotto

Chicken and Corn Risotto with Croûtons

Chicken and Grape à la Veronique

Duck, Pomegranate, and Wild Rice Risotto

Risotto alla Cacciatori

Chicken and Ginger Risotto

Chicken and Zucchini Risotto

Chicken, Cardamom and Cashew Risotto

Creamy Chicken Risotto with Garlic and White Wine

Turkey, Sausage, Cranberry, and Bacon Risotto

Coq au Vin Risotto

Chicken, Tarragon, and Mushroom Risotto

Chicken and Asparagus Risotto

Chinese Chicken Risotto

Chicken with caramelized Apples and Brandy

Chicken and Lemon Risotto

Creamy Spinach and Chicken Risotto

Turkey and Prosciutto Risotto

Duck and Blackberry Risotto

Thai Coconut Risotto

Thai cookery uses coconut to flavor many of its dishes. Coupled with the blend of spices and red chilies it makes a delicious meal.

3¾ cups chicken broth	1 tsp ground coriander
¼ cup butter	1 tsp ground cumin
10 oz boneless, skinned chicken, cut into strips	1 tsp turmeric
1 onion, finely chopped	1 tsp chili powder
2 garlic cloves, minced	2 cups arborio rice
1 tsp freshly chopped lemon grass	2 red chilies, seeded and sliced
	1¼ cups coconut milk
	1 tbsp chopped fresh cilantro

Pour the broth into a saucepan and bring to a boil. Reduce the heat to a gentle simmer.

Meanwhile, melt the butter in a large skillet and cook the chicken gently for 2–3 minutes until sealed. Add the onion, garlic, lemon grass, coriander, cumin, turmeric, and chili powder and cook, stirring, for 2 minutes. Add the rice and cook, stirring, for a further 2 minutes until the rice is well coated in butter

Add a ladleful of broth and cook gently, stirring, until the liquid is absorbed. Continue adding small quantities of broth until half of the broth is used and the rice is creamy. Stir in the chilies.

Mix the coconut milk into the broth and continue adding until the risotto is thick but not sticky, about 25 minutes. Stir in the cilantro and serve in a warm bowl.

Duck and Orange Risotto

SERVES 4

*D*uck is rich in flavor and is complemented by tangy citrus fruits.

4 duck breasts	1 onion, finely chopped
1 tbsp soy sauce	1 garlic clove, minced
2 tbsp liquid honey	2 cups arborio rice
2 tsp ground ginger	salt and ground black pepper
3¾ cups chicken broth	1 large orange, peeled and sectioned
1¼ cups orange juice	
¼ cup butter	2 tbsp chopped fresh parsley

● Heat the oven to 400°F. Cut slits in the duck breasts with a knife and put on a rack over a roasting pan. Mix the soy sauce, honey, and 1 teaspoon of the ginger together and brush over the duck. Roast the duck for 25–30 minutes until cooked through.

● Meanwhile, pour the broth and orange juice into a saucepan and bring to a boil. Reduce the heat to a gentle simmer.

● Meanwhile, melt the butter in a large skillet. Add the onion and garlic and cook, stirring, for 2 minutes until the onion is softened but not browned. Stir in the rice and cook, stirring, for 2 minutes until the rice is well coated in butter.

● Add a ladleful of the broth and orange juice mixture and cook gently, stirring, until absorbed. Continue to add small quantities of broth to the rice until half of the broth mixture is used and the rice is creamy. Season and add the remaining ginger.

● Continue adding broth until the risotto is thick but not sticky, about 25 minutes. Stir in the orange sections and parsley and serve topped with cooked duck breasts.

Chicken and Artichoke Risotto

SERVES 4

Artichokes are a type of thistle, and are quite awkward to eat although the taste is worth it. For simplicity, use either prepared artichoke hearts in flavored oil or canned artichokes, in place of fresh.

4 cups chicken broth

⅔ cup dry white wine

¼ cup butter

1 tbsp oil

4 boneless, skinned chicken breasts

1 onion, finely chopped

2 garlic cloves, minced

2 cups arborio rice

salt and ground black pepper

juice of 1 lemon

1 celery stalk, chopped

8 artichokes in oil, drained and halved

2 tbsp pimientos in brine, drained and cut into strips

3 tbsp chopped fresh mixed herbs

3 tbsp freshly grated Parmesan cheese

Pour the broth and wine into a saucepan and bring to a boil. Reduce the heat to a gentle simmer

Meanwhile, melt the butter in a large skillet with the oil and cook the chicken gently for 5 minutes, turning until browned. Add the onion and garlic and cook for 2 minutes, stirring, until the onion has softened but not browned. Stir in the rice and cook, stirring, for 2 minutes until the rice is well coated in butter.

Add a ladleful of broth and wine and cook gently, stirring, until all of the liquid is absorbed. Continue adding small quantities of broth mixture until half of the broth has been used and the rice is creamy. Season and add the lemon juice and celery.

Continue adding broth for a further 20 minutes. Stir in the artichokes and pimientos. Continue cooking for a further 5 minutes, adding broth until the risotto is thick but not sticky.

Just before serving, stir in the herbs and cheese and serve in a warm bowl.

Smoked Chicken and Mango Risotto

SERVES 4

Smoked chicken has a wonderful flavor which is good with exotic fruits such as mango.

5 cups chicken both

¼ cup butter

1 onion, cut into eight

1 garlic clove, minced

2 cups arborio rice

salt and ground black pepper

12 oz smoked chicken, shredded

a few sprigs of thyme

1 cup wiped and quartered button mushrooms

¼ cup blanched almonds

1 large mango, peeled and diced

fresh thyme sprigs, to garnish

Pour the broth into a saucepan and bring to a boil. Reduce the heat to a gentle simmer.

Meanwhile, melt the butter in a large skillet and gently cook the onion and garlic for 2 minutes, stirring, until the onion has softened but not browned. Stir in the rice and cook, stirring, for a further 2 minutes until the rice is well coated in butter.

Add a ladleful of broth and cook gently, stirring, until the liquid has been absorbed. Continue adding small quantities of broth until half of the broth has been used and the rice is creamy. Season and add the chicken, thyme sprigs, mushrooms, and almonds.

Continue adding broth until the risotto becomes thick but not sticky, about 25 minutes. Gently stir in the mango pieces and fresh thyme. Serve in a warm bowl.

Chicken and Corn Risotto with Croûtons

SERVES 4

This recipe is made extra special with garlic croûtons which add extra crunch and flavor.

5 cups chicken broth

½ cup butter

1 tbsp oil

4 boneless chicken thighs, skinned and halved

1 onion, finely chopped

4 garlic cloves, minced

2 cups arborio rice

salt and ground black pepper

few drops of hot pepper sauce

2 tomatoes, seeded and chopped

4 oz baby corn, halved

2 thick slices white bread, crusts removed, cubed

1 tbsp chopped fresh cilantro

2 tbsp freshly grated Parmesan cheese

Pour the broth into a saucepan and bring to a boil. Reduce the heat to a gentle simmer.

Meanwhile, melt half of the butter in a large skillet with the oil and cook the chicken for 5 minutes over a gentle heat until browned. Add the onion and half of the garlic and cook, stirring, for 2 minutes until the onion has softened but not browned. Stir in the rice and cook, stirring, for 2 minutes until the rice is well coated in butter.

Add a ladleful of broth and cook, stirring, until the liquid is absorbed. Continue to add small quantities of broth until half of the broth has been used and the rice is creamy. Season and add the hot pepper sauce and tomatoes.

Continue adding broth until the risotto becomes thick but not sticky, about 25 minutes. Meanwhile, cook the corn in boiling water for 5 minutes, drain, and add to the risotto. Melt the remaining butter in a skillet and add the remaining garlic. Cook the bread cubes for 2–3 minutes, turning until browned.

Just before serving, sprinkle with herbs, stir the cheese into the risotto, turn into a warm serving dish, and top with croûtons.

Chicken and Grape à la Véronique

*V*éronique sauce is used in other recipes such as sole Véronique and consists of green seedless grapes, cream, lemon, and herbs as the basic ingredients. It is perfect with poultry, with the grapes adding a really fresh taste.

3¾ cups chicken broth	1 bay leaf
1¼ cups dry white wine	few parsley sprigs
¼ cup butter	salt and ground black pepper
1 tbsp oil	¾ cup halved green seedless grapes
4 boneless, skinned chicken breasts	1 tbsp lemon juice
1 onion, finely chopped	3 tbsp light cream
2 cups arborio rice	fresh herbs, to garnish

Pour the broth and wine into a saucepan and bring to a boil. Reduce the heat to a gentle simmer.

Meanwhile, melt the butter in a large skillet with the oil and gently cook the chicken for 5 minutes, turning until browned. Add the onion and cook for 2 minutes, stirring, until the onion has softened but not browned. Stir in the rice and cook, stirring, for 2 minutes until the rice is well coated in butter.

Add a ladleful of broth and cook gently, stirring, until the liquid is absorbed. Add the herbs and seasoning and continue adding broth until half of the broth has been used and the rice is creamy.

Continue adding broth until the risotto is thick but not sticky, about 25 minutes. Season and stir in the grapes, lemon juice, and cream. Turn the risotto into a warmed serving dish, garnish and serve.

Duck, Pomegranate, and Wild Rice Risotto

SERVES 4

The pomegranate grows in California, Asia, and Mediterranean countries. It is one of the most ancient fruits with a wonderful color and flavor.

4 boneless duck breasts

1 tbsp olive oil

2 garlic cloves, minced

2 tbsp lime juice

1 tbsp acacia honey

4 cups chicken broth

⅔ cup dry vermouth

¼ cup butter

1 onion, halved and sliced

2 garlic cloves, minced

2 cups arborio rice

⅓ cup wild rice

2 large open mushrooms, peeled and sliced

salt and ground black pepper

juice of 1 lime

2 pomegranates, halved

lime zest, to garnish

Heat the oven to 400°F. Cut slits in one side of the duck breasts. Mix together the oil, garlic, lime juice, and honey and use to brush over the duck. Cook the duck in the oven for 25–30 minutes, until cooked through.

Meanwhile, pour the broth and vermouth into a saucepan and bring to a boil. Reduce the heat to a simmer.

Meanwhile, melt the butter in a large skillet and gently cook the onion and garlic for 2 minutes until the onion has softened but not browned. Add the rice and cook, stirring, for 2 minutes until the rice is well coated in butter.

Add the wild rice and mushrooms and a ladleful of broth. Cook, stirring, until the liquid is absorbed. Continue adding broth until half of the broth has been used and the rice is creamy. Season and add the lime juice.

Continue adding broth until the risotto is thick but not sticky, about 25 minutes. Squeeze the pomegranates over a juicer and stir into the risotto; serve in a warmed bowl garnished with pared lime zest.

Risotto alla Cacciatori

SERVES 4

This recipe combines the flavors of fresh lemon, wine, tomatoes, mushrooms, and brandy to give a delicious risotto, perfect with tender chicken.

4 chicken breast fillets

½ lemon

3 cups chicken broth

⅔ cup dry white wine

¼ cup butter

1 tbsp oil

1 onion, finely chopped

1 garlic clove, minced

2 cups arborio rice

salt and ground black pepper

14 oz can chopped tomatoes and their juice

2¼ cups wiped and sliced button mushrooms

2 tbsp brandy

2 tbsp chopped fresh parsley

Rub the chicken with the lemon and reserve. Pour the broth and wine into a saucepan and bring to a boil. Reduce the heat to a simmer.

Meanwhile, melt the butter in a large skillet with the oil. Gently fry the chicken for 5 minutes, turning until browned. Add the onion and garlic and cook for 2 minutes until the onion has softened but not browned. Add the rice and cook, stirring, until the rice is well coated in butter.

Add a ladleful of broth and wine and cook gently, stirring, until the liquid is absorbed. Continue adding broth until half of the broth has been used and the rice is creamy. Season and stir in the tomatoes and mushrooms.

Continue adding broth until the risotto is thick but not sticky, about 25 minutes. Stir in the brandy and parsley and serve in a warm bowl.

Risotto alla Cacciatori ▶

Chicken and Ginger Risotto

SERVES 4

Ginger is considered to be one of the most important spices in both the East and West. Fresh ginger is essential in many recipes and is very different in flavor to ground ginger which is mainly used in baking.

5 cups chicken broth

¼ cup butter

12 oz lean, skinned chicken, cut into strips

1 leek, cut into strips

2 garlic cloves, minced

½-inch piece fresh ginger, chopped

2 cups arborio rice

salt and ground black pepper

a large pinch of saffron

1 zucchini, cut into thin strips

8 oz can bamboo shoots, drained

Pour the broth into a saucepan and bring to a boil. Reduce the heat to a gentle simmer.

Meanwhile, melt the butter in a large skillet with the oil and cook the chicken for 2–3 minutes, stirring, until browned. Add the leek, garlic, and ginger and cook for a further 2 minutes. Add the rice and cook for 2 minutes, stirring, until the rice is well coated in butter.

Add a ladleful of broth and cook gently, stirring, until the liquid is absorbed. Continue adding broth until half of the broth is used and the rice is creamy. Season and add the saffron and zucchini.

Continue adding broth until the risotto becomes thick but not sticky, about 25 minutes. Stir in the bamboo shoots and spoon into a warm serving bowl.

Chicken and Zucchini Risotto

SERVES 4

Chicken drumsticks are cooked in a risotto that is colored by grated zucchini, with added flavor and crunch from the nuts. It looks as appealing as it tastes.

5 cups chicken broth	2 cups arborio rice
¼ cup butter	salt and ground black pepper
1 tbsp oil	3 zucchini, grated
8 chicken drumsticks	½ cup shelled pecan halves
1 onion, finely chopped	½ cup freshly grated Parmesan cheese
2 garlic cloves, minced	

◀ *Chicken and Zucchini Risotto*

Pour the broth into a saucepan and bring to a boil. Reduce the heat to a gentle simmer.

Meanwhile, melt the butter in a large skillet with the oil and gently cook the chicken for 5 minutes, turning until browned. Add the onion and garlic and cook for 2 minutes, stirring, until the onion has softened but not browned. Stir in the rice and cook, stirring, for a further 2 minutes until the rice is well coated in butter.

Add a ladleful of broth to the rice and cook, stirring, until absorbed. Continue adding small quantities of broth to the rice until half of the broth has been used and the rice is creamy. Season and stir in the zucchini and pecans.

Continue adding the broth until the risotto becomes thick but not sticky, about 25 minutes. Stir in the Parmesan cheese and serve in a warm bowl.

Chicken, Cardamom, and Cashew Risotto

SERVES 4

Cardamom is native to India. Either the whole pod or the seeds can be used. Cardamom has a spicy-sweet flavor and a pungent aroma.

5 cups chicken broth	6 cardamom pods
¼ cup butter	½ tsp chili powder
1 tbsp oil	1 tsp fennel seeds
12 oz lean boneless chicken, skinned and cut into cubes	½ cup unsalted cashew nuts
1 onion, sliced	2 cups arborio rice
2 garlic cloves, minced	a large pinch of saffron
1 tsp ground cinnamon	salt and ground black pepper
	¼ cup golden raisins

Pour the broth into a saucepan and bring to a boil. Reduce the heat to a gentle simmer.

Meanwhile, melt the butter in a large skillet with the oil and gently fry the chicken for 5 minutes, stirring. Add the onion, garlic, cinnamon, cardamom pods, chili powder, fennel seeds, and cashew nuts. Cook for 2 minutes, stirring, until the onion has softened. Add the rice and cook for 2 minutes, stirring until the rice is well coated in butter.

Add a ladleful of broth to the pan and cook, stirring, until absorbed. Continue adding small quantities of broth to the rice until half of the broth has been used and the rice becomes creamy. Sprinkle in the saffron and season. Stir in the golden raisins.

Continue adding the broth until the risotto becomes thick but not sticky, about 25 minutes. Serve in a warmed bowl.

Creamy Chicken Risotto with Garlic and White Wine

SERVES 4

Garlic, wine, and cream combine deliciously with chicken. Extra color and a slight mustard flavor is given by the watercress that is added at the end of cooking.

4 cups chicken broth

⅔ cup dry white wine

¼ cup butter

1 tbsp oil

6 boneless chicken thighs, skinned and halved

1 onion, finely chopped

3 garlic cloves, minced

2 cups arborio rice

salt and ground black pepper

½ cup shelled peas, thawed if frozen

1 bunch watercress, trimmed and chopped

⅔ cup light cream

4 tbsp freshly grated Romano cheese

Pour the broth and wine into a saucepan and bring to a boil. Reduce the heat to a gentle simmer.

Meanwhile, melt the butter in a large skillet with the oil and gently fry the chicken for 5 minutes, turning until browned. Add the onion and garlic and cook for 2 minutes, stirring, until the onion has softened. Stir in the rice and cook, stirring, for a further 2 minutes until the rice is well covered in butter.

Add a ladleful of broth to the rice and cook gently, stirring, until absorbed. Continue adding small quantities of broth to the rice until half of the broth is used and the rice becomes creamy. Season and stir in the peas.

Continue adding the broth until the risotto becomes thick but not sticky, about 25 minutes. Stir in the watercress, cream, and cheese. Serve in a warm bowl.

Turkey, Sausage, Cranberry, and Bacon Risotto

SERVES 4

A Christmas dinner all in one recipe. These traditionally complementary ingredients make a delicious dish.

5 cups chicken broth

¼ cup butter

1 tbsp oil

8 oz lean turkey meat, cut into strips

4 pork and herb sausages, cut into chunks

4 slices smoked bacon, derinded and chopped

1 onion, finely chopped

2 cups arborio rice

salt and ground black pepper

4 tbsp cranberry relish

2 tbsp chopped fresh sage or parsley

Pour the broth into a saucepan and bring to a boil. Reduce the heat to a gentle simmer.

Meanwhile, melt the butter in a large skillet with the oil and gently cook the turkey, sausages, and bacon for 3 minutes, stirring until the turkey has browned. Add the onion and cook, stirring, for 2 minutes until softened but not browned. Stir in the rice and cook, stirring, for 2 minutes until the rice is well coated in butter.

Add a ladleful of broth to the rice and cook gently, stirring, until absorbed. Continue adding broth to the rice until half of the broth has been used and the rice is creamy. Season well and add the cranberry relish.

Continue adding the broth until the risotto is thick but not sticky, about 25 minutes. Sprinkle on the herbs and serve in a warm bowl.

Coq au Vin Risotto

Ensure that the chicken joints are thoroughly cooked, by turning during cooking and testing to see if the juices run clear from the thickest part of the chicken piece. If large pieces of chicken are to be used, cook separately in the oven and serve with the risotto.

4 cups chicken broth	2 cups arborio rice
⅔ cup red wine	bouquet garni
⅓ cup butter	1 tsp red wine vinegar
1 tbsp oil	1 tsp sugar
4 chicken joints	2 cups button mushrooms, wiped
4 slices smoked back bacon, derinded and chopped	4 slices of white bread, crusts removed and cut into triangles
12 button onions	
2 garlic cloves, minced	

Pour the broth and wine into a saucepan and bring to a boil. Reduce the heat to a gentle simmer.

Meanwhile, melt ¼ cup of the butter in a large skillet with the oil and gently fry the chicken for 5 minutes, turning until browned. Add the bacon, onions, and half of the garlic and cook, stirring, for 2 minutes. Stir in the rice, and cook for a further 2 minutes, stirring, until the rice is well coated in butter.

Add a ladleful of broth mixture to the rice and cook gently, stirring, until absorbed. Continue adding small quantities of broth to the rice until half of the broth has been used and the rice is creamy. Season well and add the bouquet garni, vinegar, sugar, and mushrooms.

Continue adding broth until the risotto becomes thick but not sticky, about 25 minutes. Meanwhile, melt the remaining butter with the rest of the garlic in a frying pan and brown the bread triangles. Serve with the risotto.

Chicken, Tarragon, and Mushroom Risotto

SERVES 4

*T*arragon is a frequent flavoring for chicken. It is one of the subtlest of herbs and forms part of the <u>fines herbes</u> mixture.

5 cups chicken both	2 cups arborio rice
¼ cup butter	1 tbsp Dijon mustard
1 tbsp oil	salt and ground black pepper
4 boneless chicken breasts, skinned	2 tbsp chopped fresh tarragon or 1 tbsp dried tarragon
1 onion, finely chopped	4 tbsp light cream
2 garlic cloves, minced	½ cup freshly grated Parmesan cheese
4 large open cap mushrooms, peeled and sliced	

Pour the broth into a saucepan and bring to a boil. Reduce the heat to a gentle simmer.

Meanwhile, melt the butter in a large skillet with the oil and cook the chicken for 5 minutes, turning until browned. Add the onion, garlic, and mushrooms and cook for 2 minutes until the onion has softened but not browned. Stir in the rice and cook gently, stirring, until the rice is well coated in butter. Stir in the mustard.

Add a ladleful of broth to the rice and cook gently, stirring, until absorbed. Continue adding small quantities of broth to the rice until half of the broth is used and the rice is creamy. Season and add the tarragon.

Continue adding the broth until the risotto becomes thick but not sticky, about 25 minutes. Stir in the cream and cheese and serve in a warm bowl.

Chicken and Asparagus Risotto

SERVES 4

Tender asparagus is perfect with delicately flavored chicken. Try to use young asparagus spears and avoid any tough, large spears.

3¾ cups chicken broth

1¼ cups dry white wine

¼ cup butter

12 oz lean chicken meat, skinned and cut into strips

1 onion, finely chopped

2 garlic cloves, minced

2 cups arborio rice

salt and ground black pepper

a large pinch of saffron

4 oz small asparagus tips

¼ cup freshly grated Parmesan cheese

Pour the broth and wine into a saucepan and bring to a boil. Reduce the heat to a gentle simmer.

Meanwhile, melt the butter in a large skillet and gently cook the chicken for 2–3 minutes, stirring, until browned. Add the onion and garlic and cook for 2 minutes until the onion has softened but not browned. Stir in the rice and cook for a further 2 minutes until the rice is well coated in butter.

Add a ladleful of broth to the rice and cook gently, stirring, until absorbed. Continue adding broth to the rice until half of the broth has been used and the rice is creamy. Season well and add the saffron.

Continue adding broth until the risotto is thick but not sticky, about 25 minutes. After 20 minutes, cook the asparagus tips in boiling water for 5 minutes. Drain well and stir into the risotto with the cheese. Serve in a warm dish.

Chinese Chicken Risotto ▶

Chinese Chicken Risotto

SERVES 4

This colorful and flavorful dish is packed with Chinese spices and vegetables, and it is a complete Chinese meal in one dish.

5 cups chicken broth

¼ cup butter

1 tbsp oil

8 oz lean boneless chicken, skinned and cut into strips

1 leek, sliced

2 garlic cloves, minced

1 tsp five-spice powder

1 piece star anise, lightly crushed

1 tbsp light soy sauce

2 cups arborio rice

1 carrot, cut into matchstick strips

1 red bell pepper, seeded and cut into strips

1 green bell pepper, seeded and cut into strips

7 oz can water-chestnuts, drained

¼ cup unsalted cashew nuts

¼ cup bean sprouts

1 tbsp sesame oil

Pour the broth into a saucepan and bring to a boil. Reduce the heat to a gentle simmer.

Meanwhile, melt the butter in a large skillet with the oil and gently cook the chicken for 2–3 minutes, stirring until browned. Add the leek, garlic, five-spice powder, star anise, and soy sauce. Cook for 2 minutes, stirring. Stir in the rice and cook for a further 2 minutes, stirring, until the rice is well coated in butter.

Add a ladleful of broth and cook gently, stirring, until absorbed. Continue adding small quantities of broth until half of the broth has been used and the rice is creamy. Stir in the carrots, bell peppers, and water chestnuts.

Continue adding broth until the risotto becomes thick but not sticky, about 25 minutes. Stir in the cashew nuts, bean sprouts, and sesame oil and serve in a warm dish.

Chicken with Caramelized Apples and Brandy

SERVES 4

Cooking the apple slices in butter and brown sugar gives them a caramel flavour which complements the simple taste of the risotto. Do not overcook the apples as they will break up and lose their texture.

5 cups chicken broth

⅓ cup butter

1 tbsp oil

8 oz lean skinless chicken, cut into chunks

1 onion, cut into eight

1 garlic clove, minced

2 cups arborio rice

salt and ground black pepper

1 tbsp dark brown sugar

2 dessert apples, peeled, cored, and sliced

2 tbsp brandy

2 tbsp chopped fresh parsley

Pour the broth into a saucepan and bring to a boil. Reduce the heat to a simmer.

Meanwhile, melt ¼ cup of the butter in a large skillet with the oil and gently cook the chicken for 3 minutes, stirring, until browned. Add the onion and garlic and cook for 3 minutes, stirring. Stir in the rice and cook for a further 2 minutes, stirring, until the rice is well coated in butter.

Add a ladleful of broth to the rice and cook, stirring, until absorbed. Continue adding small quantities of broth until half of the broth has been used and the rice is creamy. Season well.

Continue adding broth until the risotto is thick but not sticky, about 25 minutes. About 5 minutes before the rice is cooked, melt the remaining butter in a separate pan, add the brown sugar and cook the apples, stirring, until browned. Stir the brandy, apples and pan juices, and herbs into the risotto. Serve in a warm dish.

Chicken and Lemon Risotto

SERVES 4

*L*emon chicken is a favorite Chinese dish. Here it takes on a different twist, with a slightly oriental flavor and a fresh lemon sauce.

4 cups chicken broth	1 tbsp cider vinegar
8 chicken drumsticks	1 tbsp light brown sugar
¼ cup butter	3 tbsp dry sherry
1 tbsp oil	1 tbsp sesame oil
2 leeks, sliced	juice of 1 lemon
2 garlic cloves, minced	salt and ground black pepper
2 cups arborio rice	1 tbsp sesame seeds
1 tbsp light soy sauce	lemon slices, to garnish

Pour the broth into a saucepan and bring to a boil. Reduce the heat to a gentle simmer.

Meanwhile, cut two diagonal slits in each of the drumsticks. Melt the butter in a large skillet with the oil and gently cook the drumsticks for 5 minutes until browned. Add the leeks and garlic and cook for 2 minutes, stirring. Stir in the rice and cook for a further 2 minutes, stirring, until well coated in butter.

Mix together the soy sauce, vinegar, sugar, sherry, sesame oil, and lemon juice and add to the pan. Add a ladleful of broth and cook, stirring, until absorbed. Continue adding small quantities of broth until half of the broth has been used and the rice is creamy. Season well and stir in the sesame seeds.

Continue adding broth until the risotto is thick but not sticky, about 25 minutes. Serve in a warm serving dish, garnished with lemon slices.

Creamy Spinach and Chicken Risotto

SERVES 4

Spinach requires very little cooking. Choose young spinach and simply rinse and quickly cook in the water that remains on the leaves. Grated nutmeg is particularly excellent with spinach and is a popular addition.

4 cups chicken broth	2 cups arborio rice
¼ cup butter	½ tsp grated nutmeg
1 tbsp oil	⅔ cup heavy cream
12 oz lean chicken, skinned and cut into chunks	5 oz spinach, trimmed and washed
1 onion, finely chopped	4 tbsp grated Parmesan cheese
1 garlic clove, minced	
¾ cup quartered chestnut mushrooms	

Pour the broth into a saucepan and bring to a boil. Reduce the heat to a gentle simmer.

Meanwhile, melt the butter in a large skillet with the oil and gently cook the chicken for 3 minutes turning until browned. Add the onion, garlic, and mushrooms and cook for 2 minutes until the onion has softened but not browned. Stir in the rice and nutmeg and cook gently, stirring, until the rice is well coated in butter.

Add a ladleful of broth to the rice and cook gently until absorbed. Continue adding broth to the rice in small quantities until half of the broth has been used and the rice is creamy. Stir in the heavy cream.

Continue adding the broth until the risotto is thick but not sticky, about 25 minutes. Meanwhile cook the spinach and drain well. Stir into the risotto with the cheese and serve.

Turkey and Prosciutto Risotto

SERVES 4

All the flavors of Italy are packed into this recipe, including prosciutto, black olives, basil, and Italian cheese. Try to use lean white turkey meat as the red meat is highly flavored.

5 cups chicken broth	ground black pepper
¼ cup butter	½ cup prosciutto, cut into strips
1 tbsp oil	½ cup pitted black olives, quartered
8 oz lean turkey meat, cut into strips	2 tbsp chopped fresh basil
1 onion, finely chopped	4 tbsp freshly grated pecorino cheese
2 garlic cloves, minced	
2 cups arborio rice	

Pour the broth into a saucepan and bring to a boil. Reduce the heat to a gentle simmer.

Meanwhile, melt the butter in a large skillet with the oil and gently cook the turkey, stirring, for 2 minutes until browned. Add the onion and garlic and cook for 2 minutes, stirring, until the onion has softened but not browned. Stir in the rice and cook gently for a further 2 minutes, stirring, until the rice is well coated in butter.

Add a ladleful of broth to the rice and cook, stirring, until absorbed. Continue adding small quantities of broth until half of the broth is used and the rice is creamy. Season with black pepper.

Continue adding broth until the risotto is thick but not sticky, about 25 minutes. Stir in the prosciutto, olives, and basil and sprinkle the cheese on top. Serve in a warm dish.

Turkey and Prosciutto Risotto ▶

Duck and Blackberry Risotto

SERVES 4

Blackberries are a really juicy, tasty bush fruit and are best used fresh. If fresh berries are unavailable, use frozen or canned fruit.

4 cups chicken broth	2 cups arborio rice
¼ cup butter	salt and ground black pepper
1 tbsp oil	⅔ cup dry vermouth
4 duck breast portions	2 tbsp chopped fresh thyme
1 onion, finely chopped	¾ cup blackberries
1 garlic clove, minced	

Pour the broth into a saucepan and bring to a boil. Reduce the heat to a gentle simmer.

Meanwhile, melt the butter in a large skillet with the oil and gently cook the duck for 5 minutes, turning until browned. Add the onion and garlic and cook for 2 minutes until the onion is softened but not browned. Stir in the rice and cook for a further 2 minutes until the rice is well coated in butter.

Add a ladleful of broth to the rice and cook gently, stirring, until absorbed. Continue adding broth to the rice until half of the broth has been used and the rice is creamy. Season well and add the vermouth and half of the thyme.

Continue adding broth until the risotto becomes thick but not sticky, about 25 minutes. Stir in the remaining thyme and blackberries and serve in a warm dish.

Risotto with Game

Guinea Hen and Yellow Bell Pepper

Rabbit and Basil Risotto

Rabbit with Mustard and Prunes

Venison with Mixed Peppercorns

Venison with Kumquats and Walnuts

Venison and Red Currant

Venison and Lemon

Honeyed Quail with Lime

Sherried Squab with Peppercorns

Brandied Quail with Bacon

Pheasant with Red Cabbage

Pheasant with Juniper

Guinea Hen and Yellow Bell Pepper

SERVES 4

The sweetness of yellow bell peppers takes the edge off the richness of this tasty main meal risotto. Serve with a fruit jelly sauce if liked.

4 × 4-oz guinea hen breasts, skinned

salt and ground black pepper

¼ cup butter

1 tbsp olive oil

5 cups chicken broth

2 shallots, peeled and finely chopped

2 yellow bell peppers, seeded and sliced

2 cups arborio rice

⅔ cup dry white wine

3 tbsp heavy cream

2 tbsp lemon juice

lemon zest and chives, to garnish

Season the guinea hen breasts on both sides. Melt the butter with the oil in a skillet until sizzling. Lay the breasts in the pan and cook for 5 minutes. Turn over and cook for a further 5 minutes or until golden and cooked through. Remove from the pan, reserving the cooking juices, and keep warm.

Pour the broth into a saucepan and bring to a boil. Reduce the heat to a gentle simmer.

Meanwhile, transfer the reserved cooking juices to a large saucepan and heat. Gently fry the shallots and yellow bell peppers for 2–3 minutes until softened. Add the rice, and cook, stirring, for 2 minutes until well coated in the vegetable mixture.

Add the wine and cook gently, stirring, until absorbed. Ladle in the broth gradually until all the liquid is absorbed and the rice is thick, creamy, and tender. This will take about 25 minutes.

Stir in the cream and lemon juice. Adjust the seasoning. Serve the risotto topped with the guinea hen breasts, garnished with lemon zest.

Rabbit and Basil Risotto

SERVES 4

The truly Italian flavors in this dish: peppery basil, rich red wine, and tangy orange, are the perfect accompaniments to rabbit.

1 lb diced rabbit	2 cups arborio rice
salt and ground black pepper	⅔ cup red wine
2 tbsp olive oil	1 tbsp dark muscovado sugar
5 cups chicken broth	finely grated zest and juice of 1 small orange
2 medium red onions, each cut into 8 portions	a small bunch of fresh basil, shredded
1 garlic clove, minced	

Season the rabbit with salt and pepper. Heat the oil in a large saucepan until sizzling and fry the diced rabbit for 8–10 minutes all over until rich golden brown.

Meanwhile, pour the broth into a saucepan and bring to a boil. Reduce the heat to a gentle simmer.

Reduce the heat under the pan with the rabbit and add the onion and garlic. Gently fry for 2–3 minutes until softened. Add the rice and cook, stirring, for a further 2 minutes.

Add the red wine and sugar and cook gently, stirring, until absorbed. Ladle the broth into the rice gradually until it is all absorbed, and the rice is thick, creamy, and tender. This will take about 25 minutes.

Stir in the orange zest and juice. Adjust the seasoning and stir in the basil before serving.

Rabbit with Mustard and Prunes

SERVES 4

This risotto combines rabbit with a rich, sharp mustard and sweet juicy prunes.

1 lb diced rabbit

salt and ground black pepper

2 tbsp wholegrain mustard

¼ cup butter

1 tbsp olive oil

5 cups chicken broth

6 shallots, quartered

2 cups arborio rice

⅔ cup dry white wine

1 tbsp chopped fresh thyme or 1 tsp dried

¾ cup no-need-to-soak dried prunes

fresh thyme, to garnish

Season the rabbit and coat with the mustard. Melt the butter with the oil in a large saucepan until sizzling, then fry the rabbit for 8–10 minutes all over until golden.

Meanwhile, pour the broth into a saucepan and bring to a boil. Reduce the heat to a gentle simmer.

Reduce the heat under the pan with the rabbit and gently fry the shallots for 2–3 minutes until just softened. Add the rice and cook, stirring, for 2 minutes until well coated in the rabbit juices.

Add the wine and thyme and cook gently, stirring, until absorbed. Ladle in the broth gradually until half is used then add the prunes. Continue ladling in the broth until it is all absorbed and the rice is thick, creamy, and tender. This will take about 25 minutes.

Adjust the seasoning and serve garnished with thyme.

Venison with Mixed Peppercorns

SERVES 4

The pungency of peppercorns and meatiness of venison give this risotto a very appetizing flavor.

4 × 5-oz venison steaks

1 tbsp mixed peppercorns, crushed

2 tbsp butter

1 tbsp olive oil

5 cups beef broth

2 cups arborio rice

4 tbsp brandy

1 tbsp red currant jelly

1 tsp pickled pink peppercorns

1 tsp pickled green peppercorns

2 tbsp chopped fresh parsley

salt to taste

flat leaf parsley, to garnish

Rub the venison steaks on both sides with the crushed peppercorns. Melt the butter with the oil in a skillet and fry the steaks for 10–12 minutes, turning occasionally, until cooked through. Remove from the pan, reserving the juices, and keep warm.

Meanwhile, pour the broth into a saucepan and bring to a boil. Reduce the heat to a gentle simmer.

Transfer the reserved cooking juices to a large saucepan and reheat. Add the rice and cook, stirring, for 2 minutes until well coated in the juices.

Add a ladleful of broth and cook gently, stirring, until absorbed. Continue ladling the broth into the rice until all the liquid is absorbed and the rice is thick, creamy, and tender. Keep the heat moderate. This should take about 25 minutes.

Stir in the brandy, red currant jelly, the peppercorns, and chopped parsley. Add salt to taste and serve with the venison steaks, garnished with parsley.

Venison with Kumquats and Walnuts

SERVES 4

Kumquats have a sharp, citrus taste making them ideal to serve with rich game like venison. This is a truly impressive risotto.

8 × 3-oz medallions of venison	5 cups beef broth
salt and ground black pepper	2 cups arborio rice
2 tbsp butter	½ cup walnut pieces
1 tbsp vegetable oil	1 tbsp walnut oil
4 oz kumquats, sliced	4 tbsp snipped fresh chives
1 tbsp superfine sugar	

● Season the medallions lightly on both sides. Melt the butter with the oil in a skillet until sizzling and fry the medallions over a moderate heat for 5–6 minutes on each side until cooked through. Remove from the pan, reserving the juices, and keep warm.

● Meanwhile, place the kumquats in a saucepan with ½ cup water and the sugar. Bring to a boil and simmer for 2 minutes. Set aside to cool in the liquid.

● Pour the broth into a saucepan and bring to a boil. Reduce the heat to a gentle simmer.

● Transfer the reserved juices to a large saucepan and reheat. Add the rice and cook, stirring, for 2 minutes until well coated in the juices.

● Add a ladleful of broth and cook gently, stirring, until absorbed. Continue ladling the broth into the rice until all the liquid is absorbed and the rice becomes thick, creamy, and tender. This will take about 25 minutes.

● Stir in the kumquats and their cooking liquid until absorbed. Then add the walnut pieces, walnut oil, and snipped chives. Adjust the seasoning and serve with the cooked venison.

Venison and Red Currant

*R*ich meat with a fruity sauce is a classic combination in this delicious risotto.

5 cups beef broth	1 bay leaf
2 tbsp butter	salt and ground black pepper
1 tbsp olive oil	3 tbsp dry sherry
1 lb venison steak, sliced into strips	1½ cups fresh or frozen red currants
2 red onions, finely sliced	2 tbsp red currant jelly
2 cups arborio rice	2 tbsp chopped fresh parsley

Pour the broth into a saucepan and bring to a boil. Reduce the heat to a gentle simmer.

Meanwhile, melt the butter with the oil and gently fry the venison and onion for 4–5 mins until browned all over. Add the rice and cook, stirring, for 2 minutes until well coated. Add the bay leaf and seasoning.

Add the sherry along with a ladleful of broth and cook gently, stirring, until absorbed. Continue ladling in the broth until half the broth is used and the rice becomes creamy. Stir in the red currants and jelly.

Continue adding the broth until the risotto becomes thick and the rice is tender. This will take about 25 minutes.

Discard the bay leaf and adjust the seasoning before serving sprinkled with chopped parsley.

Venison and Lemon

SERVES 4

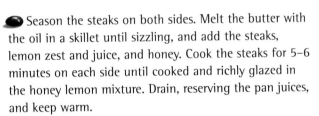

*V*enison has a strong flavor, and in this recipe it is complemented by the freshness of lemon and the delicate fragrance of lemon grass.

4 × 5-oz venison steaks

salt and ground black pepper

2 tbsp butter

1 tbsp olive oil

finely grated zest and juice of 1 lemon

1 tbsp liquid honey

5 cups vegetable broth

6 shallots, finely sliced

1 garlic clove, minced

2 cups arborio rice

1 stalk of lemon grass, bruised

1 bunch of scallions, trimmed and finely shredded

wedges of lemon, to serve

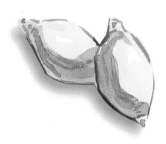

● Season the steaks on both sides. Melt the butter with the oil in a skillet until sizzling, and add the steaks, lemon zest and juice, and honey. Cook the steaks for 5–6 minutes on each side until cooked and richly glazed in the honey lemon mixture. Drain, reserving the pan juices, and keep warm.

● Meanwhile, pour the broth into a saucepan and bring to a boil. Reduce the heat to a gentle simmer.

● Transfer the pan juices to a large saucepan and reheat. Add the shallots and garlic and cook for 2–3 minutes until just softened. Add the rice and lemon grass and cook, stirring, for 2 minutes until well mixed.

● Add a ladleful of broth and cook gently, stirring, until absorbed. Continue ladling the broth into the rice until all the liquid is absorbed and the rice is thick, creamy, and tender. Keep the heat moderate. This will take about 25 minutes.

● Discard the lemon grass. Stir in the scallions and adjust the seasoning. Serve with the venison steaks, accompanied by wedges of lemon.

Honeyed Quail with Lime

SERVES 4

These little birds have a rich flavor. In this recipe they are cooked with lime and oriental ingredients.

4 × 6-oz quails

2 tbsp butter

1 tbsp vegetable oil

2 tbsp liquid honey

1 tbsp dark soy sauce

5 cups chicken broth

1 bunch scallions, trimmed and finely shredded

1 garlic clove, finely chopped

2 cups arborio rice

salt and ground black pepper

3 tbsp dry sherry

grated zest, and juice of 1 lime

2 tbsp chopped fresh cilantro

lime wedges and fresh cilantro, to garnish

Preheat the oven to 450°F.

Wash and pat dry the quails. Melt the butter with the oil in a skillet until sizzling, then fry the quails until browned on all sides. Drain, reserving pan juices, and place in a roasting pan. Mix 1 tablespoon honey with the soy sauce and brush over the quails. Bake in the oven for 5 minutes, turn them over, baste, and bake for a further 6–7 minutes until cooked through. Drain, reserving the pan juices, and keep warm.

Meanwhile, pour the broth into a saucepan and bring to a boil. Reduce the heat to a gentle simmer.

Transfer the reserved skillet juices to a large saucepan and gently fry the scallions and garlic for 2–3 minutes until softened. Add the rice and cook, stirring, for 2 minutes until well coated in the onion mixture.

Season and add the sherry, the reserved roasting juices, and a ladleful of broth. Cook gently, stirring, until absorbed. Continue ladling in the broth until all the liquid is absorbed and the rice is thick, creamy, and tender. Keep the heat moderate. This will take about 25 minutes.

Stir in the remaining honey, the lime juice and zest, and the chopped cilantro. Adjust seasoning if necessary. Serve with the roasted quail, garnished with lime zest and cilantro.

Sherried Squab with Peppercorns

SERVES 4

In this recipe, squab breast meat is soaked in sherry and added to a tasty mushroom risotto flavored with thyme.

2 × 10-oz squabs, prepared

salt and ground black pepper

2 tbsp butter

1 tbsp vegetable oil

3 tbsp medium sherry

5 cups chicken broth

6 shallots, finely sliced

1 garlic clove, minced

2 large open cap mushrooms, sliced

2 cups arborio rice

1 tbsp chopped fresh thyme or 1 tsp dried

1 tbsp pickled green peppercorns

fresh thyme, to garnish

Slice off the legs and wings from the squabs. Separate and pull out the wishbone. Pull the skin away from the breasts and back. Cut down either side of the breast bone to split the birds in half. Wash and pat dry. Lightly season on both sides. Melt the butter with the oil and gently fry the squab portions for 10–12 minutes, turning occasionally, until cooked through. Drain, reserving the pan juices, and flake the squab flesh from the bone. Place in a heatproof dish and spoon over the sherry. Cover and keep warm.

Pour the broth into a saucepan and bring to a boil. Reduce the heat to a gentle simmer.

Transfer the reserved squab juices to a large saucepan and gently fry the shallots, garlic, and mushrooms for 3–4 minutes until just softened. Add the rice and cook, stirring, for 2 minutes until well mixed.

Add a ladleful of broth and cook gently, stirring, until absorbed. Continue ladling the broth into the rice until half the broth is used and the rice becomes creamy. Stir in the thyme, peppercorns, and squab flesh.

Continue adding the broth until the risotto becomes thick and tender. This will take about 25 minutes and shouldn't be hurried. Adjust the seasoning and serve garnished with thyme.

Brandied Quail with Bacon

SERVES 4

A very rich creamy mixture of roasted quail with the flavors of bacon, brandy, and raisins.

4 × 6-oz quails, prepared	4 slices rindless bacon, chopped
2 tbsp butter	2 cups arborio rice
1 tbsp olive oil	salt and ground black pepper
5 cups chicken broth	⅓ cup seedless raisins
1 medium red onion, finely chopped	4 tbsp brandy
1 tbsp lemon juice	2 tbsp heavy cream

Preheat the oven to 450°F.

Wash and pat dry the quails. Melt the butter with the oil in a skillet until sizzling, then fry the quails until browned on all sides. Drain, reserving the pan juices, and place in a roasting pan. Bake for 5 minutes, turn over, baste, then bake for a further 6–7 minutes until cooked through. Drain, reserving any juices, and keep warm.

Meanwhile, pour the broth into a saucepan and bring to a boil. Reduce the heat to a gentle simmer.

Transfer the skillet juices to a large saucepan and heat. Fry the onion with the lemon juice and bacon for 4–5 minutes until golden. Lower the heat and add the rice. Cook, stirring, for 2 minutes until well coated. Season.

Add the raisins, brandy, cream, and a ladleful of broth and cook gently, stirring, until absorbed. Continue ladling the broth into the rice until all the liquid is absorbed and the rice becomes thick, creamy, and tender. Keep the heat moderate. This will take about 25 minutes.

Peel off the skin from the quails and discard. Flake the cooked flesh from the bones and add to the risotto. Heat through for a further 2–3 minutes until hot before serving.

Pheasant with Red Cabbage

A classic combination of red cabbage, apples, and golden raisins is combined with pan-cooked pheasant breasts in this rich risotto.

4 × 4-oz pheasant breasts

salt and ground black pepper

2 tbsp butter

1 tbsp olive oil

5 cups chicken broth

1 medium onion, finely chopped

2 cups finely shredded red cabbage

1 medium cooking apple, peeled, cored, finely diced, and tossed in 1 tbsp lemon juice

2 cups arborio rice

1 stick of cinnamon, broken

⅓ cup golden raisins

Trim each pheasant breast to remove any excess sinew and skin. Leave a neat covering of skin over each. Season lightly on each side. Melt the butter with the oil in a skillet and gently fry the breasts, skin side down, for 5 minutes. Turn over and cook for a further 6–7 minutes or until cooked through. Drain, reserving the juices, and keep warm.

Meanwhile, pour the broth into a saucepan and bring to a boil. Reduce the heat to a gentle simmer.

Transfer the reserved juices to a large saucepan and gently fry the onion, cabbage, and apple with the lemon juice for 3–4 minutes until just softening. Add the rice and cook, stirring, for 2 minutes until well mixed.

Add the cinnamon and a ladleful of broth. Cook gently, stirring, until absorbed. Continue ladling the broth into the rice until half the broth is used and the rice becomes creamy. Stir in the golden raisins.

Continue adding the broth until the risotto becomes thick and tender. This will take about 25 minutes.

Discard the cinnamon stick. Adjust the seasoning. Serve the risotto with the pheasant breasts.

Pheasant with Juniper

Juniper adds a pungent, fresh taste to a dish. The spice complements the richness of pheasant.

4 × 4-oz pheasant breasts

salt and ground black pepper

2 tbsp butter

1 tbsp olive oil

2 tsp juniper berries, crushed

2 tbsp dry gin

5 cups chicken broth

2 medium leeks, trimmed and finely shredded

1 large carrot, peeled and coarsely grated

2 cups arborio rice

⅔ cup dry white wine

juice and pared zest of 1 lemon

2 tbsp snipped fresh chives

● Trim each pheasant breast to remove any excess sinew and skin. Leave a neat covering of skin on each. Season lightly on both sides. Melt the butter with the oil in a skillet and gently fry the pheasant breasts with the juniper berries, skin side down, for 5 minutes. Turn over and cook for a further 6–7 minutes until cooked through. Drain, reserving the pan juices, discard the skin, and flake the flesh. Place in a heatproof dish, spoon over the gin and keep warm.

● Pour the broth into a saucepan and bring to a boil. Reduce the heat to a gentle simmer.

● Transfer the pheasant pan juices with the juniper to a large saucepan and gently fry the leeks and carrot for 2–3 minutes until just softened. Add the rice and cook, stirring, for 2 minutes until well mixed.

● Add the wine, lemon juice, and zest, and cook gently, stirring, until absorbed. Ladle in the broth gradually until half the broth is used and the rice becomes creamy. Stir in the pheasant.

● Continue adding the broth until the risotto becomes thick and the rice is tender. This will take about 25 minutes.

● Discard the lemon zest and stir in the chives. Adjust the seasoning before serving.

Fish Risotto

Filled White Fish Rolls with Mustard Risotto

Trout and Shrimp Risotto

Tuna and Harissa Risotto

Salmon and Caviar Risotto

Chili Monkfish Risotto

Mackerel and Orange Risotto

Sole and Fennel Risotto

Smoked Trout and Pepper Risotto

Smoked Salmon and Dill Risotto

Anchovy, Pepper, and Tomato Risotto

Colcannon Risotto

Kipper and Apple Risotto

Curried Fish Risotto

Filled White Fish Rolls with Mustard Risotto

SERVES 4

$\mathcal{F}$lounder or sole are perfect flatfish for filling and rolling. Baked separately in this recipe they are filled with a sun-dried tomato stuffing and served on a mustard risotto.

4 white flounder fillets

FOR THE FILLING

½ cup whole wheat bread crumbs

1 tbsp chopped gherkins

1 tbsp capers

2 scallions, finely chopped

2 tbsp chopped sun-dried tomatoes

salt and ground black pepper

1 egg, beaten

4 tbsp fish broth

FOR THE RISOTTO

5 cups fish broth

¼ cup butter

1 onion, finely chopped

2 garlic cloves, minced

2 cups arborio rice

3 tbsp Dijon mustard

salt and ground black pepper

2 tbsp chopped fresh parsley

3 tbsp freshly grated Romano cheese

Cut each fish fillet in half lengthwise. Combine all the stuffing ingredients except the broth, and spoon onto each fillet. Roll up the fish from head to tail. Put in a shallow ovenproof dish and pour broth around the rolls. Cook for 20 minutes at 400°F.

Meanwhile, pour the broth for the risotto into a saucepan and bring to a boil. Reduce the heat to a gentle simmer.

Melt the butter in a large skillet and gently cook the onion and garlic for 2 minutes, stirring, until the onion has softened but not browned. Stir in the rice and cook for a further 2 minutes, stirring, until the rice is well coated in butter.

Add a ladleful of broth to the rice and cook gently, stirring, until absorbed. Continue adding small quantities of broth to the rice until half of the broth has been used. Stir in the mustard and season well.

Continue adding broth until the risotto is thick but not sticky, about 25 minutes. Stir in the parsley and cheese. Spoon the risotto into a warmed dish and top with the plaice rolls.

Trout and Shrimp Risotto

SERVES 4

Smoked trout has been used in this flavorful and colorful dish. If unavailable, unsmoked trout fillets would also be delicious.

4 cups fish broth

⅔ cup dry white wine

¼ cup butter

1 leek, sliced

1 garlic clove, minced

1¼ cups arborio rice

¾ cup wild rice

1 green bell pepper, seeded and chopped

2 tsp fennel seeds

12 oz smoked trout fillets, cut into chunks

4 oz shelled cooked shrimp

1 tbsp chopped fresh parsley

2 tbsp freshly grated Parmesan cheese

lime wedges, to serve

Pour the broth and wine into a saucepan and bring to a boil. Reduce the heat to a gentle simmer.

Meanwhile, melt the butter in a large skillet and gently cook the leek and garlic for 2 minutes, stirring. Add the rices and cook gently, stirring, for 2 minutes until the rice is well coated in butter.

Add a ladleful of broth and wine mixture to the rice and cook gently, stirring, until absorbed. Continue adding small quantities of broth until half of the broth mixture has been used. Add the bell pepper and fennel.

Continue adding the broth for a further 20 minutes. Add the fish and shrimp and cook for a further 5 minutes, stirring gently, adding any remaining broth until the risotto is thick but not sticky.

Just before serving, add the parsley and cheese; serve in a warm bowl with lime wedges.

Trout and Shrimp Risotto ▶

Tuna and Harissa Risotto

SERVES 4

Harissa is a robust chili sauce which may be made and stored at home, but it is more convenient to purchase it ready-made. Alter the quantity of harissa to your liking.

5 cups fish broth

¼ cup butter

1 onion, finely chopped

2 garlic cloves, minced

2 cups arborio rice

ground black pepper

1 tbsp harissa sauce

10 oz fresh tuna, cut into large pieces

1 oz green beans, trimmed

¼ cup pitted green olives

2 tbsp freshly grated Parmesan cheese

Pour the broth into a saucepan and bring to a boil. Reduce the heat to a gentle simmer.

Meanwhile, melt the butter in a large skillet and gently cook the onion and garlic, stirring, for 2 minutes until the onion has softened but not browned. Stir in the rice and cook for a further 2 minutes, stirring, until the rice is well coated in butter.

Add a ladleful of broth to the rice and gently cook, stirring, until absorbed. Continue adding broth in small quantities until half of the broth has been used. Season with pepper and stir in the harissa sauce.

Continue adding broth for 15 minutes. Stir in the fish and beans and continue to cook for a further 10 minutes, adding broth. Stir in the olives and cheese and serve in a warm bowl.

Salmon and Caviar Risotto

SERVES 4

Lumpfish caviar is used as a caviar substitute in this dish. Lumpfish are abundant in cold seas and their eggs are collected and dyed to produce this inexpensive substitute for real caviar.

5 cups fish broth

¼ cup butter

1 onion, finely chopped

2 garlic cloves, minced

2 cups arborio rice

ground black pepper

12 oz salmon fillet, skinned, boned, and cut into large cubes

2 oz jar of black lumpfish caviar

2 scallions, sliced

4 tbsp sour cream

2 tbsp freshly grated Parmesan cheese

◀ *Salmon and Caviar Risotto*

Pour the broth into a saucepan and bring to a boil. Reduce the heat to a gentle simmer.

Meanwhile, melt the butter in a large skillet and gently cook the onion and garlic, stirring, until the onion has softened but not browned. Stir in the rice and cook gently, stirring, until the rice is well coated in butter.

Add a ladleful of broth to the rice and cook gently, stirring, until absorbed. Continue adding small quantities of broth for a further 20 minutes. Season with black pepper.

Add the salmon and cook, continuing to add the broth for a further 5 minutes until the risotto is thick but not sticky. Stir in the caviar, scallions, sour cream, and cheese and serve in a warm bowl.

Chili Monkfish Risotto

SERVES 4

Chilies and limes are synonymous with Mexico, and both appear in this hot risotto dish. For a milder recipe, reduce the number of chilies and remove the seeds before cooking.

4 cups fish broth

¼ cup butter

1 onion, finely chopped

2 garlic cloves, minced

1 tsp chili powder

2 cups arborio rice

salt and ground black pepper

7 oz can chopped tomatoes

2 green chilies, chopped

2 tbsp tomato paste

juice of 1 lime

12 oz monkfish, skinned, boned, and cut into large chunks

2 tbsp chopped fresh basil

2 tbsp freshly grated pecorino cheese

Pour the broth into a saucepan and bring to a boil. Reduce the heat to a gentle simmer.

Meanwhile, melt the butter in a large skillet and gently cook the onion, garlic, and chili powder, stirring, for 2 minutes until the onion has softened but not browned. Stir in the rice and cook gently, stirring, for a further 2 minutes until the rice is well coated in butter.

Add a ladleful of broth to the rice and cook, stirring, until absorbed. Continue adding small quantities of broth until half has been used. Season well and add the tomatoes, chilies, tomato paste, and lime juice.

Continue adding broth for a further 15 minutes. Stir in the monkfish and continue cooking and adding broth for a further 10 minutes until the risotto is thick but not sticky.

Just before serving add the basil and cheese and serve in a warm dish.

Mackerel and Orange Risotto

SERVES 4

Orange and mackerel are a classic combination, the oily fish being perfectly offset by the tangy citrus fruit.

3¾ cups fish broth

1¼ cups orange juice

¼ cup butter

1 onion, finely chopped

2 garlic cloves, minced

2 cups arborio rice

salt and ground black pepper

2 tsp fennel seeds

1 celery stalk, chopped

2 mackerel, cleaned, gutted, and halved lengthwise

1 tbsp olive oil

2 oranges, peeled and sectioned

1 tbsp chopped fresh rosemary

Pour the broth and orange juice into a saucepan and bring to a boil. Reduce the heat to a gentle simmer.

Meanwhile, melt the butter in a large skillet and gently cook the onion and half of the garlic for 2 minutes, stirring until the onion has softened but not browned. Stir in the rice and gently cook, stirring, for a further 2 minutes until well coated in butter.

Add a ladleful of broth and juice mixture and gently cook, stirring, until absorbed. Continue adding the broth and juice until half has been used. Season and add the fennel seeds and celery.

Continue adding the broth mixture until the rice is thick but not sticky, about 25 minutes. Meanwhile, brush the mackerel with the remaining garlic and oil and broil for 10 minutes, turning until cooked through. Remove as many bones as possible from the fish and cut the fish into large pieces. Gently stir into the rice with the orange sections and rosemary. Serve in a warm bowl.

Mackerel and Orange Risotto ▶

Sole and Fennel Risotto

SERVES 4

Sole is a beautiful, delicate fish which is superb with the aniseed flavor of fennel. If the fennel head is intact, use the fronds as a garnish.

3¾ cups fish broth

1¼ cups dry white wine

¼ cup butter

1 red onion, halved and sliced

1 garlic clove, minced

1¼ cups arborio rice

¾ cup wild rice

1 tbsp fennel seeds

juice and zest of 1 lime

1 fennel bulb, sliced

10 oz sole fillets, skinned and cut into strips

2 tbsp chopped fresh dill

2 tbsp freshly grated Romano cheese

lime zest, to garnish

Pour the broth and wine into a saucepan and bring to a boil. Reduce the heat to a gentle simmer.

Meanwhile, melt the butter in a large skillet and gently cook the onion and garlic, stirring, for 2 minutes until the onion has softened. Stir in the rices and cook gently, stirring, for a further 2 minutes until the rice is well coated in butter.

Add a ladleful of broth mixture to the rice and cook gently, stirring, until absorbed. Continue adding broth mixture until half has been used. Stir in the fennel seeds, lime juice and zest, and fennel slices.

Continue adding broth for 15 minutes. Stir in the sole and cook for a further 10 minutes, adding broth until the risotto is thick but not sticky.

Just before serving add the dill and cheese. Serve in a warmed dish, garnished with lime zest.

Smoked Trout and Pepper Risotto

SERVES 4

*R*ed rice and mixed peppercorns are added to this risotto for color and flavor. The pale pink flesh of the smoked trout looks and tastes wonderful with this combination of ingredients.

5 cups fish broth

¼ cup butter

1 onion, finely chopped

2 garlic cloves, minced

1 tsp ground anise

3 tbsp mixed peppercorns, coarsely crushed

½ cup blanched almonds

1¼ cups arborio rice

¾ cup wild rice or red camargue rice

salt

2 tsp almond extract

2 tbsp chopped fresh parsley

12 oz smoked trout fillets, cut into large chunks

2 tbsp freshly grated Parmesan cheese

Pour the broth into a saucepan and bring to a boil. Reduce the heat to a gentle simmer.

Meanwhile, melt the butter in a large skillet and gently cook the onion, garlic, anise, peppercorns, and almonds for 2 minutes, stirring, until the onion has softened but not browned. Stir in the rices and cook gently, stirring, for 2 minutes until the rices are well coated in butter.

Add a ladleful of broth to the rice and cook gently, stirring, until absorbed. Continue adding small quantities of broth until half has been used. Season with salt and stir in the almond extract.

Continue adding broth until the risotto is thick but not sticky, about 20 minutes. Stir in the parsley, fish, and cheese and transfer to a warm serving dish.

Smoked Salmon and Dill Risotto

Smoked salmon is enhanced by the aniseed flavor of dill in this recipe, which is an attractive and flavorful herb.

3¾ cups fish broth

1¼ cups dry white wine

¼ cup butter

2 tbsp lemon juice

1 red onion, cut into eight

2 garlic cloves, minced

2 cups arborio rice

salt and ground black pepper

1 tsp cayenne pepper

4 tbsp chopped fresh dill

10 oz smoked salmon, cut into strips

⅔ cup light cream

fresh dill sprigs, to garnish

Pour the broth and wine into a saucepan and bring to a boil. Reduce the heat to a gentle simmer.

Meanwhile, melt the butter in a large skillet and add the lemon juice. Gently fry the onion and garlic, stirring, until the onion has softened but not browned. Stir in the rice and cook gently, stirring, for 2 minutes until the rice is well coated in butter.

Add a ladleful of the broth and wine mixture to the rice and cook gently, stirring, until absorbed. Continue adding the broth mixture until half of the broth has been used. Season well and add the cayenne pepper.

Continue adding broth for a further 20 minutes. Stir in the dill, salmon, cream, and continue cooking, adding broth for a further 5 minutes until the risotto is thick but not sticky. Serve in a warm bowl, garnished with dill.

Anchovy, Pepper, and Tomato Risotto

SERVES 4

Anchovies appear in many Italian recipes. As they are very salty, do not add any extra salt to the dish. Choose good quality fillets in olive oil for this recipe.

5 cups fish broth

¼ cup butter

1 onion, finely chopped

2 garlic cloves, minced

2 cups arborio rice

ground black pepper

1 red bell pepper, seeded and chopped

1 green bell pepper, seeded and chopped

2 green chilies, chopped

1 tsp chili sauce

4 oz cherry tomatoes, halved

6 oz anchovy fillets in oil, drained

2 tbsp chopped fresh parsley

Pour the broth into a saucepan and bring to a boil. Reduce the heat to a gentle simmer.

Meanwhile, melt the butter in a large skillet and gently cook the onion and garlic, stirring, for 2 minutes until the onion has softened but not browned. Stir in the rice and cook gently, stirring, for a further 2 minutes until the rice is well coated in butter.

Add a ladleful of broth and cook gently, stirring, until absorbed. Continue adding broth to the rice until half of the stock has been used. Season well with pepper and stir in the bell peppers, chilies, and chili sauce.

Continue adding broth until the risotto is thick but not sticky, about 20 minutes. Stir in the tomatoes, anchovies, and parsley, cook for a further 5 minutes and serve in a warm dish.

Colcannon Risotto

SERVES 4

The traditional recipe for Colcannon comes from Ireland where the ingredients are potatoes, cabbage, and butter. For this risotto, the cabbage is stirred into the rice which is flavored with traditional herbs and cheese.

5 cups fish broth

¼ cup butter

2 large onions, halved and sliced

1 garlic clove, minced

2 cups arborio rice

salt and ground black pepper

1 tsp freshly grated nutmeg

2 tbsp chopped fresh parsley

12 oz smoked cod, skinned and cut into large chunks

1½ cups shredded savoy cabbage

¼ cup freshly grated Parmesan cheese

freshly chopped parsley, to garnish

Pour the broth into a saucepan and bring to a boil. Reduce the heat to a gentle simmer.

Meanwhile, melt the butter in a large saucepan and gently cook the onion and garlic, stirring, for 2 minutes. Stir in the rice and cook gently, stirring, for a further 2 minutes until the rice is well coated in butter. Add a ladleful of broth to the rice and gently cook, stirring, until absorbed. Continue adding broth until half has been used. Season well and add the nutmeg and parsley.

Continue adding broth for a further 15 minutes. Stir in the fish and cook for a further 10 minutes, adding broth until the risotto is thick but not sticky. Meanwhile, cook the cabbage in boiling water for 5 minutes. Drain well and stir into the risotto.

Just before serving, stir in the cheese and transfer to a warm serving dish. Garnish and serve.

Kipper and Apple Risotto

SERVES 4

Kippers are the most common smoked herring and are usually sold whole, in pairs. Look for undyed kippers for this recipe.

3¾ cups fish broth

1¼ cups apple juice or cider

¼ cup butter

8 button onions, halved

1 garlic clove, minced

2 cups arborio rice

ground black pepper

juice of 1 lemon

4 boned kippers, cut into strips

1 green dessert apple, sliced

3 tbsp chopped fresh sage

4 tbsp light cream

Pour the broth and apple juice or cider into a saucepan and bring to a boil. Reduce the heat to a gentle simmer.

Meanwhile, melt the butter in a large skillet and gently cook the onions and garlic for 2 minutes. Stir in the rice and cook gently, stirring, for a further 2 minutes until the rice is well coated in butter.

Add a ladleful of broth mixture and cook gently, stirring, until absorbed. Continue adding to the rice until half has been used. Season with pepper and stir in the lemon juice.

Continue adding broth for a further 20 minutes. Stir in the fish, apple, sage, and cream and cook for a further 5 minutes until the risotto is thick but not sticky. Serve in a warm dish.

Curried Fish Risotto

Fish and curry spices go very well together. This curry is relatively mild and is enhanced by the addition of ground almonds for an extra nutty flavor.

5 cups fish broth

¼ cup butter

1 onion, quartered

3 garlic cloves, minced

1 tsp ground cumin

1 tsp ground coriander

1 tsp garam masala

1 tsp chili powder

a large pinch of turmeric

2 cups arborio rice

¼ cup ground almonds

salt and ground black pepper

3 tbsp mango chutney

10 oz cod fillets, cut into large chunks

⅔ cup heavy cream

2 tbsp golden raisins

2 tbsp toasted flaked almonds

2 tbsp chopped fresh cilantro

Pour the broth into a saucepan and bring to a boil. Reduce the heat to a gentle simmer.

Meanwhile, melt the butter in a large skillet and gently cook the onion, garlic, cumin, coriander, garam masala, chili powder, and turmeric for 2 minutes, stirring, until the onion softens. Stir in the rice and gently cook for a further 2 minutes, stirring, until the rice is well coated in butter.

Add a ladleful of broth and gently cook, stirring, until absorbed. Continue adding small quantities of broth until half has been used. Add the ground almonds, seasoning, and mango chutney.

Continue adding broth for a further 15 minutes. Stir in the fish and cream, cook for a further 10 minutes adding broth until the risotto is thick but not sticky.

Just before serving stir in the golden raisins, almonds, and cilantro. Serve in a warm dish.

Seafood Risotto

Squid Provencale

Mussels with Bacon and Saffron

Mussel and Shrimp Risotto

New Zealand Mussels and Red Pesto

Garlic Mussels

Langoustine and Garlic

Chili Shrimp

Shrimp with Sun-dried Tomatoes
and Porcini

Scallops and Ginger with
Yellow Bean Paste

Scampi with Herbs

Scallops with Fennel and Parmesan

Risotto Vongole

Oriental Crab Risotto

Creamy Lobster with Cheese

Seafood and Saffron

Sweet-and-sour Shellfish

Squid Provencale

SERVES 4

*P*acked full of the sunny flavors of the Mediterranean, this delicious risotto will make a substantial main meal when served with crusty bread and a crisp salad.

3¾ cups fish broth

4 tbsp olive oil

6 shallots, finely chopped

1 garlic clove, thinly sliced

1 yellow bell pepper, seeded and diced

2 medium zucchini, trimmed and diced

1 medium eggplant, trimmed and diced

2 cups arborio rice

1 tsp dried mixed herbs

⅔ cup dry red wine

14 oz can chopped tomatoes

1 tsp superfine sugar

salt and ground black pepper

8 oz prepared baby squid, sliced into rings

a few pitted black olives

fresh herbs, to garnish

Pour the broth into a saucepan and bring to a boil. Reduce the heat to a gentle simmer.

Meanwhile, heat the oil in a large saucepan and gently fry the shallots, garlic, bell pepper, zucchini, and eggplant for 4–5 minutes until softened. Add the rice and cook, stirring, for 2 minutes until well mixed.

Add the herbs, wine, tomatoes, and sugar and cook gently, stirring, until absorbed. Gradually ladle in the broth until half is used and the rice becomes creamy. Season well and stir in the squid.

Continue adding the broth until the risotto becomes thick and tender. This will take about 25 minutes.

Sprinkle with the olives and serve garnished with fresh herbs.

Mussels with Bacon and Saffron

SERVES 4

An aromatic risotto that makes a perfect dish for an informal supper, piled high with tender fresh mussels.

5 cups fish broth

¼ cup butter

1 tbsp olive oil

1 medium onion, finely chopped

4 slices rindless lean back bacon, finely chopped

2 cups arborio rice

a large pinch of saffron

salt and ground black pepper

½ cup freshly grated Parmesan cheese

2 tbsp chopped fresh parsley

3 lb fresh mussels in their shells, scrubbed

⅔ cup dry white wine

Pour the broth into a saucepan and bring to a boil. Reduce the heat to a gentle simmer.

Meanwhile, melt 2 tbsp butter with the oil in a large saucepan and gently fry the onion and bacon for 2–3 minutes until just softened. Add the rice and cook gently, stirring, for 2 minutes until well mixed.

Add a ladleful of broth and cook gently, stirring, until absorbed. Continue ladling the broth into the rice until half the broth is used and the rice becomes creamy. Sprinkle in the saffron.

Continue adding the broth until the risotto becomes thick and tender. This will take about 25 minutes. Season and stir in the Parmesan cheese and half the parsley. Keep warm.

Place the mussels in a large saucepan with the remaining butter and the wine. Cover with a tight fitting lid and cook for 4–5 minutes, shaking the pan occasionally, until the mussels have opened. Discard any that don't open.

Serve the risotto with the mussels and cooking liquid spooned over. Sprinkle with remaining chopped parsley.

Mussels with Bacon and Saffron ▶

Mussels and Shrimp

SERVES 4

This simple risotto uses cooked mussels and shrimp, flavored with chopped dill and lemon. This would make a substantial starter or light supper dish.

5 cups fish broth

¼ cup butter

2 garlic cloves, minced

2 cups arborio rice

finely grated zest and juice of 1 lemon

6 oz shelled shrimp, thawed if frozen

6 oz cooked and shelled mussels

2 tbsp chopped fresh dill

1 tbsp capers

salt and ground black pepper

wedges of lemon, to serve

Pour the broth into a saucepan and bring to a boil. Reduce the heat to a gentle simmer.

Meanwhile, melt the butter and gently fry the garlic and rice, stirring, for 2 mins until the rice is well coated.

Add a ladleful of the broth and cook gently, stirring, until absorbed. Continue ladling the broth into the rice until half the broth is used and the rice becomes creamy. Stir in the lemon zest and juice, the shrimp, and mussels.

Continue adding the broth until the risotto becomes thick and tender. This will take about 25 minutes. Stir in the dill and capers. Season well before serving with wedges of lemon.

New Zealand Mussels and Red Pesto

SERVES 4

These large meaty morsels are mixed into a risotto that is flavored with red wine and red pesto sauce.

5 cups fish broth

2 tbsp butter

2 garlic cloves, finely sliced

1 medium red bell pepper, finely diced

2 cups arborio rice

⅔ cup red wine

3 tbsp red pesto sauce

salt and ground black pepper

16 cooked New Zealand mussels

fresh basil leaves, to garnish

Pour the broth into a saucepan and bring to a boil. Reduce the heat to a gentle simmer.

Meanwhile, melt the butter and gently fry the garlic and red bell pepper for 2–3 minutes until just softened. Add the rice and cook, stirring, for 2 minutes until the rice is well coated.

Add the red wine and cook gently, stirring, until absorbed. Gradually ladle in the broth until half is used and the rice becomes creamy. Stir in the pesto sauce, seasoning, and mussels.

Continue adding the broth until the risotto becomes thick and tender. Keep the heat moderate. This will take 25 minutes. Garnish and serve with crusty bread.

Garlic Mussels

SERVES 4

A traditional combination of mussels in their shells, white wine, garlic, and cream is garnished with chopped parsley

3¾ cups fish broth

2 cups dry white wine

¼ cup butter

4 garlic cloves, minced

6 shallots, finely chopped

2 cups arborio rice

salt and ground black pepper

4 tbsp chopped fresh parsley

3 lb fresh mussels in their shells, scrubbed

3 tbsp heavy cream

Pour the broth and 1¼ cups wine into a saucepan and bring to a boil. Reduce the heat to a gentle simmer.

Meanwhile, melt 2 tbsp butter in a large saucepan and gently fry half the garlic with the shallots for 2–3 minutes until softened but not browned. Add the rice and cook, stirring, for 2 minutes.

Add a ladleful of the broth and wine mixture and cook gently, stirring, until absorbed. Continue ladling the broth into the rice until half the broth is used and the rice becomes creamy. Season well and stir in half the parsley.

Continue adding the broth until the risotto becomes thick and tender. This will take about 25 minutes. Keep warm.

Place the mussels in a large saucepan along with the cream, remaining butter and garlic, and wine. Cover with a tight fitting lid and cook for 4–5 minutes, shaking the pan occasionally, until the mussels have opened. Discard any that don't open.

Serve the mussels and the cooking liquid spooned over the risotto. Sprinkle with the remaining parsley.

Langoustine and Garlic

SERVES 4

*L*uxuriously big juicy shrimp and slivers of garlic are flambéed with brandy and stirred into a delicate tarragon risotto.

5 cups fish broth	2 tbsp chopped fresh tarragon
¼ cup butter	finely grated zest of 1 lemon
1 medium leek, finely chopped	3 garlic cloves, finely sliced
1 bay leaf	16 raw langoustine
2 cups arborio rice	3 tbsp brandy
salt and ground black pepper	fresh tarragon, to garnish

Pour the broth into a saucepan and bring to a boil. Reduce the heat to a gentle simmer.

Meanwhile, melt half the butter in a large saucepan and gently fry the leek and bay leaf for 2–3 minutes until softened. Add the rice and cook, stirring, for 2 minutes until well coated in the leek butter.

Add a ladleful of broth and cook gently, stirring, until absorbed. Continue ladling the broth into the rice until all the liquid is absorbed and the rice is thick, creamy, and tender. Keep the heat moderate. This will take about 25 minutes. Discard the bay leaf, season well and stir in the tarragon and lemon zest. Keep warm.

Melt the remaining butter in a frying pan and gently fry the garlic and langoustine for 2–3 minutes, stirring, until the langoustine are pink all over. Warm the brandy, pour over the langoustine and carefully ignite using a taper. Once the flames have died down, transfer the langoustine to the risotto along with the juices. Serve garnished with fresh tarragon and lemon wedges.

Chili Shrimp

SERVES 4

This risotto has a flavor of Thailand with ingredients such as chilies, coconut, scallions, lemon grass, and peanuts. It would be an ideal dish to serve on a special occasion.

3¾ cups fish stock

1 tbsp vegetable oil

1 bunch scallions, trimmed and chopped

1 clove garlic, minced

1 red chili, seeded and finely chopped

2 cups arborio rice

1 stalk lemon grass, bruised

1¼ cups coconut milk

1 tbsp Thai fish sauce

8 oz shelled large shrimp, thawed if frozen

¼ cup crushed roasted peanuts

shredded scallions and red chili, to garnish

Pour the broth into a saucepan and bring to a boil. Reduce the heat to a gentle simmer.

Meanwhile, heat the oil in a large saucepan and gently fry the scallions, garlic, and red chili for 1–2 minutes, until just softened. Add the rice and cook, stirring, for 2 minutes until well coated in the scallion mixture.

Add the lemon grass, coconut milk, and fish sauce and cook gently, stirring, until absorbed. Gradually ladle in the broth until all the liquid is absorbed and the rice is thick, creamy, and tender. Keep the heat moderate. This will take about 25 minutes.

Discard the lemon grass. Stir in the shrimp and cook for a further 2 minutes.

Serve sprinkled with chopped peanuts, and garnish with scallions and red chili.

Shrimp with Sun-dried Tomatoes and Porcini

SERVES 4

*D*ried vegetables have a more intense flavor than fresh. Use the soaking liquid in the risotto for maximum seasoning.

3¾ cups fish broth

2 cups sun-dried tomatoes, soaked as directed

1 cup dried porcini mushrooms, soaked as directed

3 tbsp olive oil

2 medium red onions, finely shredded

2 cups arborio rice

⅔ cup extra-dry white vermouth

salt and ground black pepper

8 oz cooked shelled shrimp, thawed if frozen

2 tbsp chopped fresh parsley

Pour the broth into a saucepan and bring to a boil. Reduce the heat to a gentle simmer.

Meanwhile, drain the tomatoes and mushrooms, reserving the soaking liquid, and rinse well. Slice the tomatoes into thin strips, and cut up the mushrooms if large.

Heat the oil in a large saucepan and gently fry the onions, sun-dried tomatoes, and mushrooms for 5 minutes until just softened, but not browned. Add the rice and cook, stirring, until the rice is coated all over in the vegetable mixture.

Add the dry vermouth and ⅔ cup soaking liquid and cook gently, stirring, until absorbed. Gradually ladle in the broth until all the liquid is absorbed and the rice becomes thick, creamy, and tender. Keep the heat moderate. This will take about 25 minutes.

Season and stir in the shrimp. Heat through for 2 minutes. Serve sprinkled with chopped parsley.

Scallops and Ginger with Yellow Bean Paste

SERVES 4

Small scallops are used in this recipe. They are sweet and juicy and require very little cooking. They are perfect for oriental dishes.

5 cups fish broth

2 tbsp vegetable oil

1 bunch scallions, peeled and chopped

1 green chili, seeded and finely chopped

2 cups arborio rice

1 lb fresh scallops, cleaned and trimmed

1-inch piece fresh ginger, peeled and cut into thin strips

1 tbsp light soy sauce

8 oz snow peas, topped, tailed, and thinly sliced

2 tbsp yellow bean paste

1 tsp superfine sugar

Pour the broth into a saucepan and bring to a boil. Reduce the heat to a gentle simmer.

Meanwhile, heat 1 tablespoon oil in a large saucepan and gently fry the scallions and chili for 1–2 minutes until just softened. Add the rice and cook, stirring, for 2 minutes until the rice is coated in the vegetable mixture.

Add a ladleful of broth and cook gently, stirring, until absorbed. Continue ladling the broth into the rice until all the liquid is absorbed and the rice is thick, creamy, and tender. Keep the heat moderate. This will take about 25 minutes. Keep warm.

Heat remaining oil in a wok or large skillet and stir-fry the scallops and ginger for 1 minute. Add the remaining ingredients and stir-fry for a further 2–3 minutes until the scallops are cooked through.

Carefully stir the scallop mixture into the rice and serve immediately.

Scampi with Herbs ▶

Scampi with Herbs

SERVES 4

Scampi are very juicy and have a sweet taste – they require very little cooking. Here they combine with a wine and herb risotto to make a delicious supper dish.

3¾ cups fish broth

1¼ cups plus 2 tbsp dry white wine

¼ cup butter

4 shallots, finely chopped

2 cloves garlic, finely chopped

2 cups arborio rice

salt and ground black pepper

2 tbsp chopped fresh dill

1 lb raw shelled scampi

3 tbsp heavy cream

1 tsp paprika

Pour the broth and 1¼ cups wine into a saucepan and bring to a boil. Reduce the heat to a gentle simmer.

Meanwhile, melt half the butter in a large saucepan and gently fry the shallots and garlic for 2–3 minutes until softened. Add the rice and cook, stirring, for 2 minutes.

Add a ladleful of the broth and wine mixture and cook gently, stirring, until absorbed. Continue ladling the broth into the rice until all the broth is used and the rice becomes thick, creamy, and tender. Keep the heat moderate. This will take about 25 minutes. Season well and stir in the dill. Keep warm.

Melt the remaining butter in a skillet and gently fry the scampi, stirring, for 2–3 minutes until pink all over. Stir in the cream and the remaining wine and cook for another minute.

Gently mix the scampi and creamy liquid into the rice and serve sprinkled with the paprika.

Scallops with Fennel and Parmesan

SERVES 4

Scallops flavored with fennel and celery give this risotto a distinctly savory taste. This is a light risotto and would make a perfect supper dish.

2 tbsp olive oil

1 lb scallops, halved or quartered if large

1 tsp celery seeds

5 cups fish broth

2 tbsp butter

2 medium leeks, finely chopped

2 celery stalks, trimmed and finely chopped

1 bulb fennel, trimmed, finely sliced, and fronds reserved

2 cups arborio rice

celery salt and ground black pepper

½ cup freshly grated Parmesan cheese

chopped celery leaves, to garnish

Heat the olive oil in a large saucepan and gently fry the scallops and celery seeds for 3–4 minutes until cooked through. Drain, reserving pan juices, and keep warm.

Pour the broth into a saucepan and bring to a boil. Reduce the heat to a gentle simmer.

Add the butter to the reserved pan juices and melt. Gently fry the leeks, celery, and fennel for 3–4 minutes until just softened. Add the rice and cook, stirring, for 2 minutes until well mixed.

Add a ladleful of broth and cook gently, stirring, until absorbed. Continue ladling in the broth until all the liquid is absorbed and the rice is thick, creamy, and tender. Keep the heat moderate. This will take about 25 minutes.

Mix in the scallops and season. Heat through for 2 minutes. Just before serving, stir in the Parmesan cheese. Serve garnished with chopped celery leaves and reserved fennel fronds.

Risotto Vongole

SERVES 4

In Italy, vongole are very small clams usually served with spaghetti, but they adapt very well to this risotto dish.

5 cups fish broth	salt and ground black pepper
2 tbsp olive oil	3 lb clams, scrubbed and soaked
3 garlic cloves, sliced	⅔ cup dry white wine
3 small dried chilies, chopped	2 tbsp chopped fresh parsley
2 cups arborio rice	

Pour the broth into a saucepan and bring to a boil. Reduce the heat to a gentle simmer.

Meanwhile, heat the oil in a large saucepan and gently fry two-thirds of the garlic and half the chilies for 1–2 minutes until just softened but not browned. Add the rice and cook, stirring, for 2 minutes until the rice is well coated in the oil.

Add a ladleful of broth and cook gently, stirring, until absorbed. Continue ladling in the broth until all the liquid is absorbed and the rice becomes thick, creamy, and tender. Keep the heat moderate. This will take about 25 minutes. Season well and keep warm.

Place the clams in a large saucepan and pour over the wine. Add the remaining garlic and chilies. Cover with a tight fitting lid, and cook on a high heat until they open, shaking the pan constantly. Discard any clams that don't open.

To serve the risotto, spoon clams with their cooking juices over each portion of rice and sprinkle with parsley.

Oriental Crab Risotto

SERVES 4

Choose crab claws which contain a lot of meat. If smaller ones are available then use 12–16 in this recipe instead.

5 cups of fish broth	2 cups arborio rice
3 tbsp vegetable oil	8 large crab claws, cracked
1 bunch of scallions, trimmed and finely chopped	1 tsp five-spice powder
1 red bell pepper, seeded and sliced	2 tbsp dark soy sauce
1 garlic clove, finely chopped	2 cups finely shredded bok choy (Chinese cabbage)
½-inch piece fresh ginger, finely chopped	2 tsp sesame oil
	2 tbsp snipped fresh chives

Pour the broth into a saucepan and bring to a boil. Reduce the heat to a gentle simmer.

Meanwhile, heat half of the vegetable oil in a large saucepan and gently fry the scallions, red bell pepper, garlic, and ginger for 3–4 minutes until softened. Add the rice and cook, stirring, for 2 minutes until well mixed.

Add a ladleful of broth and cook gently, stirring, until absorbed. Continue to ladle in the broth until all the liquid is absorbed and the rice becomes thick, creamy, and tender. Keep the heat moderate. This will take about 25 minutes. Keep warm.

Heat the remaining oil in a wok or large skillet and stir-fry the crab claws with the five-spice powder for 1 minute. Add the soy sauce and bok choy and stir-fry for a further 2–3 minutes until the leaves are tender and wilted. Mix in the sesame oil.

Spoon the stir-fried crab mixture over the rice and serve sprinkled with snipped chives.

Oriental Crab Risotto ▶

Creamy Lobster with Cheese

SERVES 4

A luxuriously rich risotto that would make an excellent starter to a light meal. Juicy lobster is mixed with cream, cheese, herbs, and wine to give a delicious dish.

3¾ cups fish broth	8 oz cooked lobster meat, flaked
1¼ cups dry white wine	2 tbsp chopped fresh parsley
2 tbsp butter	2 tbsp chopped fresh tarragon
1 tbsp olive oil	2 tbsp chopped fresh dill
6 shallots, finely shredded	4 tbsp heavy cream
1 garlic clove, minced	salt and ground black pepper
2 cups arborio rice	½ cup freshly grated Parmesan cheese

Pour the broth and wine into a saucepan and bring to a boil. Reduce the heat to a gentle simmer.

Meanwhile, melt the butter with the oil in a large saucepan and gently fry the shallots and garlic for 2–3 minutes until softened but not browned. Add the rice and cook, stirring, for 2 minutes, until well coated in the shallot mixture.

Add a ladleful of broth and cook gently, stirring, until absorbed. Continue ladling in the broth until half is used and the rice becomes creamy. Mix in the lobster, half the herbs, and the cream.

Continue adding the broth until the risotto becomes thick, but not sticky. This will take about 25 minutes and shouldn't be hurried.

Season. Just before serving, stir in the grated cheese and serve sprinkled with remaining herbs.

Seafood and Saffron

SERVES 4

A selection of mussels, clams, shrimp, and scallops are cooked in a wine and cream sauce and served with a fragrant, golden risotto.

5 cups fish broth	4 tbsp heavy cream
⅓ cup butter	1 lb fresh mussels in their shells, scrubbed
1 medium onion, finely chopped	
2 garlic cloves, minced	1 lb fresh clams in their shells, scrubbed and soaked
2 cups arborio rice	
a large pinch of saffron	8 oz fresh scallops, cleaned and trimmed
salt and ground black pepper	8 oz large unshelled raw shrimp
⅔ cup dry white wine	2 tbsp chopped fresh parsley

Pour the broth into a saucepan and bring to a boil. Reduce the heat to a gentle simmer.

Meanwhile, melt ¼ cup butter in a large saucepan and gently fry the onion and half the garlic for 2–3 minutes until softened but not browned. Stir in the rice and cook, stirring, for 2 minutes until the rice is well coated in butter.

Add a ladleful of broth and cook gently, stirring, until absorbed. Continue ladling the broth into the rice until half the broth is used and the rice becomes creamy. Sprinkle in the saffron and seasoning.

Continue adding the broth until the risotto becomes thick, but not sticky. this will take about 25 minutes and shouldn't be hurried. Keep warm.

Pour the wine into a saucepan and add the cream and remaining garlic and butter. Add the shellfish, cover with a tight fitting lid and cook on a high heat for 5–6 minutes, shaking the pan occasionally, until the mussels and clams have opened and the shrimp are pink. Discard any mussels or clams that don't open.

Serve the risotto with the shellfish and cooking liquid spooned over, and sprinkle with the chopped parsley.

Sweet-and-sour Shellfish

SERVES 4

Use a mixture of cooked shellfish for this risotto, such as squid, shrimp, crab, mussels, and lobster.

5 cups fish broth

3 tbsp vegetable oil

4 shallots, finely chopped

2 garlic cloves, finely chopped

2 cups arborio rice

1 bunch scallions, trimmed and cut into 1-inch lengths

4 oz baby corn, sliced lengthwise

1 red bell pepper, seeded and thinly sliced

12 oz cooked, mixed shellfish, thawed if frozen

2 tbsp light soy sauce

1 tbsp tomato paste

2 tbsp red wine vinegar

2 tsp superfine sugar

2 tbsp chopped fresh cilantro

Pour the broth into a saucepan and bring to a boil. Reduce the heat to a gentle simmer.

Meanwhile, heat half the oil in a large saucepan and gently fry the shallots and garlic for 2–3 minutes until just softened, but not browned. Add the rice and cook, stirring, for 2 minutes until the rice is well coated in the oil.

Add a ladleful of broth and cook gently, stirring, until all the broth is absorbed. Continue adding the broth until all the liquid is absorbed and the rice is thick, creamy, and tender. Keep the heat moderate. This will take about 25 minutes. Keep warm.

Heat the remaining oil in a wok or large skillet and stir-fry the scallions, baby corn, and red bell pepper for 1 minute. Add the shellfish and soy sauce and continue to cook for another minute. Blend together the tomato paste, vinegar, and sugar and add to the wok. Stir-fry for 1 minute until the vegetables are just tender.

To serve, carefully mix the stir-fried shellfish and vegetables into the risotto and serve sprinkled with chopped cilantro.

Sweet Risotto

Sunshine Fruit Risotto

Chocolate and Vanilla Risotto

Summer Fruit Risotto

Apple, Pear, and Cinnamon Risotto

Cream Cheese and Apricot Risotto

Raspberry, Peach, and Hazelnut Risotto

Tiramisù Risotto

Lemon and Golden Raisin Risotto

Chocolate Orange Risotto

Sunshine Fruit Risotto

SERVES 4

This is a really colorful recipe, the different tones of the fruit complementing each other in flavor also.

5 cups pineapple juice

¼ cup butter

2 tbsp soft brown sugar

2 cups arborio rice

1 tsp ground cinnamon

1 tsp ground allspice

8 oz fresh pineapple, peeled, cored, and cubed

2 bananas, peeled and sliced

1 papaya, halved, seeded, and sliced

1 mango, peeled and sliced

Pour the pineapple juice into a saucepan and bring to a boil. Reduce the heat to a gentle simmer.

Meanwhile, melt the butter in a large skillet and stir in the sugar and rice. Add the spices and cook gently, stirring, until the rice is well coated in butter.

Add a ladleful of pineapple juice and cook gently, stirring, until absorbed. Continue adding pineapple juice in small quantities for 20 minutes. Stir in the fruit and cook for a further 5 minutes until the risotto is thick but not sticky. Serve in a warm dish.

Chocolate and Vanilla Risotto

SERVES 4

*T*his is an indulgent, rich dessert that is not for those watching calories.

4 cups milk

¼ cup butter

2 cups arborio rice

2 tbsp superfine sugar

1 vanilla pod

3 oz semisweet chocolate, grated

⅔ cup heavy cream

Heat the milk to just below boiling point. Reduce the heat to a gentle simmer.

Meanwhile, melt the butter in a large skillet and gently cook the rice for 2 minutes, stirring, until the rice is well coated in butter.

Add a ladleful of milk and cook gently, stirring until absorbed. Stir in the sugar and vanilla pod. Continue adding small quantities of milk for 20 minutes, stirring, until the milk has been used. Remove the vanilla pod.

Add the chocolate and cream and cook for a further 5 minutes. Serve in a warm dish.

Summer Fruit Risotto

SERVES 4

*N*othing quite beats the flavors of mixed summer fruits. Stir them very gently into the risotto so that they do not break up.

3¾ cups milk

1¼ cups heavy cream

¼ cup butter

2 cups arborio rice

1 tsp ground cinnamon

2 tbsp superfine sugar

2 tbsp kirsch

4 cups mixed summer fruits such as strawberries, raspberries, blueberries, red and black currants

1 tbsp chopped fresh mint

Pour the milk and cream into a saucepan and bring to a boil. Reduce the heat to a gentle simmer.

Meanwhile, melt the butter in a large skillet and gently cook the rice, stirring, until well coated in butter.

Add a ladleful of milk and cream mixture and cook gently, stirring, until absorbed. Add the cinnamon, sugar, and kirsch and continue adding small quantities of milk and cream until the risotto is thick but not sticky. Stir in the fruit and mint and serve.

Apple, Pear, and Cinnamon Risotto

SERVES 4

*T*his is a real orchard dessert, delicately flavored with cinnamon to bring out the best in the fruits.

5 cups apple juice

½ cup butter

2 tsp ground cinnamon

2 tbsp soft brown sugar

2 cups arborio rice

2 red dessert apples, cored and sliced

2 dessert pears, cored and sliced

¼ cup pecan halves

Pour the apple juice into a saucepan and bring to a boil. Reduce the heat to a gentle simmer.

Meanwhile, melt half of the butter in a large skillet and add the cinnamon, sugar, and rice. Cook gently, stirring, for 2 minutes until the rice is well coated in butter.

Add a ladleful of apple juice and gently cook, stirring, until absorbed. Continue adding apple juice in small quantities until the risotto is thick but not sticky, about 25 minutes.

Meanwhile, melt the remaining butter in a separate skillet and cook the apples, pears, and pecans for 3–4 minutes, stirring. Add the contents of the pan to the rice, mix gently, and serve.

Apple, Pear, and Cinnamon Risotto ▶

Cream Cheese and Apricot Risotto

SERVES 4

*C*heese and apricots taste good together when lightly sweetened. Use full-fat cream cheese if possible and ripe apricots for better flavor.

5 cups apricot juice

¼ cup butter

2 tsp ground allspice

2 cups arborio rice

1 cup cream cheese

2 tbsp confectioners' sugar, sifted

12 oz fresh apricots, pitted and quartered

lemon balm, to garnish

Pour the apricot juice into a saucepan and bring to a boil. Reduce the heat to a gentle simmer.

Meanwhile, melt the butter in a large skillet and gently cook the allspice and rice for 2 minutes, stirring, until the rice is well coated in butter.

Add a ladleful of apricot juice and cook gently, stirring, until absorbed. Continue adding small quantities of juice to the rice until half has been used. Stir in the cream cheese and sugar.

Continue adding the juice until the risotto is thick but not sticky, about 25 minutes. Stir in the apricots and cook for a further 5 minutes. Serve garnished with lemon balm.

Raspberry, Peach, and Hazelnut Risotto

SERVES 4

This is a colorful combination of ingredients usually found in Peach Melba. Stirred into rice sweetened with peach nectar, it is sensational.

2½ cups milk

1¼ cups heavy cream

1¼ cups peach nectar

¼ cup butter

½ cup coarsely chopped hazelnuts

2 cups arborio rice

2 tbsp confectioners' sugar

8 oz canned or fresh peach quarters

⅔ cup raspberries

mint sprigs, to decorate

◀ *Raspberry, Peach, and Hazelnut Risotto*

Pour the milk and cream into a saucepan with the peach nectar and bring to a boil. Reduce the heat to a gentle simmer.

Meanwhile, melt the butter in a large skillet and gently cook the nuts for 1 minute, stirring. Add the rice and cook, stirring, for a further 2 minutes until the rice is well coated in butter.

Add a ladleful of the milk, cream, and nectar mixture and cook gently, stirring, until absorbed. Stir in the sugar and continue adding the liquid in small quantities for a further 20 minutes.

Stir in the peaches and raspberries, cook for 4–5 minutes until the risotto is thick but not sticky. Serve in a warm dish, decorated with mint.

Tiramisù Risotto

SERVES 4

This is a traditional, rich dessert associated with, and loved by, Italians.

3¾ cups milk

1¼ cups heavy cream

¼ cup butter

2 cups arborio rice

4 tbsp strong black coffee

1 tbsp cocoa powder

2 tbsp superfine sugar

3 tbsp brandy

2 oz coarsely grated semisweet chocolate

Pour the milk and cream into a saucepan and bring to a boil. Reduce the heat to a gentle simmer.

Meanwhile, melt the butter in a large skillet and stir in the rice. Cook gently, stirring, for 2 minutes until the rice is well coated in butter. Mix the coffee, cocoa, sugar, and brandy together and stir into the rice with a ladleful of milk and cream mixture.

Cook gently, stirring, until absorbed. Continue adding the cream and milk in small quantities for a further 25 minutes. Stir in the chocolate and serve in a warm dish.

Lemon and Golden Raisin Risotto

SERVES 4

This is a tangy dessert with fresh lemon juice and zest, and flavored with nutmeg.

3¾ cups milk

1¼ cups heavy cream

⅓ cup butter

2 cups arborio rice

juice and zest of 1 lemon

1 tsp freshly grated nutmeg

2 tbsp light brown sugar

½ cup golden raisins

1 lemon, halved and sliced

Pour the milk and cream into a saucepan and bring to a boil. Reduce the heat to a gentle simmer.

Meanwhile, melt ¼ cup of the butter in a large skillet and cook the rice for 2 minutes, stirring, until the rice is well coated in butter.

Add a ladleful of milk and cream mixture with the lemon juice and zest and cook gently, stirring, until the liquid is absorbed. Stir in the nutmeg and sugar, continue adding small quantities of milk and cream for a further 20 minutes.

Stir in the golden raisins and continue cooking for a further 5 minutes until the risotto is thick but not sticky. Meanwhile, melt the remaining butter in a separate skillet and cook the lemon slices for 2–3 minutes, turning. Stir the contents of the pan into the risotto and serve in a warm dish.

Chocolate Orange Risotto

SERVES 4

Chocolate and orange are an irresistible combination. Grate the white chocolate over the risotto just before serving to prevent it melting totally.

4 cups milk	⅔ cup orange juice
¼ cup butter	2 oz milk chocolate, grated
2 cups arborio rice	2 oranges, peeled and sectioned
4 tbsp orange liqueur	1 oz white chocolate, coarsely grated

Pour the milk into a saucepan and bring to a boil. Reduce the heat to a gentle simmer.

Meanwhile melt the butter in a saucepan and gently cook the rice for 2 minutes, stirring, until the rice is well coated in butter. Stir in the orange liqueur and orange juice and cook gently, stirring, until absorbed.

Add a ladleful of milk to the rice and cook, stirring, until absorbed. Continue adding small quantities of milk for a further 20 minutes. Stir in the milk chocolate and orange sections. Continue to cook for a further 5 minutes until the risotto is thick but not sticky. Sprinkle the white chocolate over the top and serve.

Pizza

The pizza originated in Naples, an invention of Neapolitan bakers for the poverty-stricken inhabitants of the back streets of the city, to make a little food stretch a long way. Because it is still a cheap and cheerful way to eat, the pizza has become even more popular in other countries than it is in Italy and there are pizza restaurants all over the world.

The Neapolitan pizza is made with fresh tomatoes, oregano, anchovy fillets, mozzarella cheese, and olive oil. There are now countless toppings for pizzas and making them at home is an excellent way of utilizing fresh vegetables, meats, and cheese to add variety to family meals.

Salami, chicken, bacon, smoked hams, and spicy sausages can all be used as toppings with different cheeses on a tomato base.

Fish pizzas can be flavored with anchovies, clams, mussels, shrimp, and tuna on tomatoes and herbs.

Pizzas are also a great boon to vegetarians as a tomato base is ideal with mushrooms, green, red, or yellow bell peppers, eggplant, artichoke hearts, corn, herbs, black or green olives, and cheese according to preference.

Professional pizza chefs hurl the dough in the air to achieve the correct thickness but at home the dough can be rolled and molded without this particular technique. The authentic pizza texture imparted by a brick-built pizza oven cannot be recreated exactly at home. Homemade pizzas are therefore bound to be slightly different, but they are still very good and you can be sure of delicious toppings. The deep pan pizza is much easier to copy at home with the aid of a flan ring or cake pan.

Bake your own pizzas to suit your family's tastes and you will discover, as have the Neapolitan bakers, that a little does indeed go a long way. Small children, teenagers, and adults are enthusiastic pizza-eaters and pizzas are therefore always popular. A glass of wine and a pizza are really only the equivalents of a beer and a sandwich, but they always seem more exciting.

Making Pizza Dough

Making bread dough for pizzas is straightforward providing the cook who is not familiar with yeast cookery keeps the following notes in mind when using the recipes. Enough time must be allowed for the dough to rise, but during this time it requires no attention and other work may be done.

Ingredients

Bread flour is best for pizza dough as it has a high gluten content which helps to give the texture and volume associated with bread doughs. As a warm atmosphere suits yeast particularly well, it is a good idea to sift flour into a slightly warmed bowl.

Many people prefer whole grain flours today and enjoy whole wheat pizzas. It must be noted that a mixture using only whole wheat flour will be fairly solid to eat but this is a matter for individual taste. A mixture of strong white flour and whole wheat gives a more digestible pizza.

Yeast is a living organism which is used as a raising agent in bread doughs. Yeast feeds on sugars and multiplies in warm moist conditions releasing carbon dioxide which expands when heated to give dough its characteristic spongy texture. However yeast can also be killed by excessive heat and it is essential that the yeast mixture be the correct temperature around 110°F. Yeast wakes up gradually so give it time – do not be too impatient.

Salt contributes to the flavor of the dough but it can also kill yeast cells. Only use the recommended amounts and do not allow the salt to come into direct contact with the yeast. Salt should be sifted with the flour. The proportion is usually 2 tsp to 4½ cups of flour used.

Sugar, if creamed with yeast can kill it; therefore it is essential not to add more than the amounts given in the recipes. Sugar added to the measured liquid and dissolved will be enough to activate the yeast without overpowering it.

Liquids used in yeast mixtures are either milk or water or a combination of the two. It is most important for the liquid to be the correct temperature. If it is warmer than 110°F it will destroy yeast cells. Try putting a finger in the water; if it feels warm, cool it slightly. Most beginners make the liquid too hot.

It is also important to measure liquids and put in less than the recipe states as more liquid can always be added but too much cannot be removed. Add the last of it carefully to obtain a slightly sticky but not wet dough. The mixture will firm to an elastic consistency as it is kneaded. It is this process which develops the gluten in the flour to give the texture.

Rising Times

It is very difficult to give the precise time required for activating yeast – it all depends on the ambient temperature. In cold surroundings yeast grows but only slowly.

In a warm place in front of a central heating radiator or warm cupboard it will take about an hour to activate. At room temperature dough can take up to 2 hours to rise. In a cool room it will rise in about 5 hours and in a refrigerator the rising process will take about 12 hours.

These rising times are useful to remember as the process can be organized around other activities.

Step-by-Step Pizza Dough

Assembling Ingredients for Dough

1 Measure all ingredients. Sift the flour.
2 On the right of the board there is fresh yeast which can be bought from some bakers, delicatessens and specialty stores.
3 On the left of the board the jug contains dried yeast mixed with liquid and left to ferment for 15 minutes.

Adding the yeast mixture to the flour

Make a well in the center of the flour, add the oil and cover with a little flour. Pour in the yeast liquid and the remaining liquid.

Mixing the dough

Use a plastic spatula to mix the dough until all the liquid has been absorbed to make a firm but pliable dough. Add liquid carefully at the end to prevent the dough becoming too sticky. If you add too much liquid, you will have to work in more flour which spoils the consistency of the dough.

Kneading the dough

When the dough is mixed turn onto a floured board and knead vigorously for 10 minutes. The kneading motion is done by pushing with the heel of the hand and turning the dough over continuously until it is smooth.

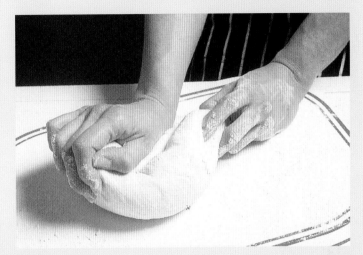

Rising the dough

Place in a bowl which has been lightly floured, or in an oiled plastic bag. If using a bowl, cover with plastic wrap or place inside a plastic bag or cover with a clean dish towel. This careful covering of the dough is to stop cooling air currents from interfering with the rising process. The dough (left) has risen and the covering has just been removed. Rising at this stage will take approximately an hour in a warm room, longer if the room is cool.

Knocking back (punching down) the risen dough

Turn the risen dough onto a floured board and knead again until the pockets of gas which are now unevenly distributed are knocked out (punched down). The dough is now smooth, firm, and elastic.

For speed, many recipes shape the pizzas at this stage but for a really delicious homemade pizza use the Pizza Dough 2 recipe (page 346). The second rising develops the real texture and the extra time is worthwhile.

Pizza Dough 1

MAKES 2 x 12-in PIZZAS OR 3 x 8-in PIZZAS

½ oz fresh or 2 tsp dried yeast

1 cup slightly warmed water

1 tsp sugar

4½ cups bread flour

1 tsp salt

1 tbsp oil

Blend fresh yeast with a little of the measured water which has the sugar dissolved in it. For dried yeast dissolve 1 tsp sugar in one third of the measured water, sprinkle the yeast onto the water and whisk. Leave to stand for 10–15 minutes until frothy.

Sift the flour and salt into a bowl and make a well in the center, add the oil, sprinkle over with a little flour.

Add the yeast liquid and most of the remaining water and mix well until the dough starts to leave the side of the bowl. If it seems too stiff add the remaining liquid slowly.

Turn onto a lightly floured board and knead well for about 10 minutes. When the dough is elastic and smooth place in a floured bowl and cover with a dish towel or plastic wrap. Alternatively leave it to rise in an oiled plastic bag until it has doubled in size. This will take approximately an hour in a warm kitchen.

The dough can then be knocked back (punched down) and shaped for pizzas.

The dough with two risings in my opinion gives the better homemade pizzas.

Pizza Dough 2

MAKES 4 x 12-in OBLONG OR ROUND PIZZAS

4½ cups flour

2 oz fresh or 2 tbsp dried yeast

2½ cups water

½ cup milk

1 tbsp salt

2 tbsp oil

Sift the flour into a large bowl and make a well in the center.

Add the yeast by crumbling into the center of the well.

Make sure that the water and milk are just at body temperature and pour most of the mixture into the well with the yeast.

Dissolve the salt in a little of the remaining liquid. Add oil. Pour them into mixture.

Knead well for about 10 minutes by hand. Place back in the bowl or in an oiled large plastic bag.

Allow to stand in a warm kitchen for about an hour or until the dough has doubled in size.

Knock back (punch down) the dough by kneading well with the heel of the hand.

Replace the dough in the bowl or bag and allow to rise again for a further hour.

Whole Wheat Pizza Dough

MAKES 2 x 12-in OR 3 x 8-in PIZZAS

½ oz fresh or 3 level tsp dried yeast

1 cup slightly warmed water

1 tsp sugar

2¼ cups whole wheat flour

2¼ cups all-purpose flour

1 tsp salt

1 tbsp oil

Cream fresh yeast with 3 tbsp measured liquid in which the sugar has been dissolved. Dried yeast should be mixed with one-third of the measured liquid with sugar dissolved in it, whisked and allowed to stand in a warm room for 10–15 minutes until frothy.

Pour the whole wheat flour into a bowl, sieve the white flour and salt on top and mix well.

Make a well in the center of the flour, pour in the oil, and cover with flour. Add the yeast mixture and most of the liquid. Mix well until dough leaves the side of the bowl, adding the remaining liquid if mixture is too dry. You may need a little extra liquid to take up the whole wheat flour but do not add too much.

Turn onto a floured board and knead well until the dough is smooth and elastic after about 10 minutes.

Put back into the bowl and cover with plastic wrap or place the dough in an oiled plastic bag. Allow to rise in a warm kitchen until doubled in size, this will take 45 minutes to an hour. Knock back (punch down) the dough and shape as required.

Garlic Dill Pizza Dough

MAKES TWO 12-INCH THIN CRUST PIZZAS OR ONE REGULAR CRUST PIZZA

The more garlic you add to this recipe, the more it tastes like garlic bread. Any topping that can be complemented by garlic does well on this crust. It is even good just topped with cheese.

1 package active dry yeast	2½ cups unbleached white flour
1 cup warm water	2 tbsp olive oil
1 tsp dried dill	½ tsp salt
2 garlic cloves, minced	

● In a large bowl, combine the yeast, warm water, dill, garlic, and 1½ cups of the flour. Mix well to blend. Add the oil, salt, and remaining flour and stir until the dough sticks together. Place the dough on a lightly floured surface. Dust your hands with flour and knead the dough until it is smooth and elastic, about 5 minutes. If the dough gets sticky, sprinkle it with a little flour.

● Roll the dough into a ball and place it in a lightly oiled bowl. Cover the bowl with a dish towel and set it in a warm, but not hot, place to rise until doubled in volume, about 1 hour.

● When the dough has risen, roll it into a ball to make one 12-inch regular crust pizza or divide it in two balls to make two thin-crust 12-inch pizzas. Before rolling out and topping the pizza, allow the dough to rest for 20 minutes.

● When ready to bake, place dough in the center of a lightly oiled pan. Roll outward toward the edges with the palm of your hand until the dough fills the pan evenly.

Chinese Pizza Dough

MAKES TWO 12-INCH THIN CRUST PIZZAS OR ONE REGULAR CRUST PIZZA

Sesame seeds and soy sauce give this dough an Oriental flavor. It is good with any stir-fry, Chinese, or Thai-style topping.

1 package active dry yeast	½ tsp salt
1 cup warm water	2 tbsp sesame seeds
1½ cups unbleached white flour	1 tbsp soy sauce
4 tsp olive oil	1 cup whole wheat flour

● In a large bowl, combine the yeast, warm water, and white flour. Mix well to blend. Add the oil, salt, sesame seeds, and soy sauce and mix thoroughly. Add the whole wheat flour and stir until the dough sticks together. Place the dough on a flat surface lightly dusted with white flour. Dust your hands with white flour and then knead the dough until it is smooth and elastic, about 5 minutes. If the dough gets sticky, sprinkle it with a little more flour.

● Roll the dough into a ball and place it in a lightly oiled bowl. Cover the bowl with a dish towel and set in a warm, but not hot, place to rise until doubled in volume, about 1 hour.

● When the dough has risen, roll it into a ball to make one 12-inch regular crust pizza or divide it in two balls to make two thin-crust 12-inch pizzas. Before rolling out and topping the pizza, allow the dough to rest for 20 minutes.

● When ready to bake, place dough in the center of a lightly oiled pan. Roll outward toward the edges with the palm of your hand until the dough fills the pan evenly.

Corn Bread Pizza Dough

Corn bread goes well with many toppings, most notably those with tomato-based sauces such as Creole, jambalaya, or Mexican-style toppings. It also goes well with cheeses.

1 cup warm water

1 package active dry yeast

1½ cups unbleached white flour

¾ cup yellow corn meal

¼ tsp salt

1 tsp sugar

2 tbsp corn oil

In a large bowl, combine the warm water, yeast, 1 cup of white flour, and ¼ cup of corn meal. Stir to mix thoroughly. Add the remaining ingredients, stirring with a wooden spoon until mixed. Place the dough on a floured surface. Dust your hands with white flour and knead the dough for 5 minutes, dusting with additional white flour if necessary to keep it from sticking. The dough should be smooth and elastic.

Place the dough in a clean bowl, cover with a dish towel, and set in a warm place to rise for about 1 hour or until doubled in size.

When dough is ready, roll into a ball and set aside to rest for 20 minutes before topping and baking.

Whole Wheat Cheese Pizza Dough

Parmesan cheese adds a sharpness to the crust. Other types of grated hard cheese can be substituted for the Parmesan, but soft cheeses melt and stick to the pan.

1 package active dry yeast

1 cup warm water

1 cup whole wheat flour

1¼ cups unbleached white flour

4 tsp olive oil

½ tsp salt

¼ cup grated Parmesan cheese

Follow instructions as for Whole Wheat Pizza Dough (see page 347), but add the Parmesan cheese to the oil and salt which will then be added to the yeast mixture.

Savory Pizzas

Pizza Napolitana Con Aglio

Deep-dish Creole Pizza

Pizza Sauce

Greek Pizza

Pizza Rarebit

Sweet and Sour Tofu Pizza

Bountiful Harvest Pizza

Pizza with Portobella Mushrooms

Pizza with Garden Vegetables

Pizza Siciliana

Pizza Caponata

Sesame Tofu Pizza

Tofu and Cashew Pizza

Breakfast Pizza

Basil and Pine Nut Pizza

Neapolitan Pizza

Beets in Orange Sauce Pizza

Pizza with Caramelized Onions

Chili Pizza

Whole Wheat Eggplant and Mozzarella Pizza

Quick Bake Calabrian Pizzas

Fennel Mornay Pizza

Pizza Verde

Sun-dried Tomatoes and Mozzarella Pizza

Eggplant Parmesan Pizza

Kung Pao Pizza

Tofu in Peanut Sauce Pizza

Deep Dish Mozzarella and Salami Pizza

Cheese and Artichoke Pizza

Deep Dish Ratatouille Pizza

Curried Tofu Pizza

Tofu and Vegetable Pizza

Deep Dish Ham and Mushroom Pizza

Family Pizza

Pizza with Roasted Peppers

Pizza Monte Carlo

Deep Dish Mushroom and Prosciutto Pizza

Blue Cheese and Broccoli Pizza

Split Pea Pizza

Pizza Romano

Pizza with Tomato and Three Cheeses

Pizza Paella

Barbecued Pizza

Taco Pizza

Swiss Green Bean Pizza

Sesame Vegetable Pizza

Beef Pizza Pie

Hi-speed Pizzas

Jambalaya Pizza

Deep-dish Artichoke Heart and Bacon Pizza

Herbed Brussels Sprouts and Carrot Pizza

Reuben Pizza

Pizza Stroganoff

Pizza Primavera

Spinach and Cheese Pizza

Whole Wheat Pepper and Caper Pizza

Four Cheese Pizza

Pizza Napolitana Con Aglio

SERVES 6-8

2¼ cups flour, sifted

½ oz fresh yeast

½ tsp sugar

tepid water to mix

½ tsp salt

2¼ cups ripe tomatoes, skinned, seeded, and coarsely chopped

ground black pepper

2 tsp finely chopped fresh basil

2–3 garlic cloves, finely chopped

12 anchovy fillets

1½ cups thinly sliced mozzarella cheese

1½ tsp olive oil

● Preheat oven to 450°F. Put the flour into a large bowl and make a well in the center.

● Mix the yeast, sugar, and 2 tbsp tepid water in a cup and pour into the flour. Add the salt and mix well, adding enough tepid water to make a stiff dough.

● Knead on a well-floured board until light and elastic. Cover with a clean dish towel and leave in a warm place for 2-2½ hours until doubled in size.

● Roll the dough into a circle ¼ in thick, and put it onto a large, well-oiled baking sheet. Leave to rise for 10 minutes.

● Top with the tomatoes, plenty of pepper, garlic, and basil followed by the anchovies and sliced mozzarella cheese. Finally sprinkle oil over the top.

● Bake for 25 to 35 minutes, until the dough is cooked and the cheese bubbles.

Deep-dish Creole Pizza

Creole dishes tend to be spicy tomato and vegetable mixtures, and this pizza is no exception. You can try using fresh okra if it is available. Boil the whole fresh okra until tender. Then chop it to use in this recipe.

½ quantity Whole Wheat Pizza Dough (page 347)

2 × 14½ oz cans tomatoes

1 tsp oregano

1 tsp thyme

½ tsp basil

½ tsp cayenne pepper

2 garlic cloves, minced

2 celery stalks, chopped

1 small onion, chopped

2 cups cut frozen okra, thawed

Preheat oven to 500°F.

Place the dough in the center of a lightly oiled 13 × 9 × 2-inch pan. Using your fingers, gently spread the dough until it covers the bottom of the pan evenly and goes halfway up the sides.

Put the tomatoes into a colander, drain and discard the liquid but retain the thick sauce. Cut the tomatoes into quarters. Place the tomatoes and sauce in a bowl. Add the herbs, spice, and garlic. Chop the celery and onion into small pieces and add them to the bowl. Finally, add the okra and stir gently to mix.

To assemble, spread the tomato and okra mixture onto the pizza dough and bake for 20 minutes.

◀ *Deep-dish Creole Pizza*

Pizza Sauce

Puréed tomatoes have the perfect consistency for pizza sauce. If you make extra sauce and freeze it, you'll always have some on hand.

28 oz can puréed tomatoes

1 bay leaf

1 tsp oregano

1 tsp basil

1 tsp thyme

½ tsp marjoram

Place ingredients in a pan and bring to a boil. Reduce heat, cover loosely to keep from spattering, and simmer for 30 minutes, stirring occasionally.

Greek Pizza

MAKES ONE 12-INCH DOUBLE-CRUST PIZZA

*I*f you grow mint in your garden, you know it has a tendency to take over. But when you have recipes like this to make, you don't mind having lots of it on hand.

½ quantity Whole Wheat Pizza Dough (page 347)

1½ cups loosely packed fresh mint

1 tbsp olive oil

6 oz can pitted sliced black olives

2 oz feta cheese, crumbled

● Preheat oven to 500°F.

● Roughly chop the mint leaves and place in a bowl with the olive oil; stir to coat. Set aside for a few minutes. Drain the olives and spread them over the pizza dough. Then spread the mint mixture, pouring any extra oil on the pizza. Top with the feta.

● Bake for 8 minutes.

Greek Pizza ▶

Pizza Rarebit

MAKES ONE 12-INCH DOUBLE-CRUST PIZZA

*B*eer gives a special flavor to this adaptation of an old Welsh dish. The original version can be served on grilled tomatoes, but in this recipe, tomatoes are the topper.

½ quantity Whole Wheat Pizza Dough (page 347)

¼ cup butter

¼ cup flour

½ tsp vegetarian Worcestershire sauce

½ tsp salt

½ tsp pepper

½ tsp dry mustard

⅓ cup milk

⅓ cup beer

1¼ cups grated Cheddar cheese

½ large tomato, sliced

½ tsp paprika

● Preheat oven to 500°F. Bake pizza dough for 5 minutes and remove from oven.

● Melt the butter in a saucepan over medium heat. Add the flour, Worcestershire sauce, salt, pepper, and dry mustard and stir until blended. Add the milk and cook, stirring constantly, until mixture is smooth and thick. Add the beer and stir until mixture is again smooth. Simmer for 3 or 4 minutes. Add the Cheddar cheese until melted and blended in.

● Spread the mixture over the prebaked crust, leaving a ¹/₂-inch edge. Slice the tomato into thin rounds and arrange about 8 slices on top of the pizza. Sprinkle with paprika and bake for 5 minutes.

Sweet and Sour Tofu Pizza

MAKES ONE 12-INCH DOUBLE-CRUST PIZZA

Sweet and sour dishes are popular Chinese fare that go just as easily on pizza crust as they do on rice. This adaptation of the stir-fry favorite is a colorful medley of fruit, vegetables, and tofu in a tangy sauce.

½ quantity Chinese Pizza Dough
(page 348)

FOR THE TOPPING

2 tsp soy sauce

2 tsp sugar

2 tsp white wine vinegar

1 tsp cornstarch

¼ tsp ground ginger

2 tsp ketchup

2 tsp peanut oil

8 oz tofu

1 onion, chopped

1 tomato, chopped

1 cup green bell pepper,
chopped

½ cup canned pineapple, drained
and chopped

Preheat the oven to 500°F.

Combine the soy sauce, sugar, vinegar, cornstarch, ginger, ketchup, and oil in a bowl and stir to mix well. Dice the tofu into small cubes and add to the sauce, stirring gently to coat. Coarsely chop the onions, tomato, and green bell pepper and add them to the tofu. Chop the pineapple into bite-sized pieces and stir into the tofu mixture. Pile onto the pizza dough and bake for 10 minutes.

Bountiful Harvest Pizza

MAKES ONE 12-INCH DOUBLE-CRUST PIZZA

This is a basic vegetarian pizza with a variety of colors and textures. Experiment by adding whichever of your favorite vegetables are in season.

½ quantity Whole Wheat Pizza Dough (page 347)

FOR THE TOPPING

⅔ cup Pizza Sauce (page 353)

1 small onion, chopped

½ green bell pepper, chopped

½ red bell pepper, chopped

½ cup mushrooms, sliced

¾ cup broccoli florets

½ cup shredded mozzarella cheese

½ cup grated Romano cheese

◄ *Bountiful Harvest Pizza*

● Preheat oven to 500°F.

● Spread the pizza sauce onto the pizza dough, within ½ inch of the edge. Spread the chopped onions, green and red bell peppers, sliced mushrooms, and broccoli florets over the sauce. Finish with the mozzarella and then the Romano cheese. Bake for 10 minutes.

Pizza with Portobella Mushrooms

MAKES ONE 12-INCH DOUBLE-CRUST PIZZA

Some vegetarians consider the large portobella mushroom a good substitute for meat. Basted and cooked in a very hot oven, they can taste almost like a steak.

½ quantity Whole Wheat Pizza Dough (page 347)

FOR THE TOPPING

6 garlic cloves, unpeeled

¾ cup Pizza Sauce (page 353)

1 medium onion, chopped

½ cup mozzarella cheese

½ cup Monterey Jack cheese

6 oz portobella mushrooms

3–4 tbsp olive oil

1 tsp parsley flakes

● Preheat oven to 500°F.

● Boil the unpeeled garlic in water for about 20 minutes. When cool enough to touch, squeeze one end and the cooked mushy garlic will pop out.

● Spread the garlic around the pizza dough. Top with the pizza sauce. Sprinkle the chopped onions over the sauce. Spread the mozzarella and then the jack cheese. Slice the mushrooms into ¼-inch thick pieces. Brush liberally with the oil. Arrange on top of the cheese and finally sprinkle on the parsley flakes.

● Bake for 10 minutes.

Pizza with Garden Vegetables

SERVES 4-6

This is a simple pizza from Spain. The combination of bread, vegetables, and olive oil is delicious. Sometimes fresh sardines or slices of local sausage are used as a topping and there are sweet versions for festivals.

1 Spanish onion, finely chopped

6 tbsp extra virgin olive oil

2 small green bell peppers, seeded and chopped

1 large beefsteak tomato, skinned and seeded

salt and ground black pepper

FOR THE DOUGH
(or use 1 package pizza dough)

about ¾ cup milk

2 tbsp fresh yeast or 1½ tsp dried yeast

½ tsp sugar (optional)

2¼ cups bread flour, plus extra for kneading

1 tsp salt

3 tbsp olive oil, plus extra

First make the pizza dough. Warm the milk to blood heat (test with a clean finger). Cream fresh yeast with the sugar and half the milk in a cup and leave in a warm place until bubbling – about 10 minutes. For dried yeast follow the package instructions.

Sift the flour into a food processor (or big bowl) and add the salt. Add the dried yeast, or yeast mixture, and oil to the bowl, and work in enough of the remaining warm milk to make a dough. If using a processor, beat for 3–4 minutes, stopping every minute to break the dough up. Or turn the dough out onto a floured surface and knead, pushing it out with the heel of one hand to a tongue shape, then folding and slapping it into a mound again. Continue kneading until the dough becomes elastic. Shape it into a ball, put into an oiled bowl, cover with a dish towel, and leave in a warm place for 30 minutes.

Preheat the oven to 425°F. Meanwhile soften the onion in ¼ cup of oil.

When the dough has doubled in bulk, put it in the center of an oiled 12-inch pizza plate. Press down with your knuckles to fit the plate, leaving a slight rim round the edge. Oil the edges of the dough and spread the onion over the dough. Distribute the peppers and tomato over the top and season with salt and pepper. Sprinkle another 1 tablespoon of oil over the top. Bake for 25–30 minutes.

Pizza Siciliana

SERVES 2–4

½ quantity Pizza Dough
  (page 346)

⅝ cup tomato sauce

4 tomatoes, skinned and sliced

½ tsp oregano

salt and ground pepper

⅓ cup grated Parmesan cheese

1 can anchovies

½ cup pitted black olives

Preheat oven to 425°F. Shape the dough into a rectangular shape 12 × 8 inches, or use a fluted flan pan or large jelly roll pan.

Paint the dough with a pastry brush dipped in oil and then cover the surface with the tomato sauce.

Place the sliced tomatoes on top and sprinkle with oregano and seasoning.

Sprinkle with Parmesan cheese.

Drain the can of anchovies and arrange the halved fillets in a lattice design. Place an olive in the center of each lattice.

Paint over with the remaining oil and bake in a hot oven for 15 minutes. Turn the heat down to 375°F and bake for 10 minutes more.

Pizza Caponata

Caponata, an eggplant-based mixture, is good served either hot or cold. The flavor seems to improve when it is marinated overnight. You can make it ahead of time and serve it hot, or on a precooked crust as a pizza salad.

½ quantity Pizza Dough
    (page 346)

FOR THE CAPONATA

1 medium eggplant, peeled and
    chopped

6 tbsp olive oil, divided

1 large garlic clove, minced

1 onion, chopped

2 tbsp water

2 celery stalks, diced

¼ cup Pizza Sauce (page 353)
    (or use canned tomato sauce)

2 tbsp capers

2 oz pimiento-stuffed olives,
    drained and halved

2 tsp sugar

1 tbsp red wine vinegar

Preheat the oven to 500°F.

Peel and dice the eggplant and sauté it in 4 tablespoons of the oil for about 5 minutes until slightly browned. Remove from the pan. Heat the remaining oil and sauté the garlic and onion until the onion is limp. Add the diced celery, pizza sauce, and water. Simmer until celery is soft, about 10 minutes. Return the eggplant to the pan. Stir in the capers, olives, sugar, and vinegar. Simmer for another 5 minutes.

Spread the caponata onto the pizza dough. Bake for 10 minutes.

Sesame Tofu Pizza

MAKES ONE 12-INCH DOUBLE-CRUST PIZZA

The sesame-coated tofu squares that top this pizza are crunchy on the outside, tangy and soft on the inside. The canned baby corn, cut into thin rounds, looks like edible flowers.

½ quantity Chinese Pizza Dough (page 348)

FOR THE TOPPING

6 oz tofu

⅓ cup teriyaki sauce

¼ cup whole wheat flour

¼ cup sesame seeds

¼ cup oil

4 oz canned baby corn

4 scallions

Preheat the oven to 500°F.

Drain the tofu and cut into domino-sized pieces (1 × 1½ × ¼ inches). Marinate in the teriyaki sauce for 15 minutes, turning to coat. In a separate bowl, mix the flour and sesame seeds.

When the tofu has marinated, remove with a slotted spoon, saving the marinade for later use. Coat the tofu pieces with the sesame seed mixture. Heat the oil in a pan and then fry the coated tofu until lightly brown, 2 or 3 minutes per side.

Using a slotted spoon, remove the tofu from the pan and place on top of the unbaked pizza crust. Sprinkle with the corn and the chopped scallions. Spoon 3 tablespoons of the marinade over the dough. Bake at 500°F for 10 minutes.

Tofu and Cashew Pizza

MAKES ONE 12-INCH DOUBLE-CRUST PIZZA

Be sure to use fresh grated ginger in this recipe because it adds a distinctive flavor. Cashews are added in the last five minutes of baking to prevent them from burning.

½ quantity Chinese Pizza Dough (page 348)

FOR THE TOPPING

juice of 1 lemon

4 tsp tomato paste

4 tsp honey

3 tbsp soy sauce

3 garlic cloves, minced

1 tbsp grated fresh ginger

10 oz tofu

6 scallions, whites and greens

4 carrots, peeled

4 oz salted cashews

Preheat the oven to 500°F.

In a bowl, squeeze the lemon juice and add the tomato paste, honey, soy sauce, minced garlic, and grated fresh ginger. Slice the tofu into small cubes and add to the sauce, stirring gently to coat. Chop the scallions and slice the carrots into rounds and add them to the tofu mixture. Spread over the pizza dough. Bake for 5 minutes. Then top with the cashews and bake for 5 more minutes taking care not to burn them.

Breakfast Pizza

MAKES ONE 9 × 13-INCH DEEP DISH PIZZA

This filling entrée is like omelet and toast together. Serve with hot coffee and fresh fruit for a delicious brunch for six.

½ quantity Whole Wheat Pizza Dough (page 347)

1½ tsp butter

small onion, diced

½ cup diced mushroom

6 eggs

¼ tsp salt

⅓ cup half and half

¾ cup grated Cheddar cheese

Preheat oven to 500°F.

Spread the dough in a greased pan 9 × 13 × 2 inches. Prick the base in a few places with a toothpick or fork. Bake for 5 minutes.

Melt the butter and sauté the onions for about 3 minutes, until they begin to turn opaque. Add the mushrooms and sauté for 3 minutes more. Remove from the heat.

In a bowl, beat the eggs well, using a fork. Add the salt and half and half and beat again.

Lower the oven temperature to 450°F.

In the bottom of the prebaked crust, spread the Cheddar cheese. Pour the egg mixture over that and bake for 25 minutes.

Breakfast Pizza ▶

Basil and Pine Nut Pizza

MAKES ONE 12-INCH DOUBLE-CRUST PIZZA

Pine nuts, also known as piñon nuts or pignoli, come from the cones of certain pine trees. An ingredient in pesto sauce, they naturally go well with fresh basil. This is another pizza that can be assembled very quickly.

½ quantity Pizza Dough (page 346)

FOR THE TOPPING

handful fresh basil

¼ cup pine nuts

⅔ cup feta cheese, crumbled

Preheat oven to 500°F.

Wash and dry the basil and chop it into bite-sized pieces. Spread the basil over the pizza dough, leaving a ½-inch edge. Spread the pine nuts over the basil. Top with the crumbled feta cheese. Bake for 5–8 minutes.

Neapolitan Pizza

MAKES ONE 12-INCH PIZZA

½ quantity Pizza Dough
(page 346)

1 tbsp olive oil

1 garlic clove, minced

6 tomatoes, peeled and sliced

½ tsp oregano

4 chopped basil leaves

Preheat oven to 450°F. Roll the dough into a round shape, kneading the round out to the large 12-inch size with floured knuckles. Make sure that it is not too thick. Any left-over dough can be allowed to rise and cooked as a bread roll.

◀ *Neapolitan Pizza*

A large flan pan is ideal for this type of pizza or place on a greased baking tray.

Brush the dough with the olive oil and rub the whole surface with the well crushed garlic clove.

Arrange the tomatoes over the surface and sprinkle with herbs. Fresh parsley may be used if basil is unobtainable. Season well.

Place in a hot oven for 20-25 minutes.

This is the basic tomato pizza but most people prefer to add extra ingredients.

Beets in Orange Sauce Pizza

MAKES ONE 12-INCH DOUBLE-CRUST PIZZA

Beets, while not a popular vegetable, are an excellent source of beta carotene. When topped with a sweet orange sauce and piled on a corn bread crust, they become a delicious dish.

1 quantity Corn Bread Pizza
Dough (page 349)

FOR THE SAUCE

1 lb fresh beets, greens removed

2 tbsp cornstarch

1 cup orange juice

6 tbsp sugar

⅛ tsp salt

sprig of mint, to garnish

Preheat the oven to 500°F.

Boil the beets for about 40 minutes until they can be easily pierced with a fork. Allow them to cool before peeling. Thinly slice and arrange on the pizza dough.

In a separate pan, mix the cornstarch, orange juice, sugar, and salt. Bring to a boil, stirring constantly until mixture thickens, about 5 minutes. Pour the sauce over the beets. Bake for 15 minutes. Garnish with a sprig of mint before serving.

Pizza with Caramelized Onions

MAKES ONE 12-INCH DOUBLE-CRUST PIZZA

Caramelized onions are cooked slowly in oil until they are golden brown and very soft. They add a wonderful flavor to this pizza. Make them ahead of time and store them in the refrigerator until ready to use.

½ quantity Whole Wheat Pizza Dough (page 347)

FOR THE TOPPING

2 large onions

3 tbsp olive oil

½ tsp salt

2 tsp red wine vinegar

¾ cup Pizza Sauce (page 353)

¾ cup grated fontina cheese

Preheat the oven to 500°F.

Slice both ends off the onions but do not peel. Cut the onions in quarters. Place them skin side down in a roasting pan. Brush each onion with 1 tablespoon of the oil and sprinkle with salt. Cover the pan with foil and bake for 30 minutes. After 30 minutes, remove the foil and brush the onion with the remaining oil. Sprinkle with the vinegar. Turn the onion quarters on one side and return to the oven for 1 hour. Occasionally turn the onions and baste with the oil from the pan. When cooked, allow to cool or store in the refrigerator for later use.

When ready to assemble the pizza, slice the onion quarters into strips. Spread the pizza sauce over the pizza dough. Spread sliced onion over the top and top with cheese. Bake for 10 minutes.

Chili Pizza

Chili pizza is perfect to serve at a Super Bowl party because it combines two favorite football foods, pizza and chili. You can increase the heat by adding more jalapeños, or by using "Hot Mexican" chili powder.

1 quantity Corn Bread Pizza
    Dough (page 349)

FOR THE CHILI SAUCE

1 tbsp olive oil

1 onion, chopped

¾ cup chopped green peppers

2 large garlic cloves, minced

1 jalapeño pepper, minced

1 lb can peeled tomatoes,
    drained, ¼ cup liquid reserved

1 tbsp chili powder

½ tsp cumin

½ tsp oregano

½ tsp salt

½ tsp curry powder

6 oz tofu

1 cup canned dark red kidney
    beans, drained

⅔ cup grated Cheddar cheese

Preheat the oven to 500°F.

Heat the oil in a pan and sauté the chopped onions, green bell peppers, garlic, and jalapeños until the onions are soft. Drain the tomatoes, reserving the liquid, and chop them into small pieces. Add them to the pan along with ¼ cup of the reserved liquid. Add the spices. Dice the tofu into pieces about 1-inch square. Add to the pan and simmer for about 5 minutes, until most of the liquid is evaporated. Remove from the heat and add the kidney beans.

Spread the chili on the corn bread pizza dough. Top with Cheddar cheese and bake for 15 minutes at 500°F.

Whole Wheat Eggplant and Mozzarella Pizza

MAKES ONE 8-INCH PIZZA

½ quantity Whole Wheat Pizza Dough (page 347)

2 tbsp oil

1 small eggplant, sliced

salt and ground pepper

⅝ cup tomato sauce

1 small red bell pepper, seeded

3 stuffed olives, halved

½ cup sliced mozzarella cheese

Preheat oven to 425°F.

Shape the dough into an 8-in round and rub a little oil over the dough.

Sprinkle the sliced eggplant with salt and let stand for a few minutes. Spread the tomato sauce over the dough. Cut 6 rings of red bell pepper.

Heat the remaining oil in the skillet. Drain the eggplant slices of juice on paper towels and fry for about 30 seconds on each side.

Arrange the eggplant slices on the pizza with a ring of red bell pepper on top and half an olive in the center. Place the slices of mozzarella between the eggplant slices and cook in a hot oven for 15 minutes. Turn the heat down to 375°F for the final 10 minutes.

Whole Wheat Eggplant and Mozzarella Pizza ▶

Quick-Bake Calabrian Pizzas

SERVES 6

These pizzas are full of the zesty flavors of southern Italy – strong, pungent, and exciting. Serve as an appetizer or main dish or as cocktail nibbles, cut into wedges and served warm.

2 cups whole wheat flour

1 tsp salt

1 package active dry yeast

1 tbsp olive oil

¾ cup warm water

6 tsp tapenade

1 onion, sliced finely

12 halves sun-dried tomatoes in oil, chopped

1 tbsp basil leaves, roughly torn

salt and ground black pepper

2 oz can anchovy fillets, chopped

4 oz mozzarella cheese, sliced

Mix together the flour, salt, and yeast in a bowl and make a well in the center. Add the oil and most of the water, then mix to a soft but manageable dough, adding more water if necessary. Knead well until smooth and elastic.

Preheat the oven to 425°F. Divide the dough into 6 parts and roll out into circles 6 inches in diameter. Fold the edges of the dough over to form a lip, then place the bases on lightly greased baking sheets. Cover and leave in a warm place for 20–25 minutes, until the dough rises.

Spread each pizza base with 1 teaspoon of tapenade, then arrange the onion over the bases and scatter with the chopped sun-dried tomatoes. Add the torn basil leaves with plenty of salt and pepper, then scatter the chopped anchovies over the pizzas. Arrange the mozzarella slices over the pizzas then spoon the oil from the anchovies over the cheese.

Bake the pizzas in the preheated oven for 15 minutes, until the bases are crisp and the cheese has melted. Serve immediately.

Fennel Mornay Pizza

MAKES ONE 12-INCH DOUBLE-CRUST PIZZA

Fennel has been used for years in Italian cooking, but only recently has it become available in supermarkets in the U.S. This anise-flavored bulb blends smoothly with a mornay sauce made from Gruyère cheese.

½ quantity Whole Wheat Pizza Dough (page 347)

FOR THE TOPPING

1 fennel bulb

6 carrots

3 tbsp butter

3 tbsp flour

¾ cup liquid from vegetables

⅓ cup half and half

3 oz Gruyère cheese, chopped

⅓ cup Parmesan cheese

¼ tsp salt

¼ tsp white pepper

2 tsp dried thyme

◀ *Fennel Mornay Pizza*

Preheat oven to 500°F.

Cut and discard the fennel tops and coarsely chop the bulb and stalk. Peel the carrots. Put the fennel and carrots in a pot and cover them with water. Boil the vegetables until tender, 10–15 minutes. Drain the vegetables, reserving ¾ cup of the liquid. Allow to cool and chop into small pieces.

To make the sauce, melt the butter in a saucepan over low heat. Add the flour and stir until smooth. Add the reserved liquid from the vegetables and turn up the heat to high. Bring to a boil and add the half and half, stirring frequently to blend. Cook for several minutes until thickened. Add the Gruyère and Parmesan and stir while the cheeses melt. Stir in the salt and pepper.

To assemble the pizza, spread the fennel and carrot mixture over the pizza dough. Pour the sauce over the vegetables and sprinkle with the dried thyme. Bake at 500°F for 10 minutes.

Pizza Verde

MAKES ONE 12-INCH DOUBLE-CRUST PIZZA

The tomatillo is a familiar ingredient in Southwestern cuisine and is the basis for green sauces. Its name means "little tomato" in Spanish, and it looks like a small green tomato in a brown, papery husk. Although tomatillos aren't actually tomatoes, they have a similar taste to green tomatoes, which can be substituted in this recipe.

½ quantity Whole Wheat Cheese Pizza Dough (see page 349)

FOR THE TOPPING

1½ lb fresh tomatillos

¼ cup vegetable oil

2 large garlic cloves, minced

2 tsp cumin

1 small dried red pepper, crushed

1 onion, chopped

¼ tsp sugar

⅛ tsp ground cloves

3 Roma tomatoes, thinly sliced

¾ cup grated white Cheddar cheese

Preheat oven to 500°F.

Soak the tomatillos in warm water for about 10 minutes until husks are softened. Remove husks and rinse the tomatillos clean under cool water. Cut them in slices about ⅛–¼ inch thick.

In a pan, heat the oil over medium heat. Add the garlic, cumin, and red pepper and stir until well mixed and aromatic, about 3 minutes. Add the onions and sauté until limp, about 5 minutes. Add the tomatillos, sugar, and cloves and cook over low heat for about 20 minutes. The tomatillos should be limp, but still retain their shape.

To assemble the pizza, spread the sauce over the pizza dough. Place the tomatoes on top of the sauce. Top with the white Cheddar cheese. Bake for 10 minutes.

Sun-dried Tomatoes and Mozzarella Pizza

MAKES ONE 12-INCH DOUBLE-CRUST PIZZA

This pizza is simple to make, yet elegant enough for a party. For best results, allow the tomatoes to marinate overnight in the refrigerator.

½ quantity Pizza Dough
   (page 346)

FOR THE TOPPING

3 oz sun-dried tomatoes

3 tbsp extra virgin olive oil

4 cloves garlic, crushed

4 oz round mozzarella cheese,
   sliced

½ tsp dried basil

● Chop the sun-dried tomatoes into bite-sized pieces. Then put the tomatoes, olive oil, and garlic in a container and marinate at room temperature for 30 minutes or overnight in the refrigerator. Slice the mozzarella into thin rounds.

● Preheat the oven to 500°F. Bake the dough for 5 minutes and remove from oven.

● To assemble the pizza, place the mozzarella rounds on the prebaked crust, leaving room between each slice. Spread the sun-dried tomato mixture over the cheese, pouring the olive oil on as well. Sprinkle with dried basil. Bake for 4–5 minutes or until the tomatoes begin to brown.

Sun-dried Tomatoes and Mozzarella Pizza ▶

Eggplant Parmesan Pizza

MAKES ONE 12-INCH DOUBLE-CRUST PIZZA

Eggplant is a wonderfully versatile vegetable, worth growing in a backyard garden. Soaking the sliced eggplant in salted water before cooking eliminates any bitterness.

½ quantity Whole Wheat Pizza
   Dough (page 347)

1 medium eggplant

1 tbsp salt

¾ cup Pizza Sauce (page 353)

3 oz mozzarella cheese, sliced

1 tbsp olive oil

¼ cup grated Parmesan cheese

2 tsp parsley

● Preheat oven to 500°F. Bake the crust for 5 minutes and remove from oven.

● Peel the eggplant and slice into thin rounds for quick cooking. Place the eggplant in a bowl of water with the salt and soak for 20 minutes. You may need to weight the eggplant down with a glass jar. After soaking, rinse thoroughly and squeeze it between paper towels to remove moisture.

● To assemble pizza, spread the pizza sauce on the prebaked crust, to within ½ inch of the edge. Next, arrange the mozzarella slices over the sauce. Top them with eggplant slices. Sprinkle the olive oil over the eggplant. Spread the Parmesan cheese over the eggplant and finally sprinkle on the parsley. Bake for 10 minutes.

Kung Pao Pizza

*I*f you like hot and spicy Chinese food, this pizza should satisfy you. This vegetarian version of a very hot dish eliminates only the meat, not the heat.

½ quantity Chinese Pizza Dough (page 348)

2 cups broccoli florets

2 cups cauliflower florets

2 scallions, chopped

1 small tomato, chopped

¼ cup peanuts

2 tsp sugar

2 tsp cider vinegar

2 tsp cornstarch

2 tbsp soy sauce

½ tsp crushed dried hot red pepper

6 dried whole hot red peppers

1 tbsp peanut oil

Preheat oven to 500°F. Bake crust for 5 minutes and remove from oven.

Cut the broccoli and cauliflower into small florets, discarding stalks, and place in a bowl. Add the chopped scallions, chopped tomato, and peanuts.

In a separate container, add the sugar, vinegar, cornstarch, soy sauce, and crushed red pepper and stir to mix thoroughly. Pour the liquid over the vegetables, coating well. Marinate for about 5 minutes.

To assemble the pizza, spread the marinated vegetables over the crust, adding any of the liquid not absorbed. Attractively arrange the whole red peppers on top. Sprinkle the pizza with peanut oil and bake for 5 minutes.

Tofu in Peanut Sauce Pizza

MAKES ONE 12-INCH DOUBLE-CRUST PIZZA

Peanut butter and coconut milk combine to make a delicious peanut sauce from Thailand in this pizza variation. Chow mein noodles, added right before serving, add crunch to the cooked vegetables and tofu.

½ quantity Chinese Pizza Dough
  (page 348)

FOR THE TOPPING

⅓ cup unsweetened coconut
  milk

¼ cup smooth peanut butter

2 tsp sugar

1 tsp grated fresh ginger

2 garlic cloves, minced

2 cups spinach, shredded

2 tsp peanut oil

½ cup alfalfa sprouts

4 scallions, chopped

4 oz firm-style tofu

⅔ cup chow mein noodles, to
  garnish

● Preheat the oven to 500°F.

● In a small pan, heat the coconut milk, peanut butter, sugar (omit sugar if using sweetened coconut milk), grated ginger, and garlic until blended. Allow to simmer, stirring frequently, while assembling the vegetables.

● Wash and tear the spinach into small pieces. Pour the oil over the spinach and toss. Add the alfalfa sprouts and chopped scallions. Add the tofu, sliced into ½-inch squares. Toss gently to mix.

● Spread the tofu and vegetables over the pizza dough. Top with the sauce. Spread it over the tofu mixture with the back of a spoon. Bake for 10 minutes.

● Remove from the oven when done. Plunge the chow mein noodles into boiling water, about 3 minutes, and drain. Arrange on top of the pizza. Serve immediately.

Deep Dish Mozzarella and Salami Pizza

MAKES TWO 8-INCH PIZZAS

½ quantity Pizza Dough
(page 348)

1½ cups canned tomatoes,
drained

2 tsp oil

12 slices Italian salami

2 tbsp grated Parmesan cheese

1 tsp oregano

12 thin slices mozzarella cheese

salt and ground pepper

½ cup pitted black olives

🫒 Preheat oven to 425°F. Shape the dough into two 8-inch rounds. Either place on a baking sheet or into two cake pans.

🫒 Mash down the tomatoes and add a little of the drained juice.

🫒 Brush the dough with oil and arrange the tomatoes on the bottom.

🫒 Roll the salami into rounds. Sprinkle a little Parmesan cheese on the tomato and then the oregano. Arrange the salami rolls on the pizza.

🫒 Place the slices of mozzarella cheese alternately with salami. Season well.

🫒 Sprinkle with the remaining Parmesan and sprinkle the black olives over the pizza.

🫒 Brush with oil and cook in a hot oven for 20 minutes. Reduce the heat to 375°F for a further 5–10 minutes.

Deep Dish Mozzarella and Salami Pizza ▶

Cheese and Artichoke Pizza

MAKES ONE 12-INCH DOUBLE-CRUST PIZZA

Artichoke hearts bottled in olive oil are already marinated. There is little the cook has to do but assemble the ingredients and bake them to produce a perfectly seasoned pizza.

½ quantity Whole Wheat Pizza
Dough (page 347)

FOR THE TOPPING

10-oz bottle artichoke hearts

⅔ cup shredded mozzarella
cheese

⅔ cup grated fresh Romano
cheese

2 garlic cloves, minced

2 oz jar sliced pimientos, drained

🫒 Preheat oven to 500°F.

🫒 Drain the artichoke hearts, reserving the liquid. Finely chop the artichoke and place in a bowl. Add both cheeses, garlic, and drained pimientos. Measure ¼ cup of the reserved liquid from the artichoke hearts and add it to the bowl. Stir to mix.

🫒 Top the pizza dough with the artichoke and cheese mixture and bake for 10 minutes, until the cheese is melted.

Deep Dish Ratatouille Pizza

MAKES ONE 9 × 13-INCH DEEP-DISH PIZZA

Ratatouille is a casserole made with eggplant and zucchini. In this recipe, it is used as a pizza topping. Most of the ingredients, including the fresh basil, can be grown in a backyard garden.

½ quantity Whole Wheat Pizza Dough (page 347)

FOR THE RATATOUILLE

1 small eggplant, chopped

1 tbsp plus ½ tsp salt

1 small green bell pepper

1 small onion, chopped

1 medium zucchini

1 large tomato

2 garlic cloves, minced

¼ cup fresh basil leaves

¼ tsp pepper

¼ cup olive oil

Preheat oven to 500°F.

Peel the eggplant. Slice into ½-inch thick rounds. Soak in a bowl of water and 1 tablespoon salt for 20 minutes. Then rinse well and press between paper towels to dry. Dice the eggplant into pieces about ½-inch square. Dice the green bell pepper and onion. Slice the zucchini into rounds, and then cut each round into quarters. Coarsely chop the tomato.

Put the chopped and diced vegetables in a bowl and stir in the minced garlic. Add the fresh basil chopped or torn into small pieces. Then add ½ teaspoon salt, pepper, and olive oil. Stir gently to mix.

Place the dough in the center of a lightly oiled 13 × 9 × 2-inch pan. Using your fingers, gently spread the dough until it covers the bottom of the pan evenly and goes halfway up the sides.

Empty the contents of the bowl onto the dough and spread evenly over the bottom. Bake for 20 minutes.

Curried Tofu Pizza

MAKES ONE 12-INCH DOUBLE-CRUST PIZZA

Curry sauce is always spicy, but can be either hot or mild. This version uses mild curry powder, but use a hotter variety if you prefer it.

½ quantity Pizza Dough
(page 346)

¼ cup butter

2 onions, chopped

4 tsp turmeric

4 tsp curry powder

½ tsp cloves

1 tsp white pepper

2 tsp salt

2 tsp dried mint

2 tbsp crystallized ginger, finely
chopped

juice of 2 limes

¼ cup coconut milk (preferably
unsweetened)

12 oz tofu, diced

4 tbsp raisins

Preheat the oven to 500°F. Bake the pizza dough for 5 minutes.

Melt the butter in a pan and sauté the onions until soft, about 5 minutes. Remove from the heat and add the spices, salt, mint, finely chopped ginger, lime juice, and coconut milk. Return to the heat and simmer for about 5 minutes, stirring until mixture is blended and slightly thick. Remove from the heat and add the tofu and raisins, stirring gently to coat the tofu completely.

Spread the curried tofu mixture on the prebaked crust, to within ¹/₂-inch of the edge. Bake for 5 minutes.

Tofu and Vegetable Pizza

MAKES ONE 12-INCH DOUBLE-CRUST PIZZA

*T*ofu with vegetables is a popular vegetarian combination in Vietnamese cooking and makes a satisfying meal on a pizza crust.

½ quantity Garlic Dill Pizza Dough (page 348)

¼ cup soy sauce

3½ tbsp rice wine vinegar

2 garlic cloves, minced

¼ tsp cumin

1 tsp fresh grated ginger

2 tsp peanut oil

6 oz tofu

2 broccoli florets

2 carrots, peeled and sliced

½ cup water chestnuts, sliced

Preheat the oven to 500°F. Bake the pizza dough for 5 minutes.

Mix the soy sauce, vinegar, minced garlic, cumin, fresh ginger, and peanut oil together. Dice the tofu into ½-inch squares and place in a bowl. Pour the soy sauce mixture over the tofu, stirring to coat.

Add the broccoli florets, sliced carrots, and sliced chestnuts to the tofu mixture, stirring to coat. Spread the mixture over the crust and bake for 5 minutes.

Deep Dish Ham and Mushroom Pizza

MAKES TWO 8-INCH PIZZAS

½ quantity Pizza Dough
(page 346)

1 tbsp oil

1¼ cups béchamel sauce

2 cups mushrooms, washed and
sliced

1½ cups canned tomatoes,
drained

salt and ground pepper

½ tsp oregano

6 slices of cooked ham

1 cup mozzarella cheese, thinly
sliced

Preheat oven to 425°F. Shape the risen dough into two 8-inch pizza bases.

Brush over the dough with oil and divide the béchamel sauce between the two bases.

Arrange half the sliced mushrooms on the béchamel sauce.

Chop the canned tomatoes and divide between the two bases. Season well and sprinkle with oregano.

Cut the slices of ham in two and roll them up, placing 6 rolls on each pizza, alternating with thin slices of mozzarella cheese. Garnish with sliced mushrooms.

Bake in a hot oven for 15 minutes and then reduce the heat to 375°F for a further 10 minutes.

Family Pizza

½ quantity Pizza Dough
(page 346)

olive oil for brushing

1 green bell pepper, diced

1 tsp oregano

¾ cup grated Cheddar cheese

3 pork sausages

Preheat oven to 425°F. Shape the dough into a rectangular shape 12 × 8 inches, or use a fluted flan pan.

Paint the dough with a pastry brush dipped in oil.

Blanch the green bell pepper for 2 minutes, then drain. Scatter the dough with the pepper and oregano, then add the cheese. Slice the sausages diagonally and arrange over the pizza.

Bake in a hot oven for 15 minutes. Turn the heat down to 375°F and bake for 10 minutes more.

Pizza with Roasted Peppers

Roasting peppers enhances their flavor, and once you've tried them on pizza, they'll become a favorite. Because they are also good in salads and on sandwiches, roast more than you need and store any extra covered with olive oil in glass jars.

½ quantity Garlic Dill Pizza Dough (page 348)

FOR THE TOPPING

1 red bell pepper

1 green bell pepper

1 yellow bell pepper

¾ cup Pizza Sauce (page 353)

¾ cup fontina cheese, grated

Preheat the oven to 500°F.

Cut the tops off the bell peppers and remove the seeds. Cut the bell peppers in half and then squash them so that they lie relatively flat. Place the bell peppers, skin side up, in a broiler pan and broil for about 8 minutes until blackened. Using tongs, place the peppers in a plastic bag. Seal and allow to cool. Once cooled, the skin will peel right off. Discard the skins. Slice the roasted peppers in long strips.

Spread the pizza sauce on the pizza dough. Then decorate it with the pepper strips, alternating colors. There may be extra bell pepper strips, but cover them in olive oil, store in the refrigerator, and they'll keep for several days (use them on other pizzas or in salads). Lightly cover the peppers with the cheese. The cheese should not be so thick that the colorful peppers are covered.

Bake for 10 minutes.

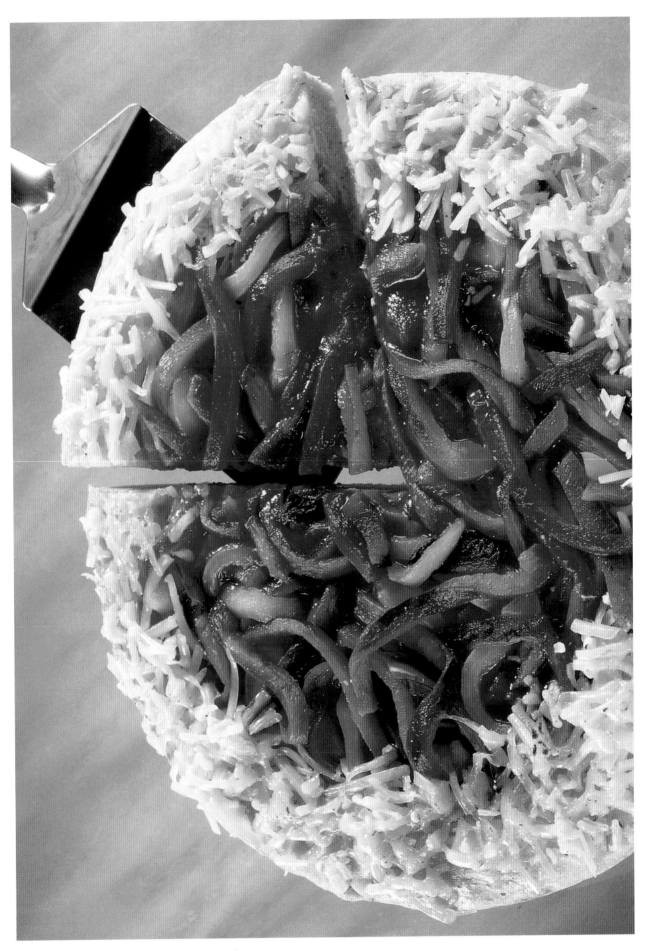

Pizza Monte Carlo

MAKES ONE 12-INCH DOUBLE-CRUST PIZZA

This pizza is named after Monte Carlo because of its class, not its richness. Asparagus is one of the tastiest vegetables to eat fresh. If it is not in season, however, you can substitute a 9-ounce package of frozen asparagus pieces. Thaw to room temperature before rolling in the cheese.

½ quantity Whole Wheat Pizza Dough (page 347)

FOR THE TOPPING

1 tbsp olive oil

2½ cups chopped mushrooms

2 oz jar diced pimientos, drained

1 lb fresh asparagus

⅓ cup grated Romano cheese

juice of ½ lemon

Preheat oven to 500°F.

Heat the oil in a pan and sauté the mushrooms for about 5 minutes until limp. Remove from the heat and stir in the drained pimientos.

Snap off the tough ends of the asparagus and steam until crisp-tender. Chop into 2-inch pieces and roll them in the Romano cheese.

To assemble the pizza, spread the mushroom mixture over the pizza dough. Top with the asparagus and cheese. Squeeze the lemon juice over the pizza. Bake for 10 minutes.

Deep Dish Mushroom and Prosciutto Pizza

½ quantity Whole Wheat Pizza Dough (page 347)

1 tbsp oil

1½ cups canned tomatoes, drained

4 tomatoes, skinned and peeled

1 tsp oregano

salt and ground pepper

2 tbsp Parmesan cheese

1 tbsp butter

6 cups sliced mushrooms

8 slices prosciutto

Preheat oven to 425°F. Shape the dough as for deep dish pizza (see page 386).

Paint the shaped dough with a pastry brush dipped in oil.

Arrange the tomatoes on the bases of the pizza dough. Sprinkle with oregano, salt, and pepper.

Sprinkle half the cheese over the tomato mixture.

Melt the butter and the remaining oil in a skillet and allow the mushrooms to cook over a low heat for about 4 minutes.

Spread the mushrooms on top of the pizzas and arrange the ham on top. Sprinkle with the remaining cheese.

Cook in a hot oven for 15 minutes, before turning the oven down to 375°F for the last 10 minutes.

Blue Cheese and Broccoli Pizza

MAKES ONE 12-INCH DOUBLE-CRUST PIZZA

When creamy blue cheese melts on the top of this pizza, it turns ordinary broccoli into a treat. The pecans add to the delight.

½ quantity Garlic Dill Pizza Dough (page 348)

FOR THE TOPPING

1 small head of broccoli, separated into florets

1 small white onion, thinly sliced

1 tbsp olive oil

⅓ cup pecans, chopped

4 oz blue cheese, crumbled

● Preheat oven to 500°F.

● Remove the stem from the broccoli; separate the head into small florets. You need about 2 cups. To assemble the pizza, first lay the thinly sliced onion over the pizza dough. Then add the broccoli. Sprinkle the olive oil over the vegetables. Add the pecans and top with the crumbled blue cheese.

● Bake in the lower half of the oven for about 6 minutes.

Split Pea Pizza

MAKES ONE 12-INCH DOUBLE-CRUST PIZZA

This pizza makes a hearty dinner on a cold winter night. A tossed salad and a cold beer completes the meal.

1 quantity Corn Bread Pizza Dough (page 349)

½ cup dried split peas

2¼ cups water, divided

¼ cup vegetable oil

¼ cup whole wheat flour

½ tsp salt

¼ tsp nutmeg

¼ tsp dry mustard

½ tsp vegetarian Worcestershire sauce

1 tbsp tomato paste

1 cup sharp Cheddar cheese, grated

2 oz jar chopped pimientos, drained

Preheat oven to 500°F. Bake the pizza dough for 5 minutes and remove from the oven.

Rinse the dried peas in cold water. Put them in a pan with 1 cup of water and bring to a boil. Reduce to low and simmer for about 20 minutes until peas are soft but not mushy. Liquid should be absorbed, but drain the peas if necessary.

In a separate pan, heat the oil and add the flour, stirring to make a roux. Slowly add the remaining 1¼ cups water and stir, mixing well. Add the salt, nutmeg, mustard, Worcestershire sauce, and tomato paste. Simmer for 5 minutes, stirring frequently. Sauce should be fairly thick. Add the cheese, stirring until it melts. Stir in the drained peas and remove from heat.

Top the prebaked crust with the peas, leaving ½-inch around the edge. Dot the split peas with the drained pimientos. Bake for 10 minutes.

Pizza Romano

Polenta, an Italian version of corn meal, was used for a topping for pizza in hard times when other ingredients weren't available. But even in good times this one is worth eating. The cheese, corn meal, and sauce make a tasty and hearty meal.

½ quantity Pizza Dough
   (page 346)

FOR THE TOPPING

½ cup corn meal

¼ tsp salt

1½ cups cold water

1 egg

½ cup Parmesan cheese, grated

⅔ cup Pizza Sauce (page 353)

● Preheat oven to 500°F.

● Put the corn meal and salt in a pan. Add the cold water a little at a time, whisking it in to remove all lumps. Place over moderate heat and continue whisking until corn meal thickens. When it gets too thick to whisk, switch to a wooden spoon. Continue stirring for about 5 minutes after the corn meal thickens. Remove from the stove. Beat the egg with ¼ cup of Parmesan cheese. Stir into the corn meal mixture.

● To assemble the pizza, spread the pizza sauce over the pizza dough. Spread the corn meal mixture on top of the sauce, using the back of a spoon to mash it down. Top with the remaining Parmesan. Bake at 500°F for 10 minutes.

Pizza with Tomato and Three Cheeses

The mellow creaminess of fontina and mozzarella combines with the sharpness of Parmesan for a rich cheese pizza. Use a garlic dill crust to add even more flavor.

½ quantity Garlic Dill Pizza
   Dough (page 348)

FOR THE TOPPING

⅔ cup Pizza Sauce (page 353)

½ cup grated mozzarella cheese

½ cup grated fontina cheese

¼ cup grated Parmesan cheese

● Preheat oven to 500°F.

● Spread the pizza sauce onto the pizza dough, leaving a ½-inch edge. Spread the mozzarella, the fontina, and then the Parmesan cheese over the sauce. Bake for 10 minutes.

Pizza Paella

MAKES ONE 12-INCH DOUBLE-CRUST PIZZA

In this vegetarian version of classic Spanish paella, leeks replace the fish and meat. But the traditional flavoring of saffron, garlic, and onions is retained.

½ quantity Pizza Dough (page 346)

1½ onions, chopped

2 leeks, chopped

2 tbsp olive oil

2 large garlic cloves, minced

1 tbsp lemon zest, cut in strips

large pinch of saffron

½ tsp salt

½ tsp cayenne pepper

½ cup frozen peas, thawed

2–3 Roma tomatoes, chopped

2¼ oz jar sliced black olives, drained

Preheat oven to 500°F.

Coarsely chop the onions. Chop the leeks into 1-inch pieces and clean thoroughly to remove dirt. Heat the oil in a pan over medium heat and add the onions, leeks, garlic, lemon zest, saffron, salt, and cayenne pepper. Sauté for 5 minutes or so, stirring frequently, until onions and leeks are wilted.

Remove from the heat and stir in the peas and tomatoes. Spread the mixture on the pizza dough. Top with the drained olives. Bake for 10 minutes.

Barbecued Pizza

MAKES ONE 12-INCH DOUBLE-CRUST PIZZA

Pizza can go on a picnic as easily as any other cook-out meal. Use a prebaked crust, or make your own stove-top, no-yeast crust, in a cast iron pan on top of a campfire. The smoky flavor you get when cooking outdoors enhances the flavor of the vegetables.

½ quantity Whole Wheat Pizza Dough (page 347)

wooden skewers

½ tsp brown sugar

½ tsp molasses

½ tsp vegetarian Worcestershire sauce

¾ cup Pizza Sauce (page 353)

½ cup large mushrooms

½ medium red bell pepper

½ medium green bell pepper

¼ cup grated Romano cheese

¼ cup scallions, chopped

¾ cup mozzarella cheese, grated

If you are making the pizza crust, preheat oven to 500°F and bake the pizza dough for 25–30 minutes then remove from the oven.

Soak the wooden skewers in water to make them burn resistant.

To make the sauce, stir the brown sugar, molasses, and Worcestershire sauce into the pizza sauce.

Light the barbecue grill and allow the coals to get white hot. When the coals are ready, push them to the edge of the grill, leaving a clear 12-inch circle in the center.

Cut the mushrooms in half and chop both bell peppers into pieces approximately 1 inch square. Run the skewers through them, leaving a little space between each to speed up cooking. Place the skewered vegetables in the center of the grill, cover, and barbecue 5–7 minutes, turning once. Remove from the grill and set aside.

Place the pizza crust in the center of the grill. Cover and barbecue for 5 minutes. Turn the crust over. Quickly sprinkle the Romano over the crust. On top of that pour the pizza sauce. Then arrange the barbecued vegetables over the sauce. Top with the scallions and, finally, with the mozzarella. Cover and barbecue 5–7 minutes or until cheese is melted.

Taco Pizza

MAKES ONE 12-INCH DOUBLE-CRUST PIZZA

*M*exican food has long been a favorite, and its ingredients go well on top of a pizza. In this vegetarian version, bean dip replaces the traditional ground beef.

1 quantity Corn Bread Pizza Dough (page 349)

1¼ cups sour cream

¼ cup mayonnaise

2 tbsp chili powder

¼ tsp cumin

½ tsp garlic powder

¼ tsp onion powder

¼ tsp salt

4–5 Roma tomatoes, chopped

8–10 scallions, chopped

10 oz can bean dip

¾ cup grated Cheddar cheese

Preheat oven to 500°F. Cook the pizza dough for 5 minutes and remove from the oven. Prepare the topping.

In a bowl, combine the sour cream, mayonnaise, spices, and salt. Mix thoroughly and set aside. Chop the tomatoes and scallions and set aside.

To top, first spread the bean dip over the dough using a rubber spatula. Next spread the sour cream mixture. Then spread the tomatoes and onions over the sour cream. Top with Cheddar cheese. Bake for 10 minutes.

Swiss Green Bean Pizza

MAKES ONE 12-INCH DOUBLE-CRUST PIZZA

Try this pizza when green beans are in season, especially if they come from your own garden. It turns an ordinary vegetable into a treat.

½ quantity Whole Wheat Pizza Dough (page 347)

FOR THE TOPPING

1 lb fresh green beans

2 tbsp olive oil

½ cup sliced almonds

1 cup grated Swiss cheese

Preheat the oven to 500°F.

Wash and snap off the ends of the green beans. Steam them for 5–7 minutes, until crisp-tender. Then arrange the beans on the pizza dough. Sprinkle the olive oil over the beans. Next, sprinkle on the sliced almonds and top with the Swiss cheese. Bake for 10 minutes.

Swiss Green Bean Pizza ▶

Sesame Vegetable Pizza

MAKES ONE 12-INCH DOUBLE-CRUST PIZZA

½ quantity Garlic Dill Pizza Dough (page 348)

FOR THE TOPPING

½ medium cucumber, seeded

2 carrots, chopped

¼ head cauliflower

1 tbsp olive oil

1 tbsp soy sauce

2 tsp sesame seeds

Preheat oven to 500°F.

Cut the peeled cucumber in half lengthwise and scoop out the seeds. Thinly slice across into semicircles. Peel and slice the carrots into thin circles. Separate the cauliflower into small florets.

To assemble arrange the cucumber over the pizza dough. Add the carrots and then the cauliflower. Sprinkle the olive oil and then the soy sauce over the vegetables. Finish with the sesame seeds.

Bake for about 10 minutes.

Beef Pizza Pie

SERVES 8

$\mathscr{F}$illed with spicy beef and peppers, this double pizza has an interesting twist.

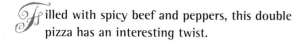

2 tbsp olive oil	1 oz all-purpose flour
2 onions, chopped	2 tbsp tomato paste
1 garlic clove, minced	⅔ cup beef broth
12 oz ground beef	2 tbsp dark soy sauce
1 small red bell pepper, chopped	14 oz can chopped tomatoes
1 small green bell pepper, chopped	1 tbsp chopped fresh oregano
1 tsp chili powder	10 oz package pizza dough mix
	1 egg, beaten

Heat the oil and fry the onions 3–4 minutes. Add the garlic and beef and fry 5 minutes, stirring. Add the bell peppers and chili powder and cook 3–4 minutes.

Add the flour, mix well, and cook 1 minute. Stir in the tomato paste, broth, soy sauce, tomatoes, and oregano. Bring to a boil, reduce the heat, and simmer for 30 minutes. Leave to cool slightly.

Heat the oven to 425°F. Make up the pizza dough according to package instructions; knead until smooth. Roll out two thirds of the dough on a lightly floured surface and line a greased 2-inch deep loose-based pan. Let the dough overhang the pan edge slightly.

Spoon the beef filling into the dough-lined pan. Roll out remaining dough in a circle large enough to cover the top of the pan. Brush edges with water and place on top, sealing with the overhanging dough by rolling the edge over. Brush with egg. Cook until golden, 30 minutes. Leave to cool. Remove and serve.

Hi-speed Pizzas

MAKES 4 SMALL PIZZAS

2¼ cups flour

½ tsp salt

1 tsp baking powder

4 tbsp olive oil

water to mix

1 cup tomato sauce

1 tsp fresh marjoram or ½ tsp dried oregano

⅓ cup black olives

1½ cups thinly sliced Cheddar cheese

1 garlic clove, finely chopped

VARIATION

You can add chopped ham, crisp bacon, strips of salami, sliced button mushrooms, or sliced red bell pepper.

Preheat oven to 450°F. Sift together the flour, salt, and baking powder, and add the oil and enough water to make a very sticky dough.

Divide into four and press each piece into a well-oiled 6-inch round pizza or pie pan.

Top each with the tomato sauce, marjoram or oregano, olives, and cheese, and sprinkle with the garlic.

Bake for 15 to 20 minutes until the dough is cooked and the cheese is browned and bubbling.

Jambalaya Pizza

MAKES ONE 12-INCH DOUBLE-CRUST PIZZA

*T*his spicy Cajun pizza makes use of the delicious meatless sausages now on the market.

1 quantity Corn Bread Pizza Dough (page 349)

FOR THE TOPPING

1 tbsp olive oil

2 garlic cloves, minced

2 medium onions, chopped

4 × 4 oz meatless sausage patties

½ red bell pepper, chopped

½ green bell pepper, chopped

½ tsp oregano

¼ tsp white pepper

½ tsp salt

½ tsp cayenne pepper

½ tsp thyme

14½ oz can tomatoes, drained, liquid reserved

¼ cup grated Cheddar cheese

Preheat oven to 500°F.

Heat the oil in a pan and add the minced garlic and chopped onion. Sauté a few minutes until the onions begin to turn opaque. Then crumble the sausages into the pan. Add the red and green bell peppers and the oregano, thyme, peppers, and salt, and sauté for 5 minutes over high heat, stirring constantly. Drain the tomatoes and reserve ½ cup of the liquid. Chop the tomatoes and add them to the pan along with ½ cup of juice. Simmer, stirring occasionally, until most of the liquid is absorbed (about 5 minutes).

To assemble the pizza, spread the jambalaya mixture over the pizza dough. Sprinkle the cheese lightly over the top. Bake for 15 minutes. Serve immediately.

Deep Dish Artichoke Heart and Bacon Pizza

MAKES TWO 8-INCH PIZZAS

½ quantity Pizza Dough (page 346)

1 tbsp olive oil

1¼ cups tomato sauce

1 can artichoke hearts

12 slices bacon

1 tbsp Parmesan cheese

1 tbsp chopped fresh basil or parsley

Preheat oven to 425°F. Shape the risen dough into flan rings or cake pans.

Brush over the dough with the oil and divide the tomato sauce between the two bases.

Drain the artichoke hearts.

Roll up the slices of bacon and cook under the broiler or in the oven for a few minutes.

Sprinkle the pizzas with Parmesan cheese and herbs.

Arrange the artichoke hearts alternately with the bacon rolls. Brush over with the remaining oil.

Cook in a hot oven for 15–20 minutes before reducing the heat to 375°F for a further 5 minutes.

Herbed Brussels Sprouts and Carrot Pizza

This colorful pizza combines Brussels sprouts and carrots. Serve it as an appetizer, a side dish, or as part of a buffet.

½ quantity Pizza Dough (page 346)	juice of 1 lemon
	2 tbsp olive oil
7–8 oz Brussels sprouts	1 tsp dried tarragon
4 oz baby carrots, peeled	¼ tsp ground nutmeg

Preheat the oven to 500°F. Bake the pizza dough for 3 minutes.

Rinse the Brussels sprouts, remove the stems and cut in half lengthwise. Slice any baby carrots that are larger than about ¼-inch in diameter in half lengthwise. Steam vegetables for 4 minutes.

In a separate bowl, whisk together the lemon juice, olive oil, tarragon, and nutmeg.

Arrange the Brussels spouts and carrots alternately on the prebaked crust in a colorful pattern. Pour the lemon juice mixture over the vegetables. Bake for 7–8 minutes.

Reuben Pizza

You don't miss the corned beef at all in this vegetarian-pizza version of a Reuben sandwich. A little chili powder gives it color and spice.

½ quantity Pizza Dough
(page 346)

FOR THE TOPPING

1 cup mayonnaise

¼ cup chili sauce

8 oz can sauerkraut

½ tsp caraway seeds (optional)

1 small onion

1¼ cups grated Swiss cheese

½ tsp mild chili powder

Preheat oven to 500°F.

In a bowl, mix mayonnaise and chili sauce together. Spread the mixture over the pizza dough, within ½ inch of the edge. Drain the sauerkraut and squeeze to eliminate as much moisture as possible. Spread the sauerkraut over the sauce. If using caraway seeds, spread them over the sauerkraut. Slice the onion and separate into rings. Place the rings on the sauerkraut. Top with the grated Swiss cheese. Sprinkle the mild chili powder over the pizza. Bake for 10 minutes.

Reuben Pizza ▶

Pizza Stroganoff

Meatless stroganoff made with mushrooms, broccoli, and onions is a hearty topping for a pizza. Sour cream and Monterey Jack make a rich sauce, and sunflower seeds add a little crunch.

½ quantity Whole Wheat Pizza
Dough (page 347)

1 tbsp butter

1½ onions, chopped

2 cups chopped mushrooms

1 tsp basil

1 tsp salt

juice of 1 lemon

1 cup sour cream

1 cup shredded Monterey Jack
cheese

3 cups broccoli florets

2 tbsp sunflower seeds

Preheat the oven to 500°F.

Melt the butter in a pan and sauté the chopped onions, mushrooms, basil, and salt over medium heat until vegetables are soft. Remove from the heat and add the lemon juice, sour cream, and cheese. Stir to blend.

Wash and drain the broccoli. To assemble the pizza, spread the broccoli over the pizza dough. Sprinkle the sunflower seeds over the broccoli. Top with the sour cream mixture. Bake for 10 minutes.

Pizza Primavera

MAKES ONE 12-INCH DOUBLE-CRUST PIZZA

Although this pizza has a rich sauce made of heavy cream and cheese, it's also full of healthy fresh vegetables.

½ quantity Whole Wheat Pizza Dough (page 347)

3 tsp olive oil

3 tsp flour

1 cup heavy cream

½ cup loosely packed basil leaves, finely chopped

2 garlic cloves, minced

2 scallions, chopped

½ cup grated Parmesan cheese

8 oz fresh asparagus, chopped

½ large red bell pepper

1 small onion, chopped

1 small zucchini

Preheat oven to 500°F.

Bake the pizza dough for 3 minutes and remove from oven.

To make the sauce, heat the olive oil in a pan and add the flour, stirring to blend. Allow to cook for 2–3 minutes until bubbling. Slowly add the cream, stirring to mix. When the flour mixture is smooth, add the basil, garlic, and scallions. Bring to a boil and then simmer over low heat for 5 minutes, stirring frequently. Remove from the heat and stir in the Parmesan cheese.

Wash the asparagus and snap off the ends, and then chop diagonally into 2-inch pieces. Seed and chop the bell pepper into 2-inch squares. Chop the onions and zucchini into fairly small pieces. Toss the vegetables in a bowl to mix.

To assemble the pizza, spread the vegetables on the pre-baked crust. Pour the sauce over the vegetables, spreading it with a back of a spoon if necessary. Bake for 7–8 minutes.

Spinach and Cheese Pizza

MAKES ONE 12-INCH DOUBLE-CRUST PIZZA

*D*ried mint and feta cheese dress up ordinary spinach in this pizza and bring to mind a Greek salad. But this dish is served hot and steaming.

½ quantity Garlic Dill Pizza
  Dough (page 348)

FOR THE TOPPING

2 tbsp olive oil

1 onion, chopped

2 large garlic cloves, minced

10 oz package frozen, chopped
  spinach, thawed

¼ tsp salt

½ tsp basil

½ tsp oregano

½ tsp dried mint

juice of 1 lemon

¾ cup grated mozzarella cheese

2 medium tomatoes, sliced

¾ cup feta cheese, crumbled

Preheat oven to 500°F.

Heat the olive oil in a pan, add the chopped onions and minced garlic, and sauté until the onions are opaque, about 5 minutes. Drain the spinach, then add to the pan along with the salt, herbs, and the lemon juice. Simmer until all of the liquid has evaporated.

Using a slotted spoon to remove it from the pan, spread the spinach mixture over the pizza dough, within $\frac{1}{2}$ inch of the edge. Layer the mozzarella over the spinach, followed by the tomatoes sliced into fairly thin rounds. Top the tomatoes with the feta.

Bake the pizza for 10 minutes.

Whole Wheat Pepper and Caper Pizza

MAKES TWO 8-INCH PIZZAS

1 quantity Whole Wheat Pizza Dough (page 347)

1 tbsp oil

1½ cups canned tomatoes

½ tsp fresh or ¼ tsp dried thyme

3 cups sliced mushrooms

1 tbsp capers, chopped

salt and ground pepper

2 tbsp Parmesan cheese

1 red bell pepper, seeded

Preheat oven to 425°F. Shape the dough into 2 × 8-inch pizzas and brush with oil.

Drain and chop the tomatoes, mix with the thyme, and spread on the pizza bases. Arrange the mushrooms on the two bases and sprinkle with chopped capers. Season well.

Sprinkle with grated cheese and arrange strips of red bell pepper on top. Bake for 15 minutes in a hot oven and then reduce the temperature to 375°F for 10 minutes more.

◀ *Whole Wheat Pepper and Caper Pizza*

Four Cheese Pizza

MAKES ONE 12-INCH PIZZA

½ quantity Pizza Dough (page 346)

1 tbsp olive oil

1 garlic clove, minced

6 tomatoes, peeled and sliced

½ tsp oregano

4 chopped basil leaves

¼ cup each of crumbled blue cheese, sliced Gruyère cheese, grated mozzarella cheese, and Cheddar cheese.

Preheat oven to 450°F. Roll the dough into a 12-inch round and place on a greased baking sheet. Brush the dough round with olive oil and sprinkle with the garlic.

Arrange the tomatoes over the dough and sprinkle with the herbs, then add the cheese, placing each variety on a quarter of the pizza. Bake for 20-25 minutes, then serve.

Pizzas with Other Bases

Pizza Cups

Individual Blue Cheese Pizzas

Potato Pan Pizza

Tuna Scone Pizza

Leek au Gratin Calzone

Hummus and Vegetable Pizza

Cheese and Guacamole Pizza Wedges

Tabbouleh Appetizer Pizzas

Wholewheat Scone Pizza

Mini Cocktail Pizzas

Spinach and Walnut Appetizer Pizzas

Three Mushrooms Calzone

Individual Pesto Pizzas

Pizza Cups

Baking miniature pizzas in muffin tins makes an interesting variation for an hors d'oeuvre. This recipe calls for a topping of onions and mushrooms, but any favorite vegetable could be used.

FOR THE DOUGH

3½ cups Bisquick

2 tbsp olive oil

½ cup milk

FOR THE FILLING

1 small onion, chopped

¾ cup mushrooms, sliced

6 tbsp Pizza Sauce (page 353)

½ cup grated mozzarella cheese

● Preheat oven to 450°F.

● In a bowl, mix 2 cups of the Bisquick with the oil and the milk. When well combined, slowly add the remaining Bisquick, kneading until a stiff dough forms. Using a rolling pin or the palm of your hand, flatten the dough until it is about ½-inch thick. Using a glass with a 2½–3 inch diameter, cut 12 circles in the dough. Rotate each circle between your fingers, pressing it until it is ⅛-inch thick and about 4 inches in diameter. Place one circle in each cup of a lightly oiled, non-stick muffin pan and push it down so that it forms a cup. (The muffin pan should make muffins approximately 3 inches in diameter.)

● Divide the onion and mushrooms equally between the 12 cups. Top with approximately 1½ teaspoons of pizza sauce and 1½ tablespoons of cheese. Bake for 15 minutes until the edges brown and the cheese melts.

Individual Blue Cheese Pizzas

MAKES FOUR 4-INCH PIZZAS

1 quantity Whole Wheat Pizza Dough (page 347)

olive oil

⅔ cup tomato sauce

1 cup crumbled blue cheese

bell pepper and pitted olives, to garnish

Preheat oven to 425°F. Shape the dough into four 4-inch rounds. Use to line four fluted flan pans or pie plates.

Brush the dough with oil, then spread the tomato sauce over each. Arrange the blue cheese over the dough and garnish with the bell pepper and olives.

Bake for 20 minutes, then serve.

Individual Blue Cheese Pizzas ▶

Potato Pan Pizza

SERVES 6

FOR THE DOUGH

6 tbsp butter

2¼ cups mashed potatoes

2¼ cups all-purpose flour

1 tsp salt

½ level tsp dried mustard

1 tsp mixed herbs

1 egg, beaten

½ cup grated cheese

⅔ cup milk

⅔ cup oil for frying

FOR THE TOPPING

1 onion, peeled and chopped

1½ cups canned tomatoes, drained

salt and pepper

1 tsp dried basil

1½ cups grated cheese

anchovies, black olives or slices of cooked ham (optional)

Preheat oven to 375°F. Mix the butter with the warm potatoes in a bowl. Weigh the potato after cooking to make sure that the proportions are correct.

Sift the flour, salt, dried mustard, and herbs, mix with the egg, add the cheese, and make a stiff dough with the milk.

Turn onto a floured board and divide the mixture into six. Roll into rounds approximately 5 inches in diameter.

Heat the oil in a deep skillet and fry the potato bases until golden brown each side.

Arrange on a baking sheet and prepare the topping.

Drain the skillet and clean out with some paper towels. Pour back a little of the strained oil and cook the finely chopped onion for 4 minutes over a low heat, add the canned tomatoes and break up in the pan. Season well and mix in the basil.

Divide the tomato filling between the potato bases and cover them with cheese. Any other topping can be added at this stage.

Cook for 10 minutes or until golden brown in the preheated oven.

Tuna Biscuit Pizza

SERVES 2-4

2¼ cups flour made into biscuit dough (page 432)

1 tsp oil

1½ cups skinned and sliced tomatoes

1 cup Cheddar cheese

scant 1 cup canned tuna

½ tsp mixed herbs

salt and pepper

7 black olives, pitted

Preheat oven to 425°F. Make the biscuit mixture and roll out to a 10-inch round.

Brush with oil and arrange the sliced tomatoes on the dough. Sprinkle with half the cheese.

Arrange the tuna evenly around the outside of the pizza and sprinkle with the mixed herbs. Season well.

Finish with a layer of cheese. Arrange the olives in a ring near the center of the circle.

Brush with oil and cook in a preheated hot oven. Turn the oven down after 10 minutes to 375°F for the remaining 15-20 minutes cooking time. Serve immediately.

Leek au Gratin Calzone

SERVES 4

These mild vegetables are well complemented by the sharp, somewhat nutty taste of the Gruyère. Leeks are often sandy at the root so make sure you wash them thoroughly.

½ quantity Whole Wheat Pizza Dough (page 347)

¼ cup olive oil

FOR THE FILLING

4 tbsp butter

4 tbsp whole wheat flour

½ cup milk

1 egg yolk

½ cup grated Gruyère cheese

1 large leek

½ tsp salt

¼ tsp pepper

● Preheat oven to 500°F.

● Melt the butter in a pan and add the flour, stirring to make a roux. Cook for 2–3 minutes and slowly add the milk. Stir until the roux thickens and bubbles. Remove from the heat and stir in the egg yolk. Add the grated cheese.

● Remove the root and then chop the leek into ½-inch pieces. Wash thoroughly to remove any dirt and drain in a colander. Pat dry and then stir into the cheese mixture. Stir in the salt and pepper.

● Divide the dough into 4 balls. Roll each one into a flat circle about 6 inches in diameter. Brush with olive oil.

● Divide the leek mixture between the 4 dough circles, placing it on one half of the circle only, Fold the dough in half until the edges meet and press slightly to seal. Brush with olive oil and poke a few holes in the top with a toothpick. Bake on a greased baking sheet for 15 minutes.

Leek au Gratin Calzone ▶

Hummus and Vegetable Pizza

MAKES 12 APPETIZER-SIZED PIZZAS

Hummus is a mixture of puréed garbanzo beans and tahini – ground sesame seed butter – and is usually served as a dip for pita bread or vegetables. It goes just as well on top of a pizza. Top with sliced vegetables and a pecan half.

12 English muffin halves

FOR THE TOPPING

1½ cups cooked garbanzo beans

¼ cup tahini

juice of 1 lemon

2 garlic cloves

2 tbsp sesame seeds

1 tsp coriander

1 tsp cumin

1 small cucumber

2 Roma tomatoes

12 pecan halves

● To make the hummus, purée the garbanzo beans in a food processor. Add the tahini, lemon juice, and garlic cloves, and purée until mixed well.

● In a separate bowl, stir together the sesame seeds, coriander, and cumin. Peel and thinly slice the cucumber and tomatoes into rounds.

● To assemble, lightly toast the muffins. Then spread a heaped tablespoon of the hummus on each muffin half. Top with about 5 cucumber rounds, slightly overlapped to look like petals. Place a slice of tomato in the center. Sprinkle on a half teaspoon of the sesame seed mixture and top with a pecan half. Bake in a toaster oven at 375° for about 5 minutes.

Cheese and Guacamole Pizza Wedges

MAKES 24 APPETIZER WEDGES

Tortillas baked with cheese are popular pizzas in the Southwest. Mexican restaurants in Arizona serve them on giant tortillas, 12 or more inches in diameter. But unless you make your own, that size is not readily available. This recipe uses 8-inch tortillas, which are easy to find, and are a good size for appetizers.

6 flour tortillas (8-inch diameter)

FOR THE TOPPING

1 ripe avocado, mashed

1 large garlic clove, minced

2 tbsp bottled pickled jalapeño peppers, chopped

2 tsp juice from pickled jalapeños

½ tsp salt

¾ cup bottled salsa

1½ cups grated Cheddar cheese

To make the guacamole, mash the avocado with a fork. Add the minced garlic and the chopped bottled jalapeño peppers, along with 2 teaspoons liquid from the bottle. Stir in the salt. Store in the refrigerator until ready to serve.

To make the pizzas, lightly toast the tortillas in a toaster oven. Remove from the oven and top each tortilla with 2 tablespoons of salsa, then ¼ cup of the grated Cheddar cheese. Broil for about 3 minutes, until cheese melts. To serve, cut each tortilla into quarters.
Top each quarter with a teaspoon of guacamole.

Tabbouleh Appetizer Pizzas

MAKES EIGHT PITA BREAD PIZZAS

This recipe combines tabbouleh, the bulgur salad with a hint of mint, and feta cheese. Because good tabbouleh needs to chill in the refrigerator, make it ahead of time. When it's time to eat, assemble and bake the appetizers in just a few minutes.

8 pita breads (6-inch diameter)	1 cup finely chopped parsley
	2 scallions, finely chopped
FOR THE TOPPING	¼ cup olive oil
⅔ cup bulgur	juice of 1 lemon
¾ cup boiling water	½ tsp salt
¼ cup finely chopped fresh mint (start with 1 cup loosely packed leaves)	2 Roma tomatoes, diced
	½ cup sliced almonds
	8 oz crumbled feta cheese

To make the tabbouleh, cover the bulgur with boiling water and set aside for 30 minutes. The water should be completely absorbed. When the bulgur is ready, add the fresh mint, parsley, and scallions. Stir in the olive oil, lemon juice, and salt. Finely dice the tomatoes and gently mix into the tabbouleh. Store in the refrigerator until ready to use.

To make the pizzas, lightly toast the pita bread. Then spread 1 tablespoon of sliced almonds on each piece. Spread approximately ½ cup of tabbouleh over the nuts on each pita. Top with 1 ounce of feta cheese. Place under hot broiler for 2–3 minutes until feta just begins to melt.

Whole Wheat Biscuit Pizza

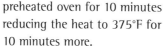

FOR THE DOUGH

1¼ cups whole wheat flour

¾ cup all-purpose flour

4 level tsp baking powder

½ tsp salt

3 tbsp butter

⅔ cup milk

FOR THE TOPPING

2 tbsp oil

1 onion, peeled and diced

1 bell pepper, seeded

2 cups sliced mushrooms

½ cup grated cheese

4 tomatoes, peeled and sliced

1 tsp chopped fresh mixed herbs

Pour the whole wheat flour into a mixing bowl, sift the white flour, baking powder, and salt into the bowl, and mix well. Rub in the butter with the tips of the fingers until the mixture resembles fine bread crumbs. Add the milk and mix to a soft dough, a further small quantity of milk may be needed to mix the dough to the correct consistency. Turn onto a lightly floured board and knead lightly into a round shape. Roll out into a 10-inch round and place on a baking sheet.

To start the topping, heat the oil in a skillet and cook the onion over a low heat for 4 minutes. Cut the pepper into thin rings and blanch in boiling water for 2 minutes. Drain. Add the mushrooms to the onion and allow to cook for a further 2 minutes.

Arrange the tomatoes on the biscuit base and sprinkle with mixed herbs and seasoning. Arrange mushrooms and onions on top of the tomatoes, and sprinkle with cheese. Finally, add the bell peppers. Cook in a preheated oven for 10 minutes reducing the heat to 375°F for 10 minutes more.

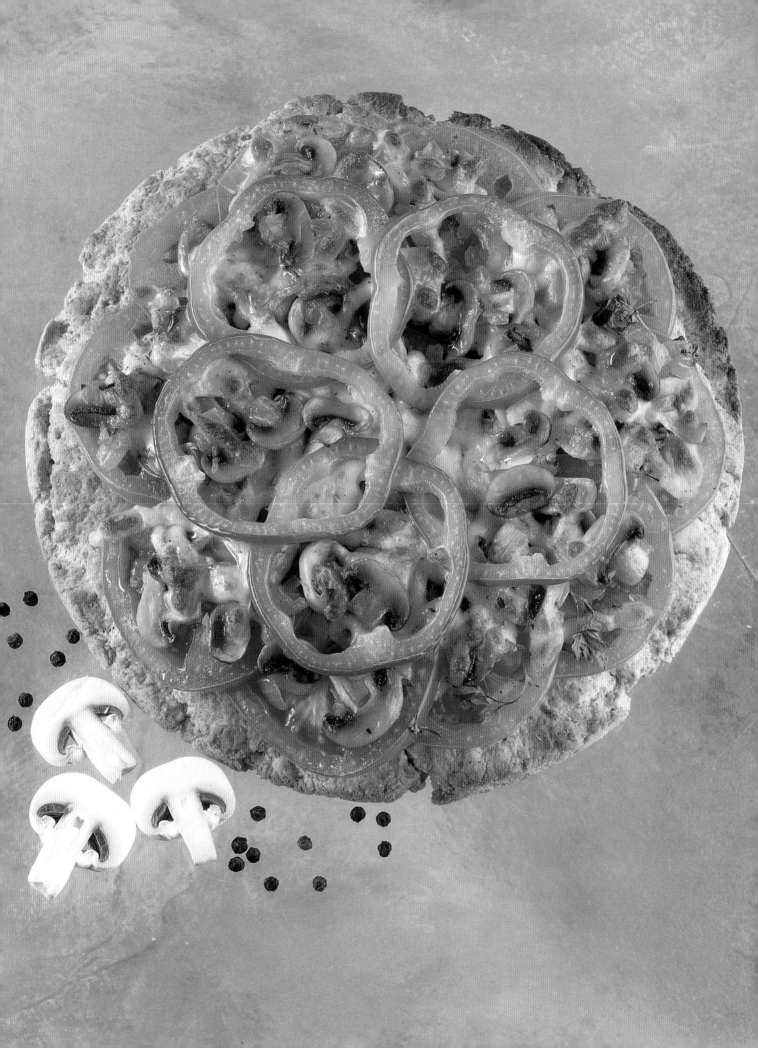

Mini Cocktail Pizzas

MAKES EIGHT MINI PIZZAS

Use English muffins as the recipe suggests, or a prebaked crust cut into small circles. These simple hors d'oeuvres are pretty to look at as well as tasty to eat.

8 English muffin halves

½ cup Pizza Sauce (page 353)

4 oz shredded Swiss cheese

1 ripe medium tomato

1 tsp olive oil

4 tsp chopped fresh parsley

Lightly toast the muffin halves. Then spread 1 tablespoon of pizza sauce on each muffin half. Top with ½ ounce Swiss cheese. Broil in a toaster oven for about 5 minutes, or until cheese is bubbly and begins to turn brown. Slice the tomato in thin, perfect rounds. Top each broiled muffin with one tomato slice. Brush with a little olive oil and sprinkle with about ½ teaspoon of parsley. Serve immediately.

◀ *Mini Cocktail Pizzas*

Spinach and Walnut Appetizer Pizzas

MAKES 12 APPETIZER PIZZAS

Walnut oil, which can be purchased in health food stores, makes an unusual vinaigrette for this appetizer pizza. Choose a good-quality Gorgonzola for the tangy, creamy topping.

½ cup walnut oil

1 cup walnut halves, broken

2 tbsp red wine vinegar

½ tsp salt

2 scallions, finely chopped

12 English muffin halves

4 oz fresh spinach, stems removed

6 oz Gorgonzola cheese

Pour the oil over the walnuts and marinate for about 15 minutes. Strain the walnuts and set aside. Mix the vinegar, salt, and finely chopped scallions into the oil.

Toast the muffins to a light brown. Wash the spinach and remove the stems. Pat dry and place about three leaves on each of the toasted muffins. Top with a scant tablespoon of the dressing, 1 tablespoon of walnuts, and top with about ½ ounce of cheese. Broil for about 3 minutes until the cheese begins to melt.

Three Mushrooms Calzone

MAKES FOUR CALZONES

Any combination of mushrooms goes well in this folded pizza, which is like a hearty sandwich. Try to use more than one variety each time for a more exciting flavor.

½ quantity Whole Wheat Pizza Dough (page 347)

¼ cup olive oil

8 oz portobella mushrooms, chopped

4 oz shiitake mushrooms, chopped

4 oz enoki mushrooms

3 tsp minced garlic

2 tsp dried sage

2 tsp dried parsley

8 oz grated fontina cheese

4 oz grated Swiss cheese

Preheat oven to 500°F.

Divide dough into 4 balls. Roll each one into a flat circle about 6 inches in diameter. Brush with olive oil. Chop the portobella and shiitake mushrooms into small pieces.

On one half of each circle of dough, place 2 ounces of portobella mushrooms (about 2 tablespoons), ½ ounce of enoki mushrooms (a clump about ½ inch in diameter) and 1 ounce (about 1 tablespoon) of shiitake mushrooms. Add ½ teaspoon minced garlic. Sprinkle with ½ teaspoon each of sage and parsley. Top with 2 ounces fontina and 1 ounce Swiss cheese.

Fold the dough in half until the edges meet and press slightly to seal. Brush with olive oil and poke a few holes in the top with a toothpick or fork.

Bake on a greased baking sheet for 15 minutes.

Individual Pesto Pizzas

MAKES FOUR 6-INCH PIZZAS

Homemade pesto is so good it's worth growing a crop of basil in your garden in order to have easy access. These pizzas make great appetizers, but are also good as the main course for lunch.

4 pieces of pita bread (6-inch diameter)

1 small red onion, thinly sliced

1 small Roma tomato, thinly sliced

4 oz feta cheese, crumbled

PESTO SAUCE:

½ cup fresh basil leaves, stems removed

1 tbsp pine nuts

1 large garlic clove, minced

¼ cup extra virgin olive oil

¼ cup Parmesan cheese

First make the pesto sauce. Put the basil, pine nuts, garlic, olive oil, and Parmesan cheese in a blender or food processor and mix until thoroughly blended. Make ahead of time and refrigerate if you wish.

To make the pizza, toast the pita bread. Then top each piece with 1 tablespoon of pesto sauce, a slice of onion, a slice of tomato, and finally, 1 ounce of feta cheese.

Cold Pizzas

Sweet and Sour Corn Pizza

Three-bean Pizza

Fruit Salad Pizza

Asian Avocado Pizza

Six-layer Pizza

Avocado and Orange Pizza

Pizza Crudité

Sweet and Sour Corn Pizza

This colorful pizza makes an unusual appetizer. It is sweet and best served in small slices. Make the topping ahead of time and store it in the refrigerator so that the flavors have time to blend.

½ quantity Pizza Dough (page 346) made with 1 cup tomato juice and 2 tbsp seeded and finely diced jalapeño peppers

½ tsp turmeric

½ tsp salt

½ tsp dry mustard

¼ cup cider vinegar

¼ cup sugar

10 oz can niblet corn

1 sweet onion, chopped

½ green bell pepper, chopped

½ red bell pepper, chopped

1 jalapeño pepper, seeded and finely chopped

1 tbsp cornstarch

8 oz feta cheese, crumbled

Add the tomato juice and chopped jalapeño peppers to the flour when making the pizza dough. Preheat the oven to 500°F. Bake the pizza dough for 25-30 minutes, remove from the oven, and allow to cool.

Put the turmeric, salt, mustard, vinegar, and sugar in a pan and stir over medium heat until the sugar and spices are dissolved. Add the corn, onion, green, red, and jalapeño peppers and bring to a boil. Reduce heat and simmer for 15 minutes, stirring occasionally.

Drain a little of the hot liquid from the mixture into a cup and add the cornstarch, stirring to a smooth paste. Stir this mixture back into the pan and cook until the corn relish thickens. Allow to cool and store in the refrigerator overnight to allow flavors to blend. (This is important as the relish is too tart when freshly made.)

To make the pizza, spread the relish over the cool crust, leaving an inch around the edge. Top with the crumbled feta and serve.

Three-bean Pizza

MAKES ONE 12-INCH DOUBLE-CRUST PIZZA

Use any three types of beans for variation. Canned beans are easy and quick, but you could use dried beans. Soak and cook them ahead of time and allow them to cool.

½ quantity Pizza Dough
   (see page 346)

⅔ cup canned pinto beans

⅔ cup canned garbanzo beans

⅔ cup canned black beans

1 red onion, sliced

½ cup green bell pepper, diced

1 medium tomato, chopped

1 tsp cider vinegar

½ tsp salt

¼ tsp pepper

1 tsp Dijon-style mustard

1 tbsp mayonnaise

● Preheat the oven to 500°F. Bake the pizza dough for 25–30 minutes, remove from oven and allow to cool.

● Drain and rinse the beans and place them in a bowl. Slice the onion into circles, separate into rings, then cut in half. Add them to the bowl. Add the diced green bell pepper and chopped tomato. In a separate container, mix the vinegar, salt, pepper, mustard, and mayonnaise. Then add this mixture to the vegetables, stirring gently to coat. Avoid mashing the beans.

● Spread the mixture on the crust and refrigerate for half an hour before serving.

◀ *Three-bean Pizza*

Fruit Salad Pizza

MAKES ONE 12-INCH DOUBLE-CRUST PIZZA

Creamy pineapple yogurt is used as a dressing to make this recipe special. Serve it during the summer when melons are at their peak of ripeness. Try other types of fruit such as papayas or mangos.

½ quantity Pizza Dough
   (page 346)

½ honeydew melon

½ cantaloupe

1 cup fresh pineapple

6 strawberries

3½ oz Gouda cheese (half a
   round), diced

½ tsp ground ginger

juice of 1 lime

8 oz pineapple yogurt

½ cup blueberries

● Preheat oven to 500°F. Bake pizza dough for about 25–30 minutes, remove from oven and allow to cool.

● Cut both melons in half and remove the seeds. Dice into small squares and place in a bowl. Peel the pineapple and remove the core. Dice in small squares and add to the bowl. Add the strawberries, stems removed, and cut in half (smaller if they are large). Cut the Gouda round in half. Remove the wax and dice the cheese. Add to the bowl. Sprinkle the ginger and squeeze the lime juice over the fruit and cheese. Gently fold in the yogurt. Store in the refrigerator until ready to serve.

● To assemble the pizza, spread the fruit mixture gently over the prebaked, cooled crust. Top with the blueberries.

Asian Avocado Pizza

MAKES ONE 12-INCH DOUBLE-CRUST PIZZA

Horseradish and capers are the ingredients that give this avocado salad an unusual kick. For an even more exotic salad, use black sesame seeds instead of white. They can be found in Asian markets.

½ quantity Chinese Pizza Dough (page 348)

1 tbsp sesame seeds

2 large ripe avocados

2 Roma tomatoes, diced

2 tbsp horseradish

2 tsp crystallized ginger, minced

2 tbsp capers

3 tbsp cider vinegar

1 tbsp sugar

Preheat the oven to 500°F. Bake pizza dough for 25–30 minutes, remove from oven, and allow to cool.

Toast the sesame seeds in a nonstick pan over medium high heat until browned, about 5 minutes. Stir frequently to keep from burning. Peel, seed, and dice the avocados and place them in a bowl. Add the diced tomatoes, horseradish, 1 teaspoon of the toasted sesame seeds, ginger, and capers. Stir gently to mix. In a separate container, mix the vinegar and sugar. Pour over the avocado mixture and gently toss.

Spread the avocado salad on the cooled crust. Top with the remaining toasted sesame seeds. Serve chilled or at room temperature.

Six-layer Pizza

MAKES ONE 12-INCH DOUBLE-CRUST PIZZA

Start with the sour cream and just layer the vegetables on top of one another. It's good for lunch or as a nutritious appetizer.

½ quantity Garlic Dill Pizza Dough (page 348)

small lettuce, shredded

1 red onion, chopped

½ cup frozen peas, thawed to room temperature

1 carrot, grated

1 small jar (2¼ oz) sliced black olives

1 cup sour cream

salt and pepper to taste

◉ Preheat oven to 500°F. Bake pizza dough for 25–30 minutes, remove from the oven and allow to cool.

◉ Prepare the vegetables: shred the lettuce, chop the onion, thaw the peas, peel and grate the carrot. Drain the olives.

◉ To assemble the pizza, spread the sour cream on the prebaked, cooled crust. Then spread the shredded lettuce on top of the sour cream. Add the onions, the carrots, the peas, and finally the olives. Season to taste. Serve cold.

◀ *Six-layer Pizza*

Avocado and Orange Pizza

MAKES ONE 12-INCH DOUBLE-CRUST PIZZA

Oranges, avocados, and onions go well together with a sweet and sour dressing. Make sure the avocado is perfectly ripe. It should be soft, but not mushy.

½ quantity Whole Wheat Pizza Dough (page 347)

1 small sweet red onion, thinly sliced and separated into rings

1 large ripe avocado, peeled and thinly sliced

11 oz can mandarin oranges, drained, 1 tbsp of the liquid reserved

1 tsp salad oil

1 tsp balsamic vinegar

⅛ tsp dried mustard

½ tsp sugar

juice of ½ lemon

⅛ tsp salt

◉ Preheat oven to 500°F. Bake the pizza dough for 25–30 minutes, remove from the oven and allow to cool.

◉ In a bowl, add red onion, avocado slices, and drained mandarin oranges. Gently toss together. In a cup, mix the oil, vinegar, mustard, sugar, reserved orange juice, lemon juice, and salt. Whisk to blend well. Pour it over the avocado mixture and gently mix together. Marinate the topping until ready to serve.

◉ To serve, spread the mixture over the cooled crust. Pour any remaining dressing on top.

Pizza Crudité

MAKES ONE 12-INCH DOUBLE-CRUST PIZZA

Fresh dill enhances the taste of the creamy sauce. Chop the vegetables very finely for best results. This pizza makes a good leftover as the flavors blend together when left overnight in the refrigerator.

½ quantity Garlic Dill Pizza
　　Dough (page 348)

6 oz cream cheese, softened

½ cup mayonnaise

1 tsp chopped fresh dill

1 garlic clove, minced

¼ tsp salt

4 medium carrots

1 medium ripe tomato

1 red onion

2¼-oz jar sliced black olives,
　　drained

Preheat the oven to 500°F. Bake the pizza dough for 25–30 minutes, remove from oven, and allow to cool.

In a bowl, cream the softened cream cheese and mayonnaise together, mashing well with a fork. Add the fresh dill, minced garlic, and salt and mix thoroughly. Using a rubber spatula, spread this mixture onto the cooled, cooked crust.

Peel the carrots and chop them very finely. Also finely chop the tomato and onion. Mix the chopped vegetables in a bowl along with the drained olives. Pile the vegetables onto the pizza and refrigerate for at least a half hour before serving.

Sweet Pizzas

Pizza Ambrosia

Pears in Port Wine Pizza

Peach and Raspberry Pizza

Chocolate Banana Pizza

Chocolate Pizza Crisp

Dessert Fruit Pizza

Apple Crisp Pizza

Cookie Pizza

Minted Melon Pizza

Pizza Ambrosia

MAKES ONE REGULAR 12-INCH PIZZA

Ambrosia is usually a mixture of winter fruits. This recipe adds nuts and a sweet sauce to make a fruity, healthy dessert pizza. Make the sauce ahead of time, if possible, because it thickens as it sits in the refrigerator.

FOR THE DESSERT PIZZA CRUST

¾ cup vegetable oil

1 cup sugar

2 eggs

1 tsp vanilla extract

1½ tsp baking powder

¼ tsp salt

2½ cups all-purpose flour

FOR THE DRESSING

1 egg

1 tbsp butter

1 tsp sugar

¼ cup orange juice

juice of 1 lemon (about 2 tbsp)

¼ cup heavy cream

2 oz cream cheese

FOR THE TOPPING

1 apple, chopped

11 oz can mandarin oranges, drained

2 bananas, sliced

1 cup pitted dates, chopped

½ cup pecan halves

3 tbsp sweetened coconut

To make the crust, preheat the oven to 375°F. In a bowl, mix the oil and sugar. Beat in the eggs and vanilla. Add the baking powder, salt, and flour and stir until well mixed. Chill the dough for 15 minutes. Lightly grease a 12-inch pizza pan. Pat out the dough on the pan until the pan is covered evenly. Bake for 15 minutes. Cool before topping.

To make the dressing, put the slightly beaten egg, butter, and sugar in the top of a double boiler and heat, stirring frequently, until cooked and thickened and smooth, about 15 minutes. Remove from the heat and add the orange and lemon juices and refrigerate. When mixture has cooled, pour into a bowl and, using an electric mixer on high, slowly add the cream and cream cheese. Beat until smooth and creamy. If there is time, refrigerate for an hour to thicken before using.

Mix the apple with the mandarin oranges, bananas, dates, and pecans. Pour enough sauce over the fruit to just cover.

Spread the fruit mixture over the baked, cooled crust. Sprinkle the coconut over the top. Serve immediately, or refrigerate for later use.

Pears in Port Wine Pizza

MAKES ONE REGULAR 12-INCH PIZZA

Marinate the pears ahead of time so that they turn a nice deep purple, and save the port marinade for an after-dinner drink! It is deliciously flavored by the fruit and spices.

1 batch Dessert Pizza Crust (page 449)

FOR THE TOPPING

4 ripe pears

½ cup raisins

1 stick cinnamon

8 whole allspice berries

1 bottle port wine

whipped cream

Select ripe pears that are no longer crisp because they absorb the wine more easily. Peel and seed them and cut into slices about ¼ inch thick. Put them in a glass jar with the raisins, cinnamon, and allspice. Add the wine, which should completely cover the fruit. Cover the jar and refrigerate overnight or for up to 3 days.

To assemble, drain the fruit, reserving the port. Discard the cinnamon stick. Spread the fruit on the baked, cooled crust in an even layer, leaving a ¼-inch edge. Pour ¼ cup of the port over the fruit. Decorate the pizza with a ring of whipped cream around the outer edge of the fruit, and another in the center.

Pears in Port Wine Pizza ▶

Peach and Raspberry Pizza

MAKES ONE REGULAR 12-INCH PIZZA

This dessert pizza offers a nice contrast between the tart berries and the sweet crust. It is a beautiful dessert to serve during the summer when fruit is at its peak of ripeness.

1 Dessert Pizza Crust (page 449)

FOR THE TOPPING

1½ cups raspberries

1 tbsp Grand Marnier liqueur

2 ripe peaches, sliced

Purée the raspberries in a food processor. Pour into a bowl, add the Grand Marnier, and stir. Cut the peaches in half and remove the pits. Cut each half in half again and slice thinly. Arrange the slices on the cooked, cooled crust so that they overlap slightly. Pour the raspberry mixture over the peaches and serve.

Chocolate Banana Pizza

MAKES ONE REGULAR 12-INCH PIZZA

The banana split inspired this dessert pizza, a combination of chocolate and bananas. A cream cheese, yogurt, and honey sauce replaces the ice cream.

FOR THE CHOCOLATE DESSERT CRUST

2 oz unsweetened chocolate

½ cup butter, softened

1 cup sugar

1 egg, beaten

1 tsp vanilla extract

1½ tsp baking powder

¼ tsp salt

1½ cups all-purpose flour

FOR THE TOPPING

4 oz cream cheese

½ cup plain yogurt

1½ tsp honey

3 large or 4 medium bananas, sliced

2 oz semisweet chocolate, shaved or grated

Make the crust. Preheat the oven to 400°F. Melt the chocolate in the top of a double boiler. Cool. In a bowl, cream together the butter and sugar. Add the egg and vanilla. Add the remaining ingredients with the chocolate and mix well. Cover and leave in the freezer for 45 minutes. Lightly grease a pizza pan and spread the dough to cover the pan evenly. Smooth out with a glass, if necessary. Bake at 400°F for 10 minutes. Cool before topping.

Soften the cream cheese to room temperature and then beat in the yogurt and honey. Slice the bananas into rounds about ¼–½ inch thick and place on the crust in a single layer. Pour the yogurt and cream cheese mixture over the bananas. Top with chocolate. Refrigerate until ready to serve.

Chocolate Pizza Crisp

MAKES ONE REGULAR 12-INCH PIZZA

This pizza is a variation of rice crispie treats. Peanuts, coconut, M&Ms®, and chocolate chips have been added to make this a chocolate lover's delight.

12 oz package semisweet chocolate chips

3 oz butter

2 cups miniature marshmallows

1–2 tbsp milk

1 cup crisp rice cereal

½ cup shredded coconut

½ cup miniature M&Ms®

½ cup unsalted dry roasted peanuts

In the top of a double boiler, melt the chocolate chips, butter, and marshmallows. When completely blended, remove from the heat and add a tablespoon or two of milk to attain a creamy mixture. Add the rice cereal and blend as thoroughly as possible. Mix in the coconut, M&Ms®, and peanuts. Spray a 12-inch pizza pan with cooking spray. Spread the chocolate mixture into the pan, pressing it down firmly. Refrigerate for 1 hour or more, until firm.

Dessert Fruit Pizza

This is the most beautiful dessert pizza you can serve and is always a hit. You can vary the fruit depending on what's in season and what you like. Follow the instructions below to arrange the fruit, or create your own designs.

1 batch Dessert Pizza Crust
(page 449)

FOR THE TOPPING

8 oz cream cheese

8 oz frozen whipped cream topping

2 kiwi fruit

5 large strawberries

11 oz can mandarin oranges, drained

Allow the cream cheese to soften to room temperature. Then mix the whipped cream topping and cream cheese together until smooth using an electric mixer. Spread the mixture over the baked and cooled dessert pizza crust. Put it in the refrigerator while you prepare the fruit.

Gently peel the two kiwis and slice one kiwi into thin rounds. Slice the second kiwi into thin rounds and then cut those in half. You will have two shapes of kiwis: circles and half circles.

Wash and slice off the tops of the strawberries. Slice them so that the pieces are more or less round. Separate the slices into large and small sizes (larger circles from the center of the berry, smaller from the ends).

To top the pizza, begin with the outer ring, using one orange section, then one half-circle kiwi. The oranges should point in toward the centre; the diameters of the kiwi should face the orange. Nestle the fruit close together. Proceed along the rim alternating the kiwi and orange sections. For the second ring, use a full-circle kiwi and a large strawberry circle. For the third ring, use orange sections and smaller strawberry circles. End with a full-circle kiwi slice for the center.

Refrigerate and serve chilled.

Apple Crisp Pizza

MAKES ONE REGULAR 12-INCH PIZZA

Apples paired with gingerbread are a delicious combination. Use any type of good, firm apple for this recipe. It can be served by itself or, like a pie, with ice cream or whipped cream.

FOR THE GINGERBREAD CRUST

¼ cup butter

¼ cup sugar

1 egg

1 tsp baking powder

½ tsp each cinnamon, ginger, and salt

1¾ cups flour

2 tbsp unsulfured molasses

1 tbsp honey

FOR THE TOPPING

2 or 3 large apples such as Red Delicious, peeled and sliced

1 cup white flour

½ cup packed dark brown sugar

1 tsp cinnamon

1 tsp ginger

½ tsp mace

½ cup butter

½ cup walnut pieces

Make the crust. Preheat the oven to 350°F. Cream the butter and sugar together. Beat in the egg, then add the baking powder, spices and salt. Add the flour, molasses, and honey and mix well. Chill for 15 minutes, then work the dough to cover a lightly greased pizza pan.

Peel the apples and remove the stem and seeds. Slice them thinly.

To make the topping, mix flour, brown sugar, cinnamon, ginger, and mace together in a bowl and stir to blend. Using two knives, cut in the butter until crumbly. Mix in the walnut pieces.

To assemble the pizza, arrange the apple slices on the gingerbread dough. Spread the topping over the apples. Bake for 15 minutes at 350°F.

◀ *Apple Crisp Pizza*

Cookie Pizza

MAKES ONE REGULAR 12-INCH PIZZA

A giant chocolate chip cookie is what this pizza really is. Because it's so rich, it should be served in small pieces.

½ cup butter, softened to room temperature

½ cup packed brown sugar

¼ cup white sugar

½ tsp baking soda

1 egg

1 tsp vanilla

1¼ cups flour

6 oz semisweet chocolate chips

¾ cup walnut pieces

Preheat oven to 350°F.

Cream the softened butter and sugars together. Mix in baking soda, egg, and vanilla. Add the flour and mix thoroughly. Add the chocolate chips and walnuts. For easier roll-out, put the dough in the refrigerator for 15–30 minutes to stiffen. Spread the dough as evenly as possible on a greased 12-inch pizza pan. Bake for 20 minutes at 350°F. Allow to cool for about 15 minutes before cutting.

Minted Melon Pizza

The sauce of this pizza has the cool flavor of mint that goes so well with berries and melon. The sauce is very sweet, and so is the crust, so don't drown the fruit.

1 Chocolate Dessert Crust (page 452), baked and cooled

FOR THE TOPPING

¼ cup sugar

½ cup water

4 or 5 fresh mint leaves

1 large ripe cantaloupe, chopped

1 cup fresh blueberries

mint leaves for garnish

In a pan, mix the sugar, water, and mint leaves. Bring to a boil and simmer for 5 minutes, reducing liquid to about ¼ cup. Remove and discard the mint leaves and cool the sugar water in the refrigerator.

Cut the cantaloupe in half, remove the seeds, and chop into small squares. Wash and sort the blueberries, removing stems and any bad berries.

To assemble, spread the melon over the crust. Sprinkle the blueberries on top. Pour the sugar water over the fruit. Garnish with mint leaves.

Index